Achieving TABE® Success in Mathematics

Level A

McGraw Hill Wright Group

Senior Editor: Diane Nieker
Executive Editor: Linda Kwil
Marketing Manager: Sean Klunder
Production Manager: Genevieve Kelley
Cover Designer: Vickie Tripp

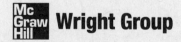 **Wright Group**

ISBN: 0-07-704470-3

Send all inquiries to:
Wright Group/McGraw-Hill
One Prudential Plaza
130 East Randolph Street, Suite 400
Chicago, IL 60601

Printed in the United States of America.

15 16 17   MAL 16 15 14

The **McGraw·Hill** Companies

Table of Contents

To the Learner

Having an understanding of math is more important than ever if you wish to compete successfully in today's global and technological world. The pages in *Achieving TABE Success in Math, Level A* provide instruction to help you increase your understanding of many basic mathematical ideas. These pages also include problems that allow you to practice and strengthen that understanding.

Start by taking the pretest on pages 1–6. Then use the answer key on page 7 to check your answers. The evaluation chart on page 7 tells you which skill area is addressed by each problem in the pretest. This chart helps you identify your areas of strength and determine skill areas that need greater attention.

The main part of the book is organized into sections by skill area: Whole Numbers; Problem Solving; Decimals; Fractions; Integers; Ratio, Proportion, and Percent; Probability, Statistics, and Data Analysis; Algebra; Geometry; and Measurement. As you complete each page, check your answers using the answer key at the back of the book. Rework problems that you miss, and be sure to check with your instructor if you find you are having difficulty. At the end of each section you will find a Skills Checkup that serves as a quiz for that section. Answers for the Skills Checkup are found in the answer key at the back of the book.

The posttest on pages 160–168 will measure your overall progress and determine whether you have mastered the skills at this level. By successfully completing *Achieving TABE Success in Math, Level A,* you will have a strong foundation on which to continue building your skills in mathematics.

Correlation Chart

Correlations Between Contemporary's Instructional Materials and TABE® Math Computation and Applied Math

Test 2 Mathematics Computation

Subskill	TABE™ Form 9	TABE™ Form 10	TABE™ Survey 9	TABE™ Survey 10	Practice and Instruction Pages			
					Achieving TABE Success in Mathematics, Level A	*GED Mathematics*	*Complete GED and Essential GED**	*GED Math Problem Solver and Top 50 Math Skills ***
Decimals								
addition	3, 7	1, 6	4	1	36	82–83	C: 733–736 E: 355–356	M: 189 T: 18–19, 141
subtraction	1, 22	13, 23	1	9	37	84–85	C: 733–736 E: 355–356	M: 189 T: 18–19, 141
multiplication	15, 20	17, 26	10	17	38–41	85–87	C: 737–738, 741–742 E: 357–358	M: 189 T: 22–23, 142
division	14, 30	15, 31	8	11	42–44	88–92	C: 739–742 E: 358–360	M: 190 T: 22–23, 142
Fractions								
addition	8, 24	7, 20	14	14	56, 58	115–117	C: 762–765 E: 372–374	M: 164–169 T: 26–27, 132–134, 140
subtraction	5, 18	5, 18	3	5	57–58	117–120	C: 762–765 E: 372–374	M: 166–169 T: 26–27, 132–134
multiplication	26, 37	34, 37	17	23	59–61, 83	120–123	C: 766–767 E: 375–376	M: 180 T: 28–29, 135
division	25, 34	33, 38	19	25	62–63, 83	123–124	C: 768–769 E: 376–377	M: 182 T: 28–29, 136–137
Integers								
addition	10, 12	12, 16	6	7	70	281–285	C: 778–781 E: 369, 380–384	M: 48–52 T: 146
subtraction	21, 29	2, 39	15	2	71	285–287	C: 778–781 E: 369, 380–384	M: 48–52 T: 146
multiplication	19, 23	4, 10, 14	13	4	72	287–289	C: 781–783 E: 384–385	M: 96–97 T: 147
division	2, 16, 27	8, 24	11, 16	6, 15	72	289–292	C: 781–783 E: 384–385	M: 96–97 T: 147

Subskill	TABE® Form 9	TABE® Form 10	TABE® Survey 9	TABE® Survey 10	Practice and Instruction Pages			
					Achieving TABE Success in Mathematics, Level A	*GED Mathematics*	*Complete GED and Essential GED**	*GED Math Problem Solver and Top 50 Math Skills ***
Percents								
percents	6, 17, 31, 35, 38	9, 25, 28, 32, 35	12, 20, 22, 24	16, 18, 21, 24	82–83	149–182	C: 793–808 E: 400–407	M: 226–237, 242–250 T: 32–33, 38–39, 140, 143–144
Order of Operations								
order of operations	13, 28, 33, 36, 40	19, 21, 27, 36, 40	9, 18, 21, 23	10, 12, 20, 22	17	43, 291	C: 714–717, 722–724 E: 343–344	M: 100–103, 104, 117–119 T: 20–21
Algebraic Operations								
computation with roots & radicals	9, 32	3, 30	5	3	16	32–36	C: 712–714 E: 341–343	M: 114–117, 121–122 T: 20–21
computation with exponents	11	11	7	8	17, 111	336–342	C: 711–712 E: 341–343, 425–428	M: 114–117 T: 20–21, 145, 148
solve equations	4	22	2	13	111, 113, 118–119, 121 123–125	294–303, 308–316, 336–342	C: 838–845 E: 412–413, 415–416	M: 30–33, 92–93, 232–234 T: 94–95, 98–99, 104–107
simplify expressions	39	29	25	19	120–122	292–294	C: 847–848 E: 408–411, 414–415, 425–428	M: 15 T: 96–97, 100–101

Test 3 Applied Mathematics

Number and Number Operations								
equivalent forms	42	48	21	——	20, 49–52, 84–85, 113	124–127	C: 749–757, 793–796 E: 341–343, 366–371	M: 88–93, 154–157 T: 30–31
factors, multiples, divisibility	3	11	——	——	55, 58, 61	20, 39–43, 339–340	C: 741–742, 864–869 E: 341–343, 426–428	M: 102–103 T: 24–25

Subskill	TABE® Form 9	TABE® Form 10	TABE® Survey 9	TABE® Survey 10	Practice and Instruction Pages			
					Achieving TABE Success in Mathematics, Level A	*GED Mathematics*	*Complete GED and Essential GED**	*GED Math Problem Solver and Top 50 Math Skills ***
percent	44	9, 43	——	3, 22	82, 90	149–155, 165–166, 165 175	C: 793–808 E: 400–407	M: 226–235, 242–250 T: 32 33, 38–39, 140, 143–144
ratio, proportion	41, 43	44	20	——	76–82	137–148, 165–166	C: 785–792 E: 386–389	M: 202–211, 214–219, 231–232 T: 34–35, 36–37, 50–51, 52–53, 138, 139
exponents, scientific notation	50	40	25	2	13–15, 33, 39–41	32–34, 93–94, 127–129	C: 711–712, 730–733 E: 341–342, 354	M: 114–117, 137–138 T: 20–21, 145, 148
Computation in Context								
decimals	——	5, 38	——	20	45	95–102	C: 725–746 E: 355–360	++ M: 188, 237 T: 18–23
fractions	16, 22	——	2	——	64–65	129–132	C: 769–774 E: 378–379	++ M: 172, 188 T: 26–29
percents	14, 29	7, 45	3	23	91	167–182	C: 800–808 E: 404–407	++ M: 234, 237 T: 38–39
Estimation								
estimation	9, 11, 26	2, 4	5, 11	1	28, 54, 65	25–28	C: 742–746 E: 360	M: 17, 59, 72–74, 94–95, 121–122, 138–139, 170–171, 181 T: x–xi, 14–15, 64, 74
rounding	2	41	1	——	18–19, 29	24–25	C: 729–730 E: 353	M: 72–74 T: xi
reasonableness of answer	——	30	——	17	103, 105–106	60–63	C: 702–710	M: 8–9, 58–59, 72–74

Subskill	TABE® Form 9	TABE® Form 10	TABE® Survey 9	TABE® Survey 10	Practice and Instruction Pages			
					Achieving TABE Success in Mathematics, Level A	*GED Mathematics*	*Complete GED and Essential GED**	*GED Math Problem Solver and Top 50 Math Skills ***
Measurement								
length, distance	30	24	——	11	145–146, 149	183–187	C: 873–883 E: 429–434	M: 89–90, T: 149
perimeter	36	——	16		153	234–240	C: 897–899 E: 443–444	M: 13–15, 105
area	38	15, 22, 36	17	18	155	240–249	C: 899–901 E: 444–446	M: 78–83, 116, 130–131 T: 62–63
rate	1	——	——	——	80		C: 785–788, 887 E: 386–387	M: 88–90, 203–204, 223 T: 46–47, 48–49, 138
convert measurement units	——	27, 37	——	19	148, 150–152	188–190	C: 873–875, 879–883 E: 429–430, 433–434	M: 77–78 T: 40–41, 44–45
circumference	46	——	23	——	154	234–240	C: 898–899 E: 443–444	M: 126–129
volume	23	——	12	——	147, 156–157	252–255	C: 902–904 E: 446–448	M: 84–85 T: 64–65
Geometry and Spatial Sense								
plane figure	——	14	——	6	136–138	231–233	C: 897–901 E: 441, 443–446	M: 78–83, 220–221 T: 58–59
angles	——	23, 26	——	12	131–133, 135	224–231	C: 904–908 E: 448–450	M: 38–41 T: 56–57
coordinate geometry	31, 37, 40	13	19	5	140	323–335	C: 854–863 E: 419–424	M: 52–55, 254–261 T: 66–67, 68–69
parts of a circle	45	——	22	——	154	232–233	C: 893–895 E: 440–441	M: 126–128
point, ray, line, plane	32	12	——	——	130–132	223–227	C: 893–894 E: 440–441	M: 44–45
transformations	39	——	18	——	141–142			
Pythagorean theorem	——	25	——	——	139	271–275	C: 908–911 E: 450–452	M: 119–121 T: 60–61

Subskill	TABE® Form 9	TABE® Form 10	TABE® Survey 9	TABE® Survey 10	Practice and Instruction Pages			
					Achieving TABE Success in Mathematics, Level A	*GED Mathematics*	*Complete GED and Essential GED**	*GED Math Problem Solver and Top 50 Math Skills ***
Data Analysis								
bar, line, and circle graph	33, 34	18, 19, 28	——	9, 15	101–103, 105	197–209	C: 275–282, 824–834 E: 396–399	M: 10, 20, 140, 178, 236, 251, 258, 284–296 T: 78–79, 80–89
table, chart, diagram	17, 18	3	7, 8	——	99–100	209–211	C: 285–286, 820–824 E: 395	M: 15, 20, 140, 173, 187, 205, 219, 236, 284–296 T: 92–93, 104–107
conclusions from data	28, 35	10, 20, 21	14	4, 10	104–106	217–222	C: 820–834 E: 393–394	M: 10, 140, 173, 178, 205, 219, 236, 251, 258 T: 74–75, 76–77, 78–79, 80–89
appropriate data display	6	6	——	——	107	197–211	C: 820–834	M: 140, 187, 258
Statistics and Probability								
probability	4, 21	39	——	——	94–95	212–216	C: 809–814 E: 390–393	M: 158–159, 167, 179 T: 90–93
statistics	15, 25	29, 34	10	16	96–98	217–222	C: 815–819 E: 393-394	M: 10, 15, 20, 140, 173, 178, 187, 205, 219, 236, 251, 258, 284–296 T: 70–71, 76–79, 80–89
sampling	——	49	——	25	98			M: 205 T: 74–75

Subskill	TABE® Form 9	TABE® Form 10	TABE® Survey 9	TABE® Survey 10	Practice and Instruction Pages			
					Achieving TABE Success in Mathematics, Level A	*GED Mathematics*	*Complete GED and Essential GED**	*GED Math Problem Solver and Top 50 Math Skills ***
Patterns, Functions, Algebra								
number pattern	24, 48	16	9, 24	7	110	36–38	C: 775–778 E: 369, 380–381	M: 48–50 T: 102–103
geometric pattern	13	1, 47	15	——	110			
variable, expression, equation	12, 19	42	6	21	114–117	292–303	C: 835–851 E: 408–413, 425	M: 14–15, 26–33, 67–68, 90–93, 129 T: 98–99, 104–111
function	——	35, 46	——	24	112			M: 141 T: 54–55
inequality	20, 47	17, 50	——	8	117, 126	304–306	C: 852–854 E: 417–418	
linear equation	49	——	——	——	118–119, 121, 123–125	329–331		M: 259–261 T: 108–109
Problem Solving and Reasoning								
solve problem	7, 10, 27	31	13	——	22–25, 73, 81, 125	51–71	C: 702–707, 841–843 E: 410–413	++ M: 30–31, 43, 79; 116, 131
identify missing/extra information	——	32	——	13	24	51–71	C: 702–707	M: 61, 144–145 T: 72–73
model problem situation, solution	8	33	4	14	26–27, 117, 124	51–71	C: 708–710	M: 28–29, 64–65 191–193
evaluate solution	5	8	——	——	102, 104	51–71	C: 702–707	M: 58–59, 72–74

* C = *The Complete GED;* E = *Essential GED*

** M = *The GED Math Problem Solver* or *The Math Problem Solver;* T = *Top 50 Math Skills for GED Success*

++ In *The GED Math Problem Solver,* all pages of "Check Your Understanding" and "GED Practice" contain computation-in-context problems.

TABE® Forms 9 and 10 are published by CTB/McGraw-Hill. TABE is a registered trademark of The McGraw-Hill Companies.

Skills Inventory Pretest

Part A: Computation

Circle the letter for the correct answer to each problem.

1. $71.8 - 0.5 =$
   A 21.8
   B 66.8
   C 713
   D 71.3
   E None of these

2. $x + x + x =$
   F $3 + x$
   G x^3
   H $3x$
   J xxx
   K None of these

3. $3.1 \times 0.06 =$
   A 186
   B 18.6
   C 1.86
   D 0.186
   E None of these

4. $\dfrac{1}{3}$
   $-\dfrac{1}{6}$
   F $\dfrac{1}{6}$ H $\dfrac{1}{18}$
   G $\dfrac{2}{3}$ J $\dfrac{1}{2}$
   K None of these

5. $8[7 - (2 + 2)] =$
   A 24   C 52
   B 56   D 42
   E None of these

6. 15% of $\$75 =$
   F $15
   G $11.25
   H $60
   J $11.05
   K None of these

7. $-15 + (-5) =$
   A 20   C 15
   B -20   D -15
   E None of these

8. $\dfrac{-30}{5} =$
   F 6
   G 5
   H -6
   J -5
   K None of these

9. $\dfrac{2}{3} + \dfrac{1}{2} + \dfrac{1}{4} =$
   A $\dfrac{1}{3}$ C $1\dfrac{1}{3}$
   B $1\dfrac{7}{12}$ D $1\dfrac{1}{2}$
   E None of these

10. 14.5% of $\square = 145$
   F 1,000
   G 100
   H 10
   J 0.001
   K None of these

11. $0.09\overline{)4.68}$
   A 52
   B 5.2
   C 0.52
   D 0.052
   E None of these

12. $\dfrac{4}{5} \times 6\dfrac{2}{3} =$
   F $6\dfrac{8}{15}$ H $4\dfrac{12}{15}$
   G $16\dfrac{8}{15}$ J $5\dfrac{1}{3}$
   K None of these

13. What percent of 360 is 30?
   A $83\dfrac{1}{3}\%$
   B 0.12%
   C 10.8%
   D 12%
   E None of these

14. $3x - y(x + 5) =$

  F $\dfrac{x}{3} - yx + 5$

  G $2x - 5y$

  H $3x - xy - 5y$

  J $3x - y + x + 5$

  K None of these

15. $3.2 + 75 + 0.006 =$

  A 113

  B 78.8

  C 377.6

  D 78.206

  E None of these

16. $4 - (-12) =$

  F 8 H -8

  G 16 J -16

  K None of these

17. $17 + 6 \times 8 \div 2^2 =$

  A 66 C 29

  B 46 D 41

  E None of these

18. $\sqrt{16} + \sqrt{9} =$

  F $\sqrt{25}$

  G 7

  H 25

  J 12

  K None of these

19. Simplify.

  $3(2y^2 + y) - 2y =$

  A $6y^2 - 3y$

  B $9y^2 - 2y$

  C $6y^3 - 2y$

  D $6y^2 + y$

  E None of these

20. Solve for n.
  $2n + 8 = -6$

  F 1 H -7

  G -5 J 4

  K None of these

21. $(4^2 + 4) - 15 \div 5 =$

  A 17

  B 1

  C $\dfrac{3}{5}$

  D $\dfrac{-3}{5}$

  E None of these

22. $|-5 - 12| =$

  F -7

  G -17

  H 7

  J 17

  K None of these

23. $8\dfrac{1}{2}\%$ of \$36 $=$

  A \$ 2.88

  B \$ 3.06

  C \$ 5.36

  D \$12

  E None of these

24. $(8 \times -4) + -7 \times 2$

  F -72

  G 46

  H -46

  J 72

  K None of these

25. What percent of 350 is 63?

  A 33% C 18%

  B 25% D 13%

  E None of these

Part B: Applied Mathematics

Circle the letter for the correct answer to each question.

1. Darren is a repairman. He drove 9.15 miles for his first service call. He drove 1.7 miles for his second call. Which numbers should Darren round to if he estimates his mileage to the nearest mile?

   A 9 and 1   **C** 9 and 2
   B 8 and 1   **D** 8 and 2

2. Selene received a $200 bonus for being the top salesperson in her group. She spent $80 of that on a new jacket. What percent of her bonus did Selene spend on the jacket?

   F 25%   **H** 40%
   G 35%   **J** 45%

3. What values of m will make the inequality true?

   $$3m + 8 < -10$$

   A $m < 6$ **C** $m < -9$
   B $m < 8$ **D** $m < -6$

4. What number is a factor of all of the numbers in the box?

   | 36 | 15 | 33 | 72 | 54 |

   F 9   **H** 6
   G 4   **J** 3

There are approximately 160 million self-described Christians living in the United States. The graph shows the percent of people who identify with some of the religious groups within that category. Study the graph. Then complete Questions 5–7.

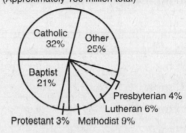

Self-Described Religious Identification of Christians in the U.S.
(Approximately 160 million total)

Catholic 32%
Other 25%
Baptist 21%
Presbyterian 4%
Lutheran 6%
Protestant 3%
Methodist 9%

U.S. Census Bureau: 2003

5. About how many Catholics are there in the United States?

   A 32 million   **C** 75 million
   B 51 million   **D** 60 million

6. If there are approximately 290 million people living in the United States, what is the ratio of Christians to non-Christians?

   F 16:29   **H** 13:29
   G 13:16   **J** 16:13

7. Approximately what fraction of Christians in the United States do not identify with one of the religions listed in the graph?

   A $\dfrac{1}{3}$ **C** $\dfrac{1}{2}$
   B $\dfrac{1}{4}$ **D** $\dfrac{1}{5}$

The "wind chill" is a measure of how cold it feels outside. It takes into account both the temperature and the wind speed. This table shows different wind chills. Temperatures are shown at the top of the table. Wind speeds are shown down the left side. Study the table. Then do Numbers 8–11.

Wind Chill

	30°F	20°F	10°F	0°F	−10°F	−20°F
5 mph	27	16	7	−5	−15	−26
10 mph	16	3	−9	−22	−34	−46
15 mph	9	−5	−18	−31	−45	−58
20 mph	4	−10	−24	−39	−53	−67
25 mph	1	−15	−29	−44	−59	−74
30 mph	−2	−18	−33	−49	−64	−79
35 mph	−4	−20	−35	−52	−67	−82
40 mph	−5	−21	−37	−53	−69	−84
45 mph	−6	−22	−38	−54	−70	−85

8. It is 20°F outside and the wind speeds rise from 10 miles per hour to 40 miles per hour. How much colder does it feel?

   F 3 degrees colder
   G 18 degrees colder
   H 21 degrees colder
   J 24 degrees colder

9. A teacher wants to show how wind chill changes as wind speeds rise. She makes a graph showing the wind chill at 10°F for different wind speeds. Which of these graphs correctly shows the relationship between wind chill and wind speed at 10°F?

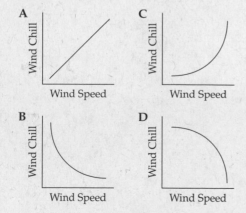

10. If the pattern of wind chill at 10 mph continues, what would be the wind chill at 10 mph and −30°F?

    F −51   H −62
    G −58   J −68

11. The weatherman reports that the wind is from the north at a speed of 25 miles per hour, and the wind chill is −44ºF. What is the actual temperature?

    A 10ºF   C −10ºF
    B   0ºF   D −20ºF

12. Shirley bought 6 pounds of chocolates for $5.11 per pound. She had the candy divided into 12 boxes, and paid $0.75 per box for gift wrapping. Which of these number sentences could you use to find how much Shirley spent in all?

    F $(6 \times \$5.11) + (\frac{6}{12} \times \$0.75) = \square$
    G $6(\$5.11 + \$0.75) = \square$
    H $12(\$5.11 + \$0.75) = \square$
    J $(6 \times \$5.11) + (12 \times \$0.75) = \square$

This map shows the first floor of a popular gym. Study the map. Then do Numbers 13–18.

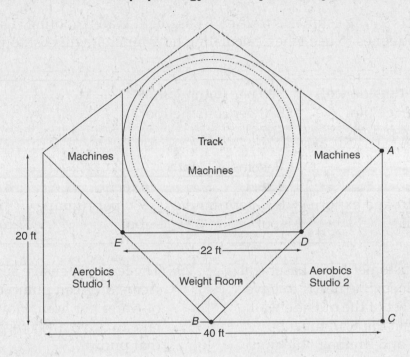

13. The two aerobics studios form congruent triangles. What is the measure of ∠*ABC*?

    A 30°   **C** 45°
    B 40°   **D** 50°

14. What type of polygon is formed by the outside walls of the gym?

    F an irregular hexagon
    G an irregular pentagon
    H a regular pentagon
    J a regular hexagon

15. What is the length of wall *AB*?

    A $\sqrt{800}$ ft   **C** 250 ft
    B 200 ft   **D** $\sqrt{400}$ ft

16. What is the circumference of the outside edge of the track? (Use $\pi = \frac{22}{7}$.)

    F $1{,}521\frac{1}{7}$ ft   **H** $250\frac{3}{7}$ ft

    G 850 ft   **J** $69\frac{1}{7}$ ft

17. What is the area of each aerobics studio?

    A 400 sq ft
    B 800 sq ft
    C 200 sq ft
    D This cannot be determined.

18. The weight room and aerobics studio 2 form similar triangles. What relationship must exist between the lengths of their walls?

    F $\dfrac{AB}{BC} = \dfrac{BD}{BE}$ **H** $\dfrac{AB}{DE} = \dfrac{BC}{BE}$

    G $\dfrac{AB}{BC} = \dfrac{BE}{DE}$ **J** $\dfrac{AB}{BC} = \dfrac{BD}{BE}$

19. Light travels at a speed of 299,792,458 meters per second, or approximately 300,000,000 meters per second. Which of these is another way to write 300,000,000?

    A 3×10^9 **C** 3×10^6
    B 3×10^7 **D** 3×10^8

Read the passage and study the chart below. Then do Numbers 20–23.

Pablo just got a job writing estimates for Acme Basement Waterproofing. The company gave him this list of guidelines to use when calculating how much it will cost to waterproof a basement wall.

		Basement Depth	
Waterproof outside wall	$20 per running foot		
Install drainage tile	$30 per running foot		
Install sump pump	$675		
		4 feet	**6 feet**	**8 feet**
Excavate dirt and expose outside wall	$60 per running foot	$80 per running foot	$100 per running foot

20. Pablo's first customer has a basement that is 6 feet deep. She needs to have 11.5 running feet of the outside wall excavated. Then the wall must be waterproofed and drainage tile must be installed. Which of the following is the best estimate of how much the entire job will cost?

   F $1,000   H $1,400
   G $1,200   J $1,800

21. Pablo's second customer has a basement that is 8 feet deep. He needs 39 running feet of drainage tile installed. He has saved $4,000 to get this done. How much more will he need for the excavation and tile installation?

   A $140   C $2,900
   B $1,070   D $5,360

22. Pablo's third customer says that her basement is $5\frac{1}{2}$ meters deep. Which of the following is the best estimate of her basement depth in feet? (Use the relationship that 1 meter is about 1.09 yards.)

   F 16 feet   H 18 feet
   G 17 feet   J 19 feet

23. The least expensive sump pump that Acme uses can pump up to 20 gallons of water per hour. How long would it take to drain a 1,000-gallon lake using that pump?

   A   8 hours 20 minutes
   B 50 hours
   C   5 hours
   D   3 hours 45 minutes

24. What number comes next in this sequence?

   1, 4, 9, 16, 25, _____

   F 30   H 42
   G 36   J 51

25. There are 62 people in the Freedom Gospel Choir. Twenty-one of those people are men. What percent of the choir is female?

   A 33.3%   C 66.1%
   B 50%   D 45%

Skills Inventory Pretest Evaluation

Use these answer keys to check your pretest. The evaluation charts match each problem in the pretest to a skill area. The charts will refer you to pages in this book that can provide information and practice to help you with problems you missed.

Answer Key—Part A: Computation

1.	D	14.	H
2.	H	15.	D
3.	D	16.	G
4.	F	17.	C
5.	A	18.	G
6.	G	19.	D
7.	B	20.	H
8.	H	21.	A
9.	E	22.	J
10.	F	23.	B
11.	A	24.	H
12.	J	25.	C
13.	E		

Evaluation Chart—Part A: Computation

Problem Number	Skill Area	Text Pages
1, 3, 11, 15	Decimals	32–44, 51–52
4, 9, 12	Fractions	48–63
7, 8, 16, 22	Integers	68–72
6, 10, 13, 23, 25	Percents	82–86
5, 17, 20, 21, 24	Order of Operations	17
2, 14, 18, 19	Algebraic Operations	113–123

Answer Key—Part B: Applied Mathematics

1.	C	14.	G
2.	H	15.	A
3.	D	16.	J
4.	J	17.	C
5.	B	18.	H
6.	J	19.	D
7.	B	20.	H
8.	J	21.	B
9.	B	22.	H
10.	G	23.	B
11.	B	24.	G
12.	J	25.	C
13.	C		

Evaluation Chart—Part B: Applied Mathematics

Problem Number	Skill Area	Text Pages
2, 4, 5, 6, 7, 19, 25	Number and Number Operations	12, 39–40, 50–52, 76–80
8, 18	Computation in Context	45, 64–65, 73, 81, 88–91, 124
1, 20, 22	Estimation	28–29, 35, 54, 146–151
13, 15, 16, 17	Measurement	145–157
14	Geometry and Spatial Sense	130–142
10, 11	Data Analysis	99–107
9	Statistics and Probability	94–98
3, 24	Patterns, Functions, Algebra	110–127
12, 21, 23	Problem Solving and Reasoning	22–29, 64–65, 81, 124

Whole Numbers

Reviewing Basic Addition Facts

Knowing basic math facts is as important to working with numbers as knowing the alphabet is to reading. To work successfully in math, you need to have quick and accurate recall of basic facts.

The **Commutative Property of Addition** states that you can change the order of the addends, and the sum will not change. This means that for each addition fact you know, you also know a related addition fact.

Example $5 + 9 = 14$ and $9 + 5 = 14$

PRACTICE

Find each sum. Work as quickly as possible. Study any facts that you do not know immediately.

1. $2 + 3 =$ _____ $3 + 3 =$ _____ $0 + 1 =$ _____ $7 + 7 =$ _____

2. $8 + 8 =$ _____ $6 + 4 =$ _____ $2 + 2 =$ _____ $9 + 6 =$ _____

3. $1 + 1 =$ _____ $6 + 5 =$ _____ $6 + 3 =$ _____ $1 + 3 =$ _____

4. $5 + 2 =$ _____ $4 + 7 =$ _____ $0 + 0 =$ _____ $4 + 1 =$ _____

5.
$$\begin{array}{r} 4 \\ + 3 \\ \hline \end{array} \qquad \begin{array}{r} 7 \\ + 8 \\ \hline \end{array} \qquad \begin{array}{r} 4 \\ + 4 \\ \hline \end{array} \qquad \begin{array}{r} 8 \\ + 9 \\ \hline \end{array} \qquad \begin{array}{r} 0 \\ + 9 \\ \hline \end{array} \qquad \begin{array}{r} 4 \\ + 0 \\ \hline \end{array}$$

6.
$$\begin{array}{r} 7 \\ + 0 \\ \hline \end{array} \qquad \begin{array}{r} 7 \\ + 5 \\ \hline \end{array} \qquad \begin{array}{r} 3 \\ + 5 \\ \hline \end{array} \qquad \begin{array}{r} 2 \\ + 4 \\ \hline \end{array} \qquad \begin{array}{r} 1 \\ + 2 \\ \hline \end{array} \qquad \begin{array}{r} 3 \\ + 0 \\ \hline \end{array}$$

7.
$$\begin{array}{r} 5 \\ + 1 \\ \hline \end{array} \qquad \begin{array}{r} 6 \\ + 2 \\ \hline \end{array} \qquad \begin{array}{r} 1 \\ + 7 \\ \hline \end{array} \qquad \begin{array}{r} 8 \\ + 4 \\ \hline \end{array} \qquad \begin{array}{r} 6 \\ + 6 \\ \hline \end{array} \qquad \begin{array}{r} 3 \\ + 7 \\ \hline \end{array}$$

8.
$$\begin{array}{r} 8 \\ + 2 \\ \hline \end{array} \qquad \begin{array}{r} 3 \\ + 8 \\ \hline \end{array} \qquad \begin{array}{r} 0 \\ + 2 \\ \hline \end{array} \qquad \begin{array}{r} 1 \\ + 8 \\ \hline \end{array} \qquad \begin{array}{r} 5 \\ + 4 \\ \hline \end{array} \qquad \begin{array}{r} 0 \\ + 5 \\ \hline \end{array}$$

9.
$$\begin{array}{r} 9 \\ + 4 \\ \hline \end{array} \qquad \begin{array}{r} 5 \\ + 5 \\ \hline \end{array} \qquad \begin{array}{r} 8 \\ + 7 \\ \hline \end{array} \qquad \begin{array}{r} 6 \\ + 1 \\ \hline \end{array} \qquad \begin{array}{r} 8 \\ + 0 \\ \hline \end{array} \qquad \begin{array}{r} 7 \\ + 6 \\ \hline \end{array}$$

10.
$$\begin{array}{r} 8 \\ + 5 \\ \hline \end{array} \qquad \begin{array}{r} 9 \\ + 3 \\ \hline \end{array} \qquad \begin{array}{r} 7 \\ + 9 \\ \hline \end{array} \qquad \begin{array}{r} 0 \\ + 6 \\ \hline \end{array} \qquad \begin{array}{r} 5 \\ + 8 \\ \hline \end{array} \qquad \begin{array}{r} 9 \\ + 9 \\ \hline \end{array}$$

Reviewing Basic Subtraction Facts

Since subtraction is the opposite of addition, you can use addition facts to recall subtraction facts.

Example $14 - 8 = 6$ because $6 + 8 = 14$

Note that the Commutative Property does not apply to subtraction. If you change the order of the numbers, the difference will *not* be the same.

PRACTICE

Find each difference. Work as quickly as possible. Study any facts that you do not know immediately.

1. $8 - 6 =$ _____ $7 - 3 =$ _____ $1 - 0 =$ _____ $10 - 5 =$ _____

2. $8 - 8 =$ _____ $6 - 4 =$ _____ $10 - 2 =$ _____ $9 - 6 =$ _____

3. $10 - 1 =$ _____ $6 - 5 =$ _____ $6 - 3 =$ _____ $3 - 1 =$ _____

4. $5 - 2 =$ _____ $7 - 4 =$ _____ $3 - 2 =$ _____ $10 - 4 =$ _____

5.
$$\begin{array}{r} 4 \\ -3 \\ \hline \end{array} \qquad \begin{array}{r} 8 \\ -7 \\ \hline \end{array} \qquad \begin{array}{r} 4 \\ -4 \\ \hline \end{array} \qquad \begin{array}{r} 9 \\ -8 \\ \hline \end{array} \qquad \begin{array}{r} 9 \\ -3 \\ \hline \end{array} \qquad \begin{array}{r} 4 \\ -0 \\ \hline \end{array}$$

6.
$$\begin{array}{r} 7 \\ -0 \\ \hline \end{array} \qquad \begin{array}{r} 7 \\ -5 \\ \hline \end{array} \qquad \begin{array}{r} 5 \\ -3 \\ \hline \end{array} \qquad \begin{array}{r} 4 \\ -2 \\ \hline \end{array} \qquad \begin{array}{r} 2 \\ -1 \\ \hline \end{array} \qquad \begin{array}{r} 3 \\ -0 \\ \hline \end{array}$$

7.
$$\begin{array}{r} 5 \\ -1 \\ \hline \end{array} \qquad \begin{array}{r} 6 \\ -2 \\ \hline \end{array} \qquad \begin{array}{r} 7 \\ -1 \\ \hline \end{array} \qquad \begin{array}{r} 8 \\ -4 \\ \hline \end{array} \qquad \begin{array}{r} 7 \\ -6 \\ \hline \end{array} \qquad \begin{array}{r} 10 \\ -3 \\ \hline \end{array}$$

8.
$$\begin{array}{r} 8 \\ -2 \\ \hline \end{array} \qquad \begin{array}{r} 8 \\ -3 \\ \hline \end{array} \qquad \begin{array}{r} 10 \\ -2 \\ \hline \end{array} \qquad \begin{array}{r} 8 \\ -1 \\ \hline \end{array} \qquad \begin{array}{r} 5 \\ -4 \\ \hline \end{array} \qquad \begin{array}{r} 5 \\ -0 \\ \hline \end{array}$$

9.
$$\begin{array}{r} 9 \\ -4 \\ \hline \end{array} \qquad \begin{array}{r} 5 \\ -5 \\ \hline \end{array} \qquad \begin{array}{r} 10 \\ -7 \\ \hline \end{array} \qquad \begin{array}{r} 6 \\ -1 \\ \hline \end{array} \qquad \begin{array}{r} 8 \\ -0 \\ \hline \end{array} \qquad \begin{array}{r} 10 \\ -9 \\ \hline \end{array}$$

10.
$$\begin{array}{r} 8 \\ -5 \\ \hline \end{array} \qquad \begin{array}{r} 9 \\ -3 \\ \hline \end{array} \qquad \begin{array}{r} 9 \\ -7 \\ \hline \end{array} \qquad \begin{array}{r} 10 \\ -6 \\ \hline \end{array} \qquad \begin{array}{r} 9 \\ -5 \\ \hline \end{array} \qquad \begin{array}{r} 7 \\ -4 \\ \hline \end{array}$$

Reviewing Basic Multiplication Facts

If you change the order of the factors, the product does not change. This rule is known as the **Commutative Property of Multiplication**. Since multiplication is commutative, if you know one multiplication fact, you know a second related multiplication fact.

Example $7 \times 8 = 56$ and $8 \times 7 = 56$

PRACTICE

Find each product. Work as quickly as possible. Study any facts that you do not know immediately.

1. $2 \times 6 =$ _____ $4 \times 4 =$ _____ $2 \times 4 =$ _____

2. $2 \times 3 =$ _____ $8 \times 4 =$ _____ $6 \times 6 =$ _____

3. $6 \times 5 =$ _____ $5 \times 3 =$ _____ $7 \times 6 =$ _____

4. $5 \times 2 =$ _____ $7 \times 4 =$ _____ $8 \times 9 =$ _____

5.
$$\begin{array}{r} 4 \\ \times\,3 \\ \hline \end{array} \qquad \begin{array}{r} 2 \\ \times\,2 \\ \hline \end{array} \qquad \begin{array}{r} 7 \\ \times\,3 \\ \hline \end{array} \qquad \begin{array}{r} 3 \\ \times\,9 \\ \hline \end{array}$$

6.
$$\begin{array}{r} 7 \\ \times\,7 \\ \hline \end{array} \qquad \begin{array}{r} 8 \\ \times\,3 \\ \hline \end{array} \qquad \begin{array}{r} 3 \\ \times\,3 \\ \hline \end{array} \qquad \begin{array}{r} 4 \\ \times\,5 \\ \hline \end{array}$$

7.
$$\begin{array}{r} 5 \\ \times\,9 \\ \hline \end{array} \qquad \begin{array}{r} 7 \\ \times\,5 \\ \hline \end{array} \qquad \begin{array}{r} 2 \\ \times\,7 \\ \hline \end{array} \qquad \begin{array}{r} 4 \\ \times\,6 \\ \hline \end{array}$$

8.
$$\begin{array}{r} 8 \\ \times\,2 \\ \hline \end{array} \qquad \begin{array}{r} 2 \\ \times\,9 \\ \hline \end{array} \qquad \begin{array}{r} 8 \\ \times\,5 \\ \hline \end{array} \qquad \begin{array}{r} 8 \\ \times\,8 \\ \hline \end{array}$$

9.
$$\begin{array}{r} 9 \\ \times\,4 \\ \hline \end{array} \qquad \begin{array}{r} 7 \\ \times\,8 \\ \hline \end{array} \qquad \begin{array}{r} 5 \\ \times\,5 \\ \hline \end{array} \qquad \begin{array}{r} 6 \\ \times\,8 \\ \hline \end{array}$$

10.
$$\begin{array}{r} 7 \\ \times\,9 \\ \hline \end{array} \qquad \begin{array}{r} 3 \\ \times\,6 \\ \hline \end{array} \qquad \begin{array}{r} 9 \\ \times\,9 \\ \hline \end{array} \qquad \begin{array}{r} 6 \\ \times\,9 \\ \hline \end{array}$$

Reviewing Basic Division Facts

Since division is the opposite of multiplication, you can use multiplication facts to recall division facts.

Example $63 \div 7 = 9$ because $7 \times 9 = 63$

In division, as in subtraction, if you change the order of the numbers, the result will *not* be the same.

PRACTICE

Find each quotient. Work as quickly as possible. Study any facts that you do not know immediately.

1. $3\overline{)12}$ = _____ $2\overline{)4}$ = _____ $3\overline{)21}$ = _____ $3\overline{)27}$ = _____

2. $7\overline{)49}$ = _____ $3\overline{)24}$ = _____ $6\overline{)42}$ = _____ $5\overline{)20}$ = _____

3. $5\overline{)45}$ = _____ $5\overline{)35}$ = _____ $7\overline{)14}$ = _____ $6\overline{)24}$ = _____

4. $\dfrac{16}{2}$ = _____ $\dfrac{18}{2}$ = _____ $\dfrac{40}{5}$ = _____ $\dfrac{64}{8}$ = _____

5. $\dfrac{36}{4}$ = _____ $\dfrac{56}{8}$ = _____ $\dfrac{25}{5}$ = _____ $\dfrac{48}{8}$ = _____

6. $\dfrac{63}{9}$ = _____ $\dfrac{18}{3}$ = _____ $\dfrac{81}{9}$ = _____ $\dfrac{54}{9}$ = _____

7. $12 \div 6$ = _____ $16 \div 4$ = _____ $8 \div 4$ = _____

8. $6 \div 3$ = _____ $32 \div 4$ = _____ $36 \div 6$ = _____

9. $30 \div 5$ = _____ $15 \div 3$ = _____ $9 \div 3$ = _____

10. $10 \div 2$ = _____ $28 \div 4$ = _____ $0 \div 5$ = _____

Computing with Whole Numbers

The problems on this page provide review and practice using whole number operations.

PRACTICE

Find each sum, difference, product, or quotient.

1. $18 + 6 + 107 =$ _____ $379 + 1{,}015 =$ _____ $1{,}585 + 273 + 131 =$ _____

2. $4{,}857 - 653 =$ _____ $370 - 128 =$ _____ $5{,}339 - 2{,}157 =$ _____

3. $9 \times 26 =$ _____ $8 \times 357 =$ _____ $562 \times 20 =$ _____

4. $486 \div 2 =$ _____ $650 \div 5 =$ _____ $411 \div 3 =$ _____

5.
```
    4,263          287        1,854          738
  +   488        + 5,660       766        + 2,264
                            +   55
```

6.
```
    4,808        3,000        5,084          543
  - 2,745      - 1,862      -  733        -  278
```

7.
```
     345           96           57           66
  ×   18        ×  75        × 108        × 482
```

8. $8\overline{)648}$ $4\overline{)576}$ $20\overline{)860}$ $35\overline{)4{,}865}$

9. $\dfrac{725}{4}$ $\dfrac{3{,}600}{30}$ $\dfrac{2{,}453}{25}$ $\dfrac{857}{44}$

Working with Exponents and Powers

Exponents

You know that multiplication is a shortcut for repeated addition: $4 \times 3 = 3 + 3 + 3 + 3$
There is also a shortcut for showing repeated multiplication: $3^4 = 3 \times 3 \times 3 \times 3$

With the shortcut for writing repeated multiplication, the number that is repeatedly multiplied is called the **base**. The small raised number is called an **exponent**. The exponent is also called a **power**. It tells you how many times to use the base as a factor.

4^2 2 ← exponent
    4 ← base

4^2 means use the base, 4, as a factor 2 times.
Write two 4s and put a multiplication sign between them.
$4 \times 4 = 16$, so $4^2 = 16$.
The expression 4^2 can be read *4 to the second power*.

To write a number using an exponent,
- check that the same factor is being used. Use that number as the base.
- count the number of times the factor appears. Use that number as the exponent.

Example $7 \times 7 \times 7 \times 7$ All of the factors are 7, so the base number is 7.
                       The base number 7 appears 4 times, so the exponent is 4.

$7 \times 7 \times 7 \times 7 = 7^4$

- A number to the 1st power uses the base number as a factor only 1 time. So 3^1 would be 3, and 5^1 would be 5, and so on. Usually, if a number is to the 1st power, no exponent is used.

- Any number to the zero power is 1. $3^0 = 1$ $52^0 = 1$ $107^0 = 1$

PRACTICE

Write each multiplication using an exponent.

1. $5 \times 5 \times 5 \times 5 \times 5 =$ _____

2. $y \times y =$ _____

3. $9 \times 9 \times 9 =$ _____

4. $7 \times 7 \times 7 \times 7 \times 7 \times 7 =$ _____

5. $25 \times 25 \times 25 =$ _____

6. 4 to the 5th power = _____

7. 8 to the 4th power = _____

8. 1 to the 10th power = _____

Write out the repeated multiplication for each expression. Then find its value.

9. $5^3 =$ _____

10. $2^4 =$ _____

11. $3^2 =$ _____

12. $10^0 =$ _____

13. $1^8 =$ _____

14. 4 to the 4th power = _____

15. 9 to the 3rd power = _____

16. 10 to the 2nd power = _____

Working with Exponents and Powers (continued)

The product of a number to the 2nd power is usually called the **square** of the number. This is because if you show the multiplication as an array with rows and columns, a square is formed.

4^2 can be read *4 to the 2nd power*, or *4 squared*.

$$4^2 = 4 \times 4 = 16$$

A number raised to the 3rd power is called the **cube** of the number. If you show the multiplication with rows and columns, a cube is formed.

2^3 can be read *2 to the 3rd power*, or *2 cubed*.

$$2^3 = 2 \times 2 \times 2 = 8$$

PRACTICE

Give the value of each of the following.

17. $9^2 =$ _____

18. 8 squared = _____

19. 11 squared = _____

20. $12^2 =$ _____

21. $5^3 =$ _____

22. 10 cubed = _____

23. 6 cubed = _____

24. $3^3 =$ _____

Powers of Ten

Our number system is a base 10 system, so our place-value columns of tens, hundreds, thousands, and so on, can be named with powers of 10. Study the relationship between the power and the number of zeros at the end of a number.

Power	Multiplication	Product	Number of Zeros
10^0	1	1	0
10^1	10	10	1
10^2	10×10	100	2
10^3	$10 \times 10 \times 10$	1,000	3
10^5	$10 \times 10 \times 10 \times 10 \times 10$	100,000	5

Notice that with powers of 10, the number of zeros after the 1 is the same as the power of 10. To show the value of 10^8, just write 1 followed by 8 zeros: $10^8 = 100,000,000$.

PRACTICE

Give the value of each power of 10.

25. $10^4 =$ _____

26. $10^6 =$ _____

27. $10^2 =$ _____

28. 10 to the 3rd power = _____

Multiplying by Powers of 10

A shortcut for multiplying by **powers of 10** is to move the decimal point one place to the right for each factor of 10. Write zeros at the end of the number as needed.

Multiply By	Move Decimal Point to Right	Examples	
10 or 10^1	1 place	$10 \times 7.5 \longrightarrow 7.5$	$10 \times 7.5 = 75$
100 or 10^2	2 places	$100 \times 0.479 \longrightarrow 0.479$	$100 \times 0.479 = 47.9$ $10^2 \times 0.479 = 47.9$
1,000 or 10^3	3 places	$1,000 \times 25 \longrightarrow 25,000$	$1,000 \times 25 = 25,000$ $10^3 \times 25 = 25,000$
10,000 or 10^4	4 places	$10,000 \times 7.68 \longrightarrow 7.6800$	$10,000 \times 7.68 = 76,800$ $10^4 \times 7.68 = 76,800$

PRACTICE

Find each product.

1. $10 \times 32 =$ _____

2. $100 \times 72 =$ _____

3. $1,000 \times 847 =$ _____

4. $10^2 \times 375 =$ _____

5. $10^3 \times 127 =$ _____

6. $10^2 \times 355 =$ _____

7. $10 \times 157 =$ _____

8. $100 \times 4 =$ _____

9. $1,000 \times 54 =$ _____

10. $10 \times 5,785 =$ _____

11. $10^4 \times 1 =$ _____

12. $10 \times 742 =$ _____

13. $10 \times 13,476 =$ _____

14. $100 \times 680 =$ _____

15. $1,000 \times 952 =$ _____

16. $10^3 \times 5 =$ _____

17. $10^2 \times 9,604 =$ _____

18. $10^5 \times 72 =$ _____

Finding a Square Root

In mathematics there are certain operations that are inverses or opposites; one operation undoes the other. For example, subtraction is the opposite of addition, and division is the opposite of multiplication.

The opposite of squaring a number is finding a **square root**. You know that $7 \times 7 = 7^2$ or 7 squared, which is 49. The square root of 49 is the number that was squared to get 49. Since 7 was squared to get 49, the square root of 49 is 7. The symbol for square root is $\sqrt{}$, so $\sqrt{49} = 7$.

- To find the square root of a number, think: *What number multiplied by itself equals the number?*

Example   Find the square root of 16.

$$4 \times 4 = 16 \text{ so } \sqrt{16} = 4$$

- The squares for the numbers 1–12 are listed in the table. Squares of integers are called **perfect squares**. Knowing perfect squares makes it easier to find square roots.

Perfect Square	1	4	9	16	25	36	49	64	81	100	121	144
Square Root	1	2	3	4	5	6	7	8	9	10	11	12

For the square root of a number that is not a perfect square, such as the number 32, the number is often left inside the square root symbol. However, you can usually estimate the square root by identifying the two perfect squares the number falls between.

Example   Estimate $\sqrt{18}$.

- Identify the perfect squares that 18 falls between. 18 is between 16 and 25.
- Find the square roots of 16 and 25.

    $\sqrt{16} = 4$ and $\sqrt{25} = 5$

- Estimate the square root.

    $\sqrt{18}$ is between 4 and 5. Since 18 is closer to 16 than to 25, the square root is closer to 4 than to 5.

$\sqrt{18}$ is a little more than 4.

PRACTICE

Find each square root.

1. $\sqrt{100} =$ _____

2. $\sqrt{81} =$ _____

3. $\sqrt{64} =$ _____

4. $\sqrt{169} =$ _____

5. $\sqrt{10,000} =$ _____

6. $\sqrt{144} =$ _____

7. $\sqrt{196} =$ _____

8. $\sqrt{4} =$ _____

Estimate each square root.

9. $\sqrt{55} =$ _____

10. $\sqrt{110} =$ _____

11. $\sqrt{8} =$ _____

12. $\sqrt{75} =$ _____

Following Order of Operations

There may be several operations involved in solving a problem. You can reach a different answer depending on the order in which you do those operations.

Example $3^2 - 2 \times 3 = 21$ or $3^2 - 2 \times 3 = 3$

$$3^2 - 2 \times 3 \qquad\qquad 3^2 - 2 \times 3$$
$$9 - 2 \times 3 \qquad\qquad 9 - 2 \times 3$$
$$7 \times 3 \qquad\qquad\qquad 9 - 6$$

In the example above, the solution on the right is correct. To make sure there is only one correct answer, mathematicians have agreed on an order in which to do the operations. This is called the **order of operations**.
- First simplify the amount inside parentheses.
- Second, calculate amounts with exponents.
- Next, work in order from left to right to multiply or divide.
- Finally, work in order from left to right to add or subtract.

Some people use the letters **PEMDAS** or the phrase *Please Excuse My Dear Aunt Sally* to remember the first letters of the operations in the order they should be done: parentheses, exponents, multiplication, division, addition, subtraction.

Example   Simplify. $30 - (6 - 3)^2 + 8 \div 2 =$ _____

P	parentheses—simplify within parentheses	$30 - (3)^2 + 8 \div 2$
E	exponents—evaluate numbers with exponents	$30 - 9 + 8 \div 2$
M D	multiply or divide—work in order from left to right	$30 - 9 + 4$
A S	add or subtract—work in order from left to right	$21 + 4 = 25$

$$30 - (6 - 3)^2 + 8 \div 2 = 25$$

PRACTICE

Simplify each expression.

1. $23 - (4 \times 5) =$ _____

2. $3^2 \times (8 - 3) =$ _____

3. $(15 - 8)^2 \times 8 =$ _____

4. $7 \times 15 \div 3 - 6 =$ _____

5. $12 + 4^2 \times 3 =$ _____

6. $34 + 6 \times (4^2 \div 2) =$ _____

Write *Yes* if the sentence is true. Write *No* if it is not. If it is not true, give the correct answer.

7. $7 \times 3 + 5 = 26$ _____

8. $3 \times (2 + 5)^2 = 147$ _____

9. $(2^3 + 5 \times 2) + 6 = 32$ _____

Use parentheses to make the sentence true.

10. $5 + 5 \times 6 = 60$

11. $36 \div 6 + 3 = 4$

12. $5^2 - 12 \div 3 \times 2^2 = 84$

13. $20 + 20 \div 4 - 4 = 21$

Rounding Whole Numbers

Sometimes you do not need an exact number; you just need to know *about* how much. This is called making an **approximation** or an **estimate**. One way of estimating is to **round** to a number that is close to the exact amount but that is easier to work with.

To round a number
- Look at the digit to the right of the place you are rounding to.
  - If that digit is 5 or greater, increase the digit in the place you are rounding to by 1.
  - If that digit is less than 5, keep the digit you are rounding to the same.
- Change each digit to the right of the place to which you are rounding to 0.

Examples

Round 45,083 to the nearest 100.

8 > 5
↓
45,083   Since 8 > 5, increase the
              hundreds digit by 1.
              Write 0 in the tens and ones
              places.

45,083 rounds to 45,100.

Round 45,083 to the nearest 1,000.

0 < 5
↓
45,083   Since 0 < 5, the thousands digit will
              remain the same.
              Write 0 in the hundreds,
              tens, and ones places.

45,083 rounds to 45,000.

You can round money to the nearest dollar, ten dollars, and so on. You can also round to the nearest dime or penny. When you are rounding to the nearest dime, the digit that represents pennies will determine what happens to the dimes, and the pennies digit will become zero. When rounding to the nearest dollar, the digit that represents dimes is the one to look at.

Examples $344.75   rounded to the nearest dime is $344.80
                           rounded to the nearest dollar is $345
                           rounded to the nearest ten dollars is $340

PRACTICE

Circle the number that completes the statement and makes it true.

1. 102 rounds to   100   110

2. 397 rounds to   390   400

3. 158 rounds to   150   160

4. $79.36 rounds to $79.30 $79.40

5. $112 rounds to $110 $120

6. 5,999 rounds to   6,000   5,990

7. 23,785 rounds to   23,000   23,800

8. 16,409 rounds to   16,000   17,000

Round each number to the indicated place.

9. 679 to the hundreds place _____

10. 1,723 to the hundreds place _____

11. 1,723 to the thousands place _____

12. 12,314 to the thousands place _____

13. $45.15 to the nearest dollar _____

14. $143.15 to the nearest
    ten dollars _____

15. $57.67 to the nearest
    ten dollars _____

16. $11.35 to the nearest dime _____

Estimating Answers

You can use rounding to estimate sums, differences, products, and quotients. One method is to round each number to the digit in the greatest place-value column. Then compute.

Examples

Addition

$$
\begin{array}{r}
375 \rightarrow 400 \\
+\ 87 \rightarrow +\ 90 \\
\hline
490
\end{array}
$$

Subtraction

$$
\begin{array}{r}
5{,}726 \rightarrow 6{,}000 \\
-\ 2{,}075 \rightarrow -\ 2{,}000 \\
\hline
4{,}000
\end{array}
$$

Multiplication

$$
\begin{array}{r}
736 \rightarrow 700 \\
\times\ 27 \rightarrow \times\ 30 \\
\hline
21{,}000
\end{array}
$$

Division

$$
22\overline{)5{,}862} \rightarrow 20\overline{)6{,}000} \quad (300)
$$

PRACTICE

Round each number and then find the estimated sum, difference, product, or quotient.

1. $5{,}744$
    $+\ 3{,}085$

2. 965
    $\times\ 28$

3. 397
    $-\ 150$

4. 726
    $\times\ 75$

5. $72{,}350 \div 67 = $ _____

6. $497 + 86 + 215 = $ _____

7. $18\overline{)4{,}236}$

8. $2{,}366$
    $-\ 987$

9. $2{,}212$
    $\times\ 367$

10. $8{,}526$
    $+\ 3{,}725$

11. $12{,}962 - 7{,}265 = $ _____

12. $227\overline{)1{,}587}$

Reading Very Large Numbers

You often see or hear large numbers in a shortened form in the news.

Example   As of March 30, 2005, the National Debt was $7.7 trillion. It is estimated that the National Debt will continue to increase an average of $2.21 billion per day!

- The number 2.21 billion means 2 billion, 210 million or 2,210,000,000.
- The number 7.7 trillion means 7 trillion, 7 hundred billion, or 7,700,000,000,000.

Very large numbers are difficult to work with. You can see that using a shortened form makes the amount easier to read and understand.

Expressing very large numbers in shortened form is somewhat similar to rounding, but you do not show all of the digits in the number. Remember, our digits are organized in families that have three members. The most familiar family names, from right to left, are ones, thousands, millions, billions, and trillions.

Example   Write 12,923,870 in shortened form.

12,923,870   Identify the greatest place-value family name of the number. In this number the 12 means 12 million.

12,923,870   Identify the next digit immediately to the right of that family. In this number, it is a 9 in the hundred thousands place.

12.9   Write the digits of the greatest place-value family with a decimal point to the right of them. Then write the greatest digit in the next family.

12.9 million Finally, write the name of the greatest place-value family after the number.

12,923,870 ≈ 12.9 million. This amount means 12 million 9 hundred thousand.

PRACTICE

Circle the letter of the number that can be correctly represented by the shortened form.

1. 3.4 million

   A 3,774,456
   B 34,583,752
   C 3,446,900
   D 3,465,832,720

2. 74.3 billion

   F 74,356,876
   G 74,356,876,489
   H 74,356
   J 743,568,764

3. 7.8 billion

   A 78,834,245
   B 78,512,642,098
   C 7, 834,245
   D 7,851,642,098

4. 234 million

   F 234,045,531
   G 234,670
   H 234,004,489,211
   J 2,340,579,900

Whole Numbers Skills Checkup

1. $\dfrac{6{,}843}{27} =$

   A 253 R12
   B 304
   C 225 R18
   D 253 R4
   E None of these

2. 5,692
    + 2,308

   F 7,990
   G 8,000
   H 8,990
   J 7,090
   K None of these

3. $10^3 \times 6.8 =$

   A 6.800
   B 68
   C 680
   D 6,800
   E None of these

4. 5,008
    − 1,359

   F 4,359
   G 4,759
   H 3,749
   J 3,649
   K None of these

5. $12 + 36 \div 4 - 2 =$

   A 19   C 32
   B 14   D 24
   E None of these

6. $\sqrt{100}$

   F 5   H 10
   G 8   J 20
   K None of these

7. $18^2 \times 3^3 =$

   A 324   C 8,748
   B 972   D 2,916
   E None of these

8. If you estimate $143 + $59 + $89 by rounding to the nearest ten dollars, what numbers should you use?

   F $142, $59, and $89
   G $140, $60, and $90
   H $143, $60, and $89
   J $150, $60, and $90
   K None of these

9. One cookie contains 83 calories. Which of these is the best estimate of the number of calories in a box of 78 cookies?

   A 5,400
   B 5,600
   C 6,400
   D 6,600
   E None of these

10. There are 28 to 31 students in each class at Taylor Grade School. If there are 17 classrooms, which of these is the best estimate of the number of students at the school?

   F 600
   G 1,200
   H 800
   J 1,000
   K None of these

11. Judy read that there were 3,100,000 households with dogs in the United States. Which of these is another way to write 3,100,000?

   A 3.1 hundred thousand
   B 3.1 billion
   C 31 thousand
   D 3.1 million
   E None of these

Problem Solving

Following a Five-Step Plan

Being able to compute accurately is important, but it is only one part of the problem-solving process. The five-step approach outlined here provides a plan that will help you solve word problems.

Identify the question.
- Read the problem. Make sure you understand all of the terms being used.
- Determine exactly what question you are being asked to answer.
- Try to restate the problem in your own words.

Identify the information.
- Read the problem again to find out what information has been given.
- Eliminate information you do not need.
- Decide if there is information missing. If so, is it information you can get?
- Look for signal words that can help you decide what operation(s) to use.

Make a plan.
- Decide what operation or operations you will use.
- Determine the steps to take; what will you do first, second, and so on?
- Set up the problem. Write a number sentence whenever possible.

Carry out your plan.
- Do the computation. Record all of your work.
- Label the answer if a label is needed.

Check your results.
- Go over your computation.
- Make sure you answered the question that was asked.
- Check that your answer is reasonable. Does it make sense?

Here are additional tips that can help you with word problems.
- Read the problem through carefully before you begin to solve.
- Underline the question being asked.
- List the information in the problem that can help you find the answer to the question.
- Cross out any information that is not needed.
- Decide whether an actual answer is needed or whether an estimate will do. Remember, words such as *about how much* or *approximately how much* generally signal that an estimate is called for.
- Look for signal words or phrases that can help you decide what operation to use. The chart on page 25 can help you.

Identifying the Question

Before you start working to find an answer, make sure you understand the question.

PRACTICE

Circle the letter of the question that best describes what the problem asks you to find.

1. In the mayoral election, Jones received 13,487 votes, Smith got 12,506 votes, and Brown had 11,092 votes. How many people cast a vote in the mayoral election?

   A How many more votes than Smith did Jones receive in the mayoral election?

   B How many fewer votes than Smith did Brown receive in the mayoral election?

   C What was the total number of votes that were cast in the mayoral election?

   D None of these

2. Five friends went out for dinner. They shared the cost equally. The meal came to $165.32, including $15.15 tax. They left a tip of $30. What was each one's share?

   F What was the total cost of the meal without tax?

   G How much money did each person pay?

   H What percent of the bill does the tip represent?

   J None of these

3. Herman has already read 70 pages of a 350-page book assigned for class. He has 7 days to finish reading the book before the quiz. He plans to divide the remaining number of pages so he can read the same number of pages each day. How many pages will Herman need to read each day to complete the book on time?

   A How many pages should Herman plan on reading each day?

   B How long did it take Herman to read the first 70 pages of the book?

   C How many pages does Herman still have to read?

   D None of these

4. Maya needs to supply cookies for 20 people. She plans to use a recipe that makes 24 cookies per batch, and takes only 45 minutes from start to finish. If she figures each person will eat 4 cookies, how many batches of cookies will she need to bake?

   F How many times will Maya need to repeat the recipe?

   G How many cookies does Maya need to bake?

   H How much time should Maya allow to bake the cookies needed?

   J None of these

Identifying Too Much or Too Little Information

It is important to read through a problem very carefully before you start working to solve it. There might not be enough information. On the other hand, there might be more information than you need.

PRACTICE

Problems 1–4 each contain unnecessary information. Draw a line through the information that is not needed to solve the problem.

1. Theo had to drive 720 miles in one day. He drove for 3 hours and then took a 20-minute break. He drove another 5 hours and then stopped for an hour for lunch. He drove 4 more hours after lunch to reach his destination. How many hours did Theo spend driving?

2. A scout leader has a project planned for the 6 girls in her troop. Each girl will need a wooden ball, a bottle of paint, a paintbrush, and 6 ounces of beads. The balls cost 45¢ each, paint is 75¢ per bottle, paintbrushes are 89¢ apiece, and beads are 65¢ an ounce. How much will it cost to buy enough beads for the project?

3. Green plants cost about $25 each. For the awards ceremony, Mrs. Sullivan wants to have green plants across the stage, which is 35 feet wide. Each plant is about 2 feet wide and weighs about 2 pounds. If 1 foot of space is left between each plant, how many plants will be needed?

4. Mark is planning to have some carpentry work done in his house. A master carpenter charges $250 a day, while an apprentice charges only $96 a day. The job will take 3 days. How much will it cost Mark to have a master carpenter do the work?

Problems 5–8 do not give enough information to be solved. Tell what additional information is needed.

5. The Darouie family's heating bill for December was $250. How many gallons of heating oil did they use?

_____

_____

6. About how much gas would Arnie's car use on a 300-mile trip?

_____

_____

7. Eleanor bought a sweater on sale for $59.95. How much less than regular price was the sale price?

_____

_____

8. During its recent fundraising drive, the radio station raised $750,000. How much more money than the last fundraiser did this one bring in for the station?

_____

_____

Deciding Which Operation to Use

After you have identified the question and have found information needed to solve the problem, you need to plan how you will use the information.

- Add to put together different amounts and find out how many in all.
- Subtract to compare amounts or find their difference.
- Multiply to put together amounts that are the same.
- Divide to separate into equal groups.

The chart below contains signal words and phrases that can help you to decide which operation to use.

Signal Words

Addition	Subtraction	Multiplication	Division
plus	minus	times	divided by
sum	difference	multiplied by	apiece
total	take away	product	each
added to	subtract	twice, three times, and so on	per
all together	left over	apiece	quotient
in all	how much change	each	how many equal groups
combined	more than		shared equally
increased by	less than		separated into equal groups
	decreased by		

Remember, words such as *about how much* or *approximately how much* generally signal that an estimate is called for.

PRACTICE

For each problem, tell whether you will add, subtract, multiply, or divide. You *do not* have to solve the problem.

1. You buy $128 worth of groceries and write a check for $140. How much change should you get back? _____

2. There will be 26 performances of *The Nutcracker*. About 450 people are expected to attend each performance. Approximately how many people will attend in all? _____

3. You buy a television for $425. Tax is $42. What is the total cost? _____

4. Your family used 1,892 gallons of water in September. About how many gallons of water does that come to per day? (September = 30 days) _____

5. If your family uses 1,892 gallons of water per month, how much will they use in a year? _____

6. You need egg cartons for a craft project. You save 14 cartons. A neighbor gives you 7, and your family collects 25 more. How many egg cartons is that in all? _____

Identifying the Steps to Follow

Each problem below requires two steps to be solved. Circle the letter of the choice that correctly describes how to solve the problem.

1. At Central Middle School there are 556 seventh graders, 397 eighth graders, and 35 teachers. How many teachers are there per student?

   A Add 556 and 397. Then divide the sum by 35.

   B Add 556 and 397. Then subtract 35 from the sum.

   C Add 556 and 397. Then add 35.

2. You need 60 ounces of nuts to make holiday candies. You buy 15 ounces of pecans, 12 ounces of walnuts, and 20 ounces of peanuts. How many more ounces of nuts do you need to buy?

   F Add 15, 12, and 20. Then multiply the sum by 60.

   G Add 15, 12, and 20. Then add the sum to 60.

   H Add 15, 12, and 20. Then subtract the sum from 60.

3. You have six $20 bills in your wallet. You spend $15.96. How much cash do you have left?

   A Multiply 20 dollars by 6. Then subtract $15.96.

   B Add 20 dollars and 6. Then subtract $15.96.

   C Subtract $15.95 from $20. Then multiply by 6.

4. John's daughter eats 2 apples a day. How many dozen apples does she eat in a year? (1 year = 365 days, and 1 dozen = 12.)

   F Add 365 to 12. Divide the sum by 2.

   G Multiply 2 by 365. Divide the product by 12.

   H Divide 365 by 2. Divide the quotient by 12.

5. Derek's living room is 150 square feet, and his family room is 300 square feet. If he buys 500 square feet of carpeting for these two rooms, how much carpet will be left over?

   A Subtract 150 from 500. Then add 300 to the difference.

   B Add 150 and 300. Then divide 500 by the sum.

   C Subtract 150 from 500. Then subtract 300 from the difference.

6. Ellen's property is 45 feet wide and 25 feet deep. How much fencing would she need to enclose all 4 sides of the yard?

   F Add 45 and 25. Then divide the sum by 4.

   G Add 45 and 25. Then multiply the sum by 2.

   H Subtract 25 from 45. Then multiply the difference by 4.

7. Mike must drive an oversized trailer a distance of 1,800 miles. He completes the trip in 3 days, driving 8 hours on Monday, 11 hours on Wednesday, and 10 hours on Thursday. On average, how many miles does he drive each hour?

   A Add 8 hours, 11 hours, and 10 hours. Then subtract 1,800 miles from the sum.

   B Add 8 hours, 11 hours, and 10 hours. Then multiply the sum by 1,800 miles.

   C Add 8 hours, 11 hours, and 10 hours. Then divide 1,800 miles by the sum.

Setting Up and Solving the Problem

Probably the most difficult part of problem solving is setting up the problem: putting together the numbers and operation signs to show the steps you will use. The problem must be set up correctly in order to get the correct solution.

PRACTICE

Circle the number sentence that is set up correctly to solve the problem. Then solve the problem. Remember to check your work and make sure you have answered the question that was asked.

1. For the first three months of last year, Jackie earned $2,500 a month. Then she got a raise and her salary was $3,000 a month. How much did Jackie make last year?

   A $(3 \times \$2,500) + (12 \times \$3,000) = \boxed{}$

   B $(9 \times \$3,000) + (3 \times \$2,500) = \boxed{}$

   C $(12 \times \$3,000) - (3 \times \$2,500) = \boxed{}$

   D $(9 \times \$3,000) - (3 \times \$2,500) = \boxed{}$

   $\boxed{} = \underline{\hspace{2cm}}$

2. There are currently 16,420 unemployed adults in Marion. The pottery factory is scheduled to close in 2 months. When that happens 1,567 adults will lose their jobs. How many adults will be out of work then?

   F $16,420 + 1,567 = \boxed{}$

   G $16,420 - 1,527 = \boxed{}$

   H $\dfrac{16,420 - 1,527}{2} = \boxed{}$

   J $\dfrac{16,420 + 1,527}{2} = \boxed{}$

   $\boxed{} = \underline{\hspace{2cm}}$

3. The drive from Wilber to Crete is 25 miles. The drive from Crete to Lincoln is 65 miles. If you drive at an average speed of 45 miles an hour, how long will it take to drive from Wilber to Lincoln by way of Crete?

   A $(25 + 65) \div 45 = \boxed{}$

   B $(25 + 65) \times 45 = \boxed{}$

   C $(25 + 65) + 45 = \boxed{}$

   D $(25 + 65) - 45 = \boxed{}$

   $\boxed{} = \underline{\hspace{2cm}}$

4. Herman has already read 70 pages of a 350-page book assigned for class. He has 7 days to finish the book before the quiz. He plans to divide the remaining number of pages so he can read the same number of pages each day. How many pages will Herman need to read each day to complete the book on time?

   F $(350 \div 7) - 70 = \boxed{}$

   G $(350 \div 70) \times 7 = \boxed{}$

   H $(350 \div 7) + 70 = \boxed{}$

   J $(350 - 70) \div 7 = \boxed{}$

   $\boxed{} = \underline{\hspace{2cm}}$

Estimating Answers for Word Problems

Sometimes a word problem does not require an exact answer; an estimated answer is enough. Words such as *almost, about,* and *approximately* usually signal that an estimate is called for.

You can often use common sense to come up with an estimate. For instance, you know from experience that a hamburger and an order of fries should cost about $5, not $50. This type of common sense is very useful when you are doing math problems. Get into the habit of using it to check whether your answers make sense.

PRACTICE

Circle the problem number of each situation below that calls for an estimate.

1. The newspaper says there are about 30 businesses downtown, but that figure seems too high to you. You decide to find out the number of businesses for yourself.

2. You just wrote a check for $65. You must subtract that amount from your old balance to find your current balance.

3. You want to know about how many fish are in the Great Lakes.

4. You want to know the approximate number of people who will be attending an annual pancake breakfast.

5. You need 35 milliliters of medicine. You want to know how many teaspoons that is.

6. You want to know the amount of money you spend each year at restaurants.

7. You sell someone a book for $18.42. He gives you a $20 bill, and you need to know how much change to give back.

Use common sense to estimate the answers for Numbers 8–13.

8. The cost of 10 gallons of milk would be about this much.
   - A $5
   - B $1.50
   - C $12
   - D $20

9. About how long would an 800-mile drive on the highway take?
   - F 12 hours
   - G 7 hours
   - H 3 hours
   - J 3 days

10. If you earn $25,000 a year, about how much do you earn in 1 month?
    - A $ 300
    - B $2,000
    - C $10,000
    - D $ 800

11. About how much would 3 ice cream cones cost?
    - F 25 cents
    - G 95 cents
    - H $ 6
    - J $18

12. An adult cat weighs about this much.
    - A 3 lb
    - B 11 lb
    - C 50 lb
    - D 75 lb

13. This is the approximate mass of a wristwatch.
    - F 30 mg
    - G 30 g
    - H 300 g
    - J 300 kg

Rounding to Solve Word Problems

When a word problem calls for estimation, set up the problem as you would any other word problem. Then round all the numbers *before* you do any figuring.

PRACTICE

Use the map below to answer Questions 1–7. Round numbers to the nearest 10, and then estimate each answer.

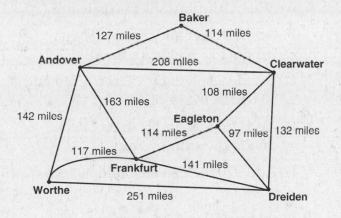

1. About how long is the trip from Clearwater to Worthe via Dreiden?

2. About how much farther is it from Clearwater to Andover than from Clearwater to Baker?

3. About how long is the trip from Dreiden to Frankfurt if you go by way of Eagleton?

4. Three times a month, Shu makes a roundtrip drive from Andover to Worthe. Approximately how many miles is that?

5. Richard must drive from Dreiden to Clearwater, from there to Frankfurt, and then back home to Dreiden. About how many miles will he drive?

6. Frank's car gets 28 miles to the gallon on the highway. About how much gas will he use on a round-trip drive between Frankfurt and Worthe?

7. Approximately how much farther is the trip from Dreiden to Andover if you go through Clearwater than if you go through Frankfurt?

Problem–Solving Skills Checkup

Circle the letter of the best answer to each problem.

1. For which of these situations would you need an exact number?

    A reporting last month's total expenses for your office

    B calculating the number of sheets of paper your office uses in a year

    C reporting the number of calls the reception desk answered last year

    D determining the number of hours workers in your office spend waiting to use the copy machine each year

2. There are 314 students at Hawthorne School. The lunchroom orders 1 pint of milk per student each day. Which of these is the best estimate of the number of pints of milk the school orders in 7 school days?

    F 2,100

    G 2,800

    H 2,500

    J 2,400

3. Hui buys a bedroom set for $5,420. He makes a down payment of $542. The rest must be paid off in 24 equal monthly payments. How much will each payment be?

    A $315

    B $256.75

    C $203.25

    D $195.75

4. AirTite weather stripping comes in 75-foot rolls. Bianca needs 220 feet of stripping to go around her windows and another 50 feet to go around her doors. Which of these shows one way she can figure out how many rolls of weather stripping she needs in all?

    F Add 220 feet and 50 feet. Then subtract 75 feet from the sum.

    G Divide 220 feet by 75 feet. Then add 50 feet to the quotient.

    H Add 220 feet and 50 feet. Then divide the sum by 75.

    J Add 220 feet, 75 feet, and 50 feet.

5. Vic saves $50 to $200 each month. At this rate, how many months will it take him to save $1,000?

    A 20 to 50 months

    B 5 to 20 months

    C 2 to 5 months

    D 5 to 10 months

6. Five crackers contains 77 calories. Which of these numbers is the best estimate of the number of calories in a box that contains 98 crackers?

    F 1,600

    G 4,000

    H 6,400

    J 7,000

7. Raul spends 43 minutes a day commuting to and from work. He worked 243 days last year. Which of these number sentences would give the best estimate of the number of hours Raul spent commuting last year? (60 minutes = 1 hour)

   A $(200 \times 40) \div 60 = \square$

   B $(240 \times 40) \div 60 = \square$

   C $(250 \times 40) \div 60 = \square$

   D $(240 \times 50) \div 60 = \square$

8. Mia planted 12 tomato plants per square yard of her tomato garden. Each plant cost $2. What additional information is needed to figure out how much the tomato plants cost?

   F the number of plants she put in each row

   G the type of tomatoes she planted

   H the number of feet of fencing around the plants

   J the number of square yards she planted with tomatoes

9. There is a toll to cross the bridge each way between Hamlet and Franklin. For cars with fewer than 3 people, the toll is $2. If there are 3 or more people, the toll is only $1.50. In one week, how much money is saved by traveling back and forth each day with 3 or more people in the car?

   A $7
   B $10
   C $15
   D $20

10. A company recorded the weight of their industrial waste products for 1 week. They found that they discarded 173 pounds of paper, 97 pounds of plastic materials, and a combined total of 227 pounds of glass, metal, and wood. If the company has about the same amount of waste each week, which is the best estimate of the number of pounds of waste they produce in 1 year? (1 year = 52 weeks)

    F   26,000
    G   40,000
    H   60,000
    J   100,000

Decimals

Reviewing Decimal Place Value

In our place-value system, amounts *less than 1* are called **decimal fractions**, or more simply, **decimals**. A **decimal point** separates decimals from whole numbers; the decimals are written to the right of the decimal point. Just as with digits of whole numbers, we identify the value of each decimal digit by its place. The names of the place-value columns on either side of the ones column are similar, but the decimal names end with *–ths*.

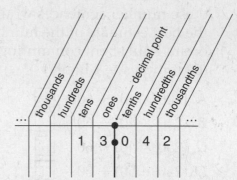

The number 13.042 is greater than 13, but it is less than 14. In this number, the 0 represents zero tenths, the 4 represents four hundredths, and the 2 represents two thousandths.

To read or write a decimal, read the number as if it were a whole number, and then add the name of the place-value column of the digit farthest to the right. The decimal portion of 13.042 is *forty-two thousandths*. The entire number is *thirteen **and** forty-two thousandths*. The word *and* represents the decimal point.

- One digit to the right of the decimal point is tenths.

- Two digits to the right of the decimal point are hundredths.

- Three digits to the right of the decimal point are thousandths.

PRACTICE

Write the number.

1. fifteen and
   six hundredths _____

2. sixty-five hundredths _____

3. forty and four tenths _____

4. nine hundred nine and
   nine hundredths _____

5. two hundred and
   five thousandths _____

6. two hundred
   five thousand _____

7. three hundred
   thousandths _____

8. five and one hundred
   twenty-two thousandths _____

Labeling Place-Value Columns

The columns in the place-value chart can be labeled with words. They can also be labeled using fractions, decimals, or powers of 10.

You know that an exponent indicates multiplication: it instructs how many times to use the base number as a factor.

- The columns for whole numbers can be named with powers of 10 — the ones column is 10^0; the tens column is 10^1; one hundred is 10×10, so the hundreds column is 10^2, and so on.

- Powers of 10 for places to the right of the decimal point have exponents with a minus sign in front of them; tenths are 10^{-1}, hundredths are 10^{-2}, thousandths are 10^{-3}, and so on.

Another way to label the decimal place-value columns is to use decimal notation. For example, 0.1 for the tenths column, 0.01 for the hundredths column, and so on.

Finally, the columns can be labeled with common fractions that have 10, 100, 1,000, and so on, in the denominator.

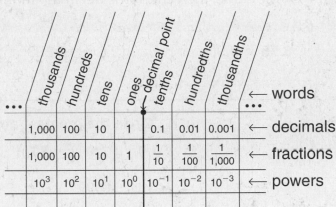

...	thousands	hundreds	tens	ones / decimal point	tenths	hundredths	thousandths	...	
	1,000	100	10	1	0.1	0.01	0.001		← words
	1,000	100	10	1	$\frac{1}{10}$	$\frac{1}{100}$	$\frac{1}{1,000}$		← decimals
	10^3	10^2	10^1	10^0	10^{-1}	10^{-2}	10^{-3}		← fractions
									← powers

PRACTICE

Circle each notation that can be used to correctly label the column named. There may be more than one correct answer for each.

1. thousandths
   - A 1,000
   - B $\frac{1}{1,000}$
   - C 10^3
   - D 0.01

2. tenths
   - F 10^1
   - G 0.1
   - H 10^{-1}
   - J 0.01

3. hundreds
   - A 10^{-2}
   - B 100
   - C 10^2
   - D 0.01

4. hundredths
   - F 10^{-2}
   - G 100
   - H 10^2
   - J 0.01

Comparing and Ordering Decimals

As you move to the right of the decimal point, the value of each digit decreases.

$1 > 0.1$ $0.1 > 0.01$ $0.01 > 0.001$, and so on

When you compare decimals, you compare the values of the digits, not how many digits there are. If one decimal number has fewer digits, you can write zeros after it to make the number of digits equal. For example, to compare 0.2 and 0.099, you can write two zeros after the 2 in 0.2 so each number has 3 digits to the right of the decimal point.

Compare the digits one place at a time.

- Start by comparing the tenths digits. $0.\underline{2} > 0.\underline{0}99$ 2 tenths is greater than 0 tenths.

- If the tenths digits are the same, check the hundredths digits. $0.2 < 0.2\underline{1}$ Each has 2 tenths. But no hundredths is less than 1 hundredth.

- If tenths and hundredths digits are the same, check the thousandths, and so on.

Of course, if there is a whole number with the decimal, compare the whole number amounts first. If the whole numbers are the same, then check the decimal amounts.

Examples
    $3.005 > 2.999$ $8.75 < 8.90$ $12.6 > 12.358$

PRACTICE

Compare. Use >, <, or =.

1. 0.05   0.1
2. 0.102   0.103
3. 0.25   1.0
4. 3.9   3.90
5. 1.01   1.1
6. 0.305   0.34
7. 0.5   0.500
8. 2.390   2.9

Circle the greatest amount in each set.

9. 4.730   4.701   4.735
10. 0.0999   0.9   0.798
11. 0.824   0.286   0.280
12. 2.95   1.886   3

Write in order from least to greatest.

13. 3.30   6.0   3.13   6.002
14. 0.475   0.49   0.46   0.477
15. 1.042   1.04   1.14   1.048
16. 6.089   6.532   6.389   6.523

Rounding Decimals

Rounding decimal numbers is similar to rounding whole numbers. When rounding to a particular place value, look at the digit to the right of that place.
- If the digit to the right is 5 or greater, the digit in the place you are rounding to will increase by 1.
- If the digit to the right is 4 or less, the place you are rounding to will remain unchanged.
- All digits to the right of the place to which you rounded should be deleted.

Examples
0.0826 rounded to the nearest tenth is 0.1.

0.0826 rounded to the nearest hundredth is 0.08.

0.0825 rounded to the nearest thousandth is 0.083.

PRACTICE

Round each number to the nearest tenth.

1. 0.35 _____

2. 4.9186 _____

3. 3.028 _____

4. 0.88 _____

5. 12.97 _____

6. 9.95 _____

Round each number to the nearest hundredth. With money, the hundredths column represents pennies.

7. 0.6419 _____

8. $8.997 _____

9. 10.004 _____

10. $17.462 _____

11. 4.531 _____

12. 10.096 _____

Round each number to the nearest thousandth.

13. 4.0065 _____

14. 11.19562 _____

15. 0.04321 _____

16. 10.2857 _____

17. 0.9995 _____

18. 0.9764 _____

Adding Decimals

When adding decimals, you add tenths to tenths, hundredths to hundredths, and so on. Write addends below one another in column form. Lining up the decimal points helps to get the digits lined up in columns.

You can write zeros after the decimal point to make the number of digits equal. Then start adding at the right and work to the left. Regroup if the sum of a column is 10 or greater. Be sure to write a decimal point in the answer.

Example   Add 0.0013 + 29 + 1.51.

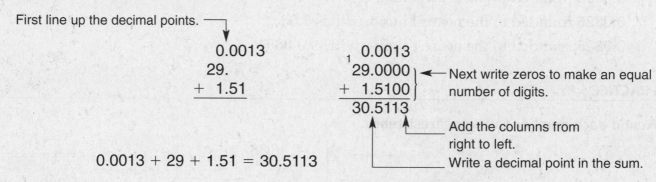

First line up the decimal points.

```
  0.0013              0.0013
 29.                1 29.0000  ← Next write zeros to make an equal
+ 1.51              + 1.5100     number of digits.
                     30.5113
```

Add the columns from right to left.

Write a decimal point in the sum.

0.0013 + 29 + 1.51 = 30.5113

PRACTICE

Rewrite each problem in column form and then find the sum. If there are dollar signs or labels, write them in the answer. Check your answers using rounded values.

1. 46 m + 1.75 m =

2. 0.003 + 0.017 =

3. 5.302 + 0.0309 =

4. 0.0703 + 0.1506 =

5. 0.19 g + 0.015 g =

6. 0.018 + 0.75 + 1.25 =

7. $0.09 + $0.13 + $0.53 =

8. $17 + $2.05 + $0.04 =

9. 129 + 8.1 + 0.03011 =

10. 0.6 + 50 + 12.42 =

11. 1.324 + 0.085 =

12. 0.59 + 0.01 =

Subtracting Decimals

When subtracting decimals, subtract tenths from tenths, hundredths from hundredths, and so on. Write the number being subtracted below the starting amount making sure to line up decimal points and digits in columns. Write a zero in each empty column to make the number of digits in each number equal. Then start subtracting at the right and work to the left. Regroup as needed. Be sure to write a decimal point in the answer.

Example   Subtract 0.16 from 12.7.

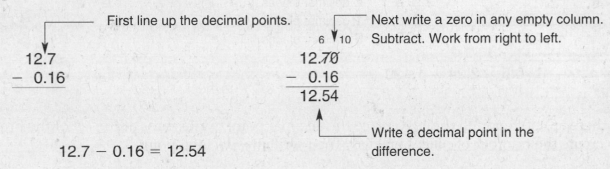

$$12.7 - 0.16 = 12.54$$

A shortcut for subtracting from a row of zeros is to write a digit 1 less than the first nonzero digit from the right. Next, write 10 over the zero farthest to the right, and then write 9 over the other zeros. Then you are ready to subtract.

$$
\begin{array}{r}
24.0000 \\
-\ \ 0.0028 \\
\end{array}
\qquad
\begin{array}{r}
3\ 9\ 9\ 9\ 10 \\
24.\cancel{0}\cancel{0}\cancel{0}\cancel{0} \\
-\ \ 0.0028 \\
\hline
23.9972 \\
\end{array}
$$

PRACTICE

Find each difference. Check your answers using addition.

1. $14.091 - 0.050 =$ _____

2. $0.157\ \ 0.03 =$ _____

3. $21.4 - 0.025 =$ _____

4. $0.145 - 0.073 =$ _____

5. $5 - 0.057 =$

6. What is 0.89 miles subtracted from 7 miles?

7. What is 0.0105 grams subtracted from 4.202 grams?

8. What is twenty-five dollars minus three cents?

9. What is 47 cents subtracted from $1.15?

10. What is 26.4 minus 0.0009?

11. What is 90 minus 0.008?

12. How much greater than 4.09 is 12.25?

13. What is the difference between 85.946 and 87?

14. How much less than 35 is 24.985?

Multiplying Decimals

When you multiply decimals, *do not* line up the decimal points. Ignore decimal points and find the product just as you would if you were multiplying whole numbers. Then count the decimal places in each factor. The total number of digits you count is the number of digits that should be to the right of the decimal point in the product.

Example   Multiply 2.24 by 0.5.

$$
\begin{array}{r}
\overset{1\ 2}{2.24} \\
\times\ 0.5 \\
\hline
1120
\end{array}
$$

$$
\begin{array}{rl}
2.24 & \leftarrow\ 2\ \text{decimal places} \\
0.5 & \leftarrow +1\ \text{decimal place} \\
\hline
1.120 & \leftarrow\ 3\ \text{decimal places} \\
\end{array}
$$
    3 2 1

$$0.5 \times 2.24 = 1.120$$

If there are not enough digits to place the decimal point, write zeros at the *left* of the product to create the number of places needed. Then write the decimal point.

Example   Multiply 0.03 by 0.02.

$$
\begin{array}{r}
0.03 \\
\times\ 0.02 \\
\hline
6
\end{array}
$$

$$
\begin{array}{rl}
0.03 & \leftarrow\ \ 2\ \text{decimal places} \\
\times\ 0.02 & \leftarrow +2\ \text{decimal places} \\
\hline
0.0006 & \leftarrow\ \ 4\ \text{decimal places} \\
\end{array}
$$
    4 3 2 1

Write zeros to the left of
the 6 to have 4 decimal places.

$$0.02 \times 0.03 = 0.0006$$

PRACTICE

For Numbers 1–4, place the decimal point in the answer.

1.
$$
\begin{array}{r}
0.0052 \\
\times\ \ \ \ 20 \\
\hline
104
\end{array}
$$

2.
$$
\begin{array}{r}
67 \\
\times\ 0.05 \\
\hline
335
\end{array}
$$

3.
$$
\begin{array}{r}
50.12 \\
\times\ \ 0.4 \\
\hline
20048
\end{array}
$$

4.
$$
\begin{array}{r}
11.2 \\
\times\ \ 0.4 \\
\hline
448
\end{array}
$$

For Numbers 5–8, write additional zeros as needed and place the decimal point to complete each product.

5.
$$
\begin{array}{r}
0.02 \\
\times\ \ 0.3 \\
\hline
6
\end{array}
$$

6.
$$
\begin{array}{r}
0.4 \\
\times\ 0.009 \\
\hline
36
\end{array}
$$

7.
$$
\begin{array}{r}
0.015 \\
\times\ 0.005 \\
\hline
75
\end{array}
$$

8.
$$
\begin{array}{r}
0.05 \\
\times\ 0.05 \\
\hline
25
\end{array}
$$

Find each product.

9.
$$
\begin{array}{r}
1.25 \\
\times\ \ 346 \\
\hline
\end{array}
$$

10.
$$
\begin{array}{r}
0.02 \\
\times\ \ 5.3 \\
\hline
\end{array}
$$

11.
$$
\begin{array}{r}
0.03 \\
\times\ 0.09 \\
\hline
\end{array}
$$

12.
$$
\begin{array}{r}
1.3 \\
\times\ 0.004 \\
\hline
\end{array}
$$

13.
$$
\begin{array}{r}
2.01 \\
\times\ 4.55 \\
\hline
\end{array}
$$

Multiplying by Powers of 10

A shortcut for multiplying by powers of 10 is to move the decimal point. For example, with $10^2 \times 15.2$, the exponent is 2, so you can move the decimal point in 15.2 two places to the right and the product will be 1,520.

However, when the power of 10 is negative (has a minus sign in front of it), the decimal point will move to the *left*. For example, the result of $10^{-2} \times 15.2$ is 0.152.

When multiplying by a negative power of 10, you can write zeros in front of the number as needed in order to move the decimal point. Remember, in a whole number the decimal point is at the right of the ones place.

Multiply by	Move decimal point to the **left**	Example	
0.1 or 10^{-1}	1 place	$0.1 \times 53 \longrightarrow 53.$	$0.1 \times 53 = 5.3$ $10^{-1} \times 53 = 5.3$
0.01 or 10^{-2}	2 places	$0.01 \times 784 \longrightarrow 784.$	$0.01 \times 784 = 7.84$ $10^{-2} \times 784 = 7.84$
0.001 or 10^{-3}	3 places	$0.001 \times 6 \longrightarrow .006.$	$0.001 \times 6 = 0.006$ $10^{-3} \times 6 = 0.006$
0.0001 or 10^{-4}	4 places	$0.0001 \times 0.12 \longrightarrow .0000.12$	$0.0001 \times 0.12 = 0.000012$ $10^{-4} \times 0.12 = 0.000012$

PRACTICE

Find each product.

1. $0.1 \times 65 =$ _____

2. $0.01 \times 7.9 =$ _____

3. $0.001 \times 3.67 =$ _____

4. $10^{-2} \times 920 =$ _____

5. $10^{-3} \times 127 =$ _____

6. $10^{-2} \times 535.6 =$ _____

7. $0.1 \times 15.7 =$ _____

8. $0.01 \times 24.5 =$ _____

9. $0.001 \times 54 =$ _____

10. $10^{-1} \times 448.5 =$ _____

11. $10^{-4} \times 1.05 =$ _____

12. $10^{-1} \times 112.8 =$ _____

13. $0.1 \times 4.76 =$ _____

14. $0.01 \times 0.68 =$ _____

15. $0.001 \times 0.52 =$ _____

16. $10^{-3} \times 0.016 =$ _____

17. $10^{-2} \times 26.23 =$ _____

18. $10^{-5} \times 0.5 =$ _____

Writing Numbers in Scientific Notation

Scientific notation is a system for writing very large or very small numbers using 2 factors. The first factor is a number between 1 and 10. The second factor is a power of 10. For example, the distance from the earth to the sun, which is approximately 93,000,000 miles, can be written in scientific notation as 9.3×10^7.

When numbers that are *greater than 10* are written in scientific notation, the exponent for the power of 10 is positive.

Example   Write 14,506,000,000,000 in scientific notation.

- Identify the power of 10 to use.
  - Count the number of digits after the digit in the greatest place value column.
  - Use the number you count as the exponent to write a power of 10. In this number there are 13 digits.
- Write the power of 10. Write 10 with an exponent of 13. 10^{13}
- Identify the number between 1 and 10 to represent the original amount.
  - Write a decimal point after the digit in the greatest place value column.   1.
  - Write each digit that follows until only zeros remain.   1.4506
    Do not write the zeros.
- Combine the power of 10 with the renamed number to express the original amount in scientific notation. 1.4506×10^{13}

$$14{,}506{,}000{,}000{,}000 = 1.4506 \times 10^{13}$$

You can check your answer by multiplying. The product should equal the original number.

PRACTICE

Circle the letter of the correct scientific notation for each number. Pay close attention to the exponents.

Write each number in scientific notation

1. 634,000,000
   - A 6.34×10^3
   - B 6.34×10^{-8}
   - C 6.34×10^9
   - D 6.34×10^8

3. 608,000,000
   - A 608×10^6
   - B 6.08×10^6
   - C 6.08×10^8
   - D 608×10^8

5. 2,000,000 = _____

6. 1,322,000,000 = _____

7. 403,000,000 = _____

2. 1,700,000,000
   - F 17×10^9
   - G 1.7×10^{-9}
   - H 1.7×10^9
   - J 1.7×10^{13}

4. 7,589,000,000,000
   - F 7.589×10^{12}
   - G 7.589×10^0
   - H 75.89×10^7
   - J 7.58×10^{12}

8. 3,057,000,000 = _____

9. 8,200,000 = _____

When numbers that are *less than 1* are written in scientific notation, the exponent for the power of 10 is negative. For example, the mass of a particle of dust, which is 0.000000000753 kg, can be written in scientific notation as 7.5×10^{-10}.

Example   Write 0.000000037 in scientific notation.

↓

- Write a decimal point to the right of the first nonzero digit.   0.00000003.7
- Identify the power of 10 to use.
  - Count the number of digits between the new decimal point and the original one.
  - Use the number you count as the exponent for a power of 10. In this number there are 8 digits. Keep in mind that the original number was less than one, so the exponent will be negative.
- Write the power of 10. Write 10 with an exponent of ⁻8. 10^{-8}
- Delete all zeros to the left of the *new* decimal point.   3.7
- Combine the power of 10 with the renamed number to express the original amount in scientific notation. 3.7×10^{-8}

$$0.000000037 = 3.7 \times 10^{-8}$$

PRACTICE

Circle the letter of the correct scientific notation for each number.

Write each number in scientific notation.

10. 0.000001873

    A 1.873×10^{6}
    B 187.3×10^{8}
    C 187.3×10^{-8}
    D 1.873×10^{-6}

12. 0.0000562

    A 5.62×10^{-6}
    B 5.62×10^{5}
    C 5.62×10^{-5}
    D 5.62×10^{6}

14. 0.00000032 = _____

15. 0.00000509 = _____

16. 0.000000077 = _____

11. 0.0008

    F 8×10^{4}
    G 8×10^{3}
    H 8×10^{-4}
    J 8×10^{-5}

13. 0.0005

    F 5×10^{4}
    G 5×10^{5}
    H 5×10^{-4}
    J 5×10^{4}

17. 0.0004 = _____

18. 0.00008351 = _____

Dividing a Decimal by a Whole Number

In division, the divisor (the number you divide by) must be a whole number. However, the dividend (the number being divided) may contain a decimal point. Place the decimal point in the quotient *before* you begin to divide. The decimal point goes directly above the decimal point in the dividend. Then divide as usual.

Example Divide 12.06 by 6.
- Write a decimal point for the quotient directly above the decimal point in the dividend.

$$6\overline{)12.06}$$

- Divide, ignoring decimal points. Remember, once you write the first digit in the quotient, there must be a digit above every remaining digit of the dividend. If a digit is less than the number you are dividing by, write a zero above that digit in the quotient.

$$
\begin{array}{r}
2.01 \\
6\overline{)12.06} \\
-12 \\
\hline
0 \\
-0 \\
\hline
6 \\
-6 \\
\hline
0
\end{array}
$$

$$12.06 \div 6 = 2.01$$

Use multiplication to check your answer.
The product for 6 × 2.01 is **12.06**, so the answer is correct.

PRACTICE

Find each quotient. Check your answers with multiplication. Remember to put a dollar sign in the quotient if money is being divided.

1. $8\overline{)0.168}$

2. $5\overline{)15.25}$

3. $4\overline{)24.52}$

4. $3\overline{)\$15.24}$

5. $7\overline{)\$211.61}$

6. $6\overline{)3.372}$

7. $14\overline{)4.2}$

8. $21\overline{)5.25}$

9. What is $\dfrac{0.391}{17}$?

10. What is $0.093 \div 3$?

11. What is 10.205 divided by 5?

12. What is $\$60.90 \div 30$? (*Remember:* Round dollar amounts to the nearest cent.)

Dividing by a Decimal

The divisor (the number you divide by) must be a whole number. If the divisor contains a decimal point, you will need to move the decimal point *before* you begin to divide. Move the decimal to the right the number of places required to have a whole number. Then, to keep the relationship between the numbers the same, move the decimal point in the dividend the same number of places and in the same direction.

Example Divide 0.429 by 0.33.

- Move the decimal point in the divisor to make the divisor a whole number. Then move the decimal point in the quotient the same way.

$$0.33\overline{)0.429}$$

- Write a decimal point in the quotient above the new decimal point location.

$$0.33\overline{)0.429}$$

- Divide.

$$\begin{array}{r} 1.3 \\ 33\overline{)42.9} \\ -33 \\ \hline 99 \\ -99 \\ \hline 0 \end{array}$$

$$0.429 \div 0.33 = 1.3$$

Use multiplication to check the answer.

If the dividend (number being divided) does not contain a decimal point, write a decimal point to the right of the ones place. Then write as many zeros as are needed to move the decimal point. Place a decimal point in the quotient above the *new* decimal point. Then divide.

Example Divide 50 by 12.5.

- Write a decimal point in the dividend. Write zeros to create additional digits. Then move the decimal points.

$$12.5\overline{)50.} \longrightarrow 12.5\overline{)50.0}$$

- Place a decimal point in the quotient above the new decimal point location. Then divide.

$$12.5\overline{)50.0} \longrightarrow \begin{array}{r} 4. \\ 125\overline{)500.} \\ \underline{500} \end{array}$$

$$50 \div 12.5 = 4$$

Use multiplication to check the answer.

PRACTICE

Find each quotient. Use multiplication to check your work.

1. $1.5\overline{)66}$

2. $0.07\overline{)42}$

3. $0.25\overline{)2.8}$

4. $0.03\overline{)\$25.89}$

5. $0.06\overline{)762}$

6. $0.022\overline{)682}$

7. $0.91\overline{)18.2}$

8. $0.03\overline{)0.6351}$

9. $0.9\overline{)63}$

Writing Zeros to Continue Dividing

When you divide, there is often a remainder. One way to show the quotient is to write the remainder as part of the answer using the letter R. Another way to show a remainder is to write a fraction. However, with decimals, you can write additional zeros in the dividend and continue to divide.

Examples   Divide 20 by 8.   Divide 20 by 12.5.

$$
\begin{array}{r}
2 \\
8\overline{)20} \\
-16 \\
\hline
4
\end{array}
\quad \longrightarrow \quad
\begin{array}{r}
2.5 \\
8\overline{)20.0} \\
-16 \\
\hline
40 \\
-40 \\
\hline
\end{array}
$$

$$20 \div 8 = 2.5$$

$$
12.5\overline{)20.0} \quad \longrightarrow \quad
\begin{array}{r}
1.6 \\
125\overline{)200.0} \\
-125 \\
\hline
750 \\
-750 \\
\hline
\end{array}
$$

$$20 \div 12.5 = 1.6$$

Sometimes as you continue dividing, the same number keeps repeating.

Example   Divide 2 by 3.

- One way to show the repeating pattern is to show a few digits and then write 3 dots.
  $2 \div 3 = 0.666\ldots$
- Another way to write a repeating decimal is to place a bar over the digit or digits that repeat.
  $2 \div 3 = 0.\overline{6}$
- Finally, you may round the quotient to the nearest tenth, or the nearest hundredth, or the nearest thousandth, and so on.

$$
\begin{array}{r}
0.666 \\
3\overline{)2.000} \\
-18 \\
\hline
20 \\
-18 \\
\hline
20 \\
-18 \\
\hline
2
\end{array}
$$

$$2 \div 3 = 0.67 \quad \text{or} \quad 0.667 \quad \text{or} \quad 0.6667$$

PRACTICE

Find each quotient. If the division does not end, divide to the thousandths place and then round the quotient to the nearest hundredth.

1. $4\overline{)6}$

2. $4\overline{)7}$

3. $3\overline{)35}$

4. $9\overline{)47}$

5. $11\overline{)39}$

6. $7\overline{)40}$

7. $11\overline{)45}$

8. $6\overline{)89}$

9. $12\overline{)4}$

Using Decimals to Solve Word Problems

Solve. Some problems can be solved in one step, but some need two steps or even three steps to find a solution. (*Note:* All dollar amounts should be rounded to the nearest cent.)

1. When Dan began driving to Cleveland, the odometer on his car read exactly 2,342.8 miles. When he got to Cleveland, it read 2,690.2. How many miles was the trip?

   _____

2. A farm produces about 3,000 eggs each day and sells them for $0.80 *per dozen*. On average, how much money does the farm get for its eggs each day?

   _____

3. The top running speed for a human is 23.13 miles per hour. A greyhound can run 39.35 miles per hour. How much faster than a human is a greyhound?

   _____

4. Gorgio paid $5.33 for 1.3 pounds of beef. How much did he pay per pound?

   _____

5. Kyoko is making an iron support for her grape plants. She needs 2 long lengths of pipe each 3.25 feet long. She also needs a shorter length of pipe 2.5 feet long. How much pipe does she need in all?

   _____

6. Three times each week Charlene runs a course that is 3.4 miles long. How many miles will she run in a year? (1 year = 52 weeks)

   _____

7. Carl earns $4.84 per hour. Ricky's hourly pay is 3.5 times higher than Carl's. How much does Ricky earn per hour?

   _____

8. Roses cost $0.89 each. How many roses can you buy for $17.80?

   _____

9. You rent a car from a company that charges 43 cents per mile. When you pick up the car, the odometer reads 11,542.5. When you return the car, the odometer reads 11,562.7. How much will you be charged for mileage?

   _____

10. A group of 27 students went to see a play. There was a $4.50 per person charge for the play, and it cost $94.50 to rent the bus. If the total cost was divided equally among the 27 students, how much did each pay?

   _____

11. Larry bought a large rug for $650. He made a down payment of $98. The remainder was paid off in 12 equal payments. How much was each payment?

   _____

12. How much change should you get from a $10 bill if you buy 2 muffins at $1.69 each, and pay $0.26 tax?

   _____

Decimals Skills Checkup

Circle the letter of the correct answer to each problem. Try crossing out unreasonable answers before you start to work.

1. $0.851 + 0.08 =$
   - A 0.931
   - B 1.651
   - C 0.859
   - D 9.31
   - E None of these

2. $11.57 - 0.7 =$
   - F 10.67
   - G 11.87
   - H 10.87
   - J 11.50
   - K None of these

3. $25.02 \times 30 =$
   - A   75.6
   - B 75,060
   - C   75.06
   - D   750.6
   - E None of these

4. $3.1\overline{)992}$
   - F 320
   - G 32
   - H   3.2
   - J   33
   - K None of these

5. $2.5 \div 0.05 =$
   - A 5
   - B 0.5
   - C   0.05
   - D 50
   - E None of these

6. Which group of numbers is in order from least to greatest?
   - F 5.619, 5.61, 5.19, 5.2
   - G 5.61, 5.619, 5.19, 5.2
   - H 5.19, 5.61, 5.619, 5.2
   - J 5.19, 5.2, 5.61, 5.619

7. You are estimating by rounding to the nearest whole number. What numbers should you use to divide 5.167 by 4.789?
   - A $5 \div 5$
   - B $5 \div 4$
   - C $5.2 \div 4.8$
   - D $5.1 \div 4.7$

8. There are 3.96 million people living in Cleveland and there are 2.2 million households. Which of these is the best estimate of the average number of people who live in each household?
   - F 2
   - G 1.5
   - H 1.3
   - J 1

9. It takes Rae Lynn about 12 minutes to make one potholder that she sells for $5.50. How much does she collect for 1 hour's worth of work? (1 = 60 min.)
   - A $6.60
   - B $25.83
   - C $27.50
   - D $11

10. One box of cereal weighs 0.781 pounds. Each carton contains 18 boxes of cereal. Which of these is the best estimate of how much each carton weighs?
    - F 10.5 pounds
    - G   7.8 pounds
    - H 14 pounds
    - J 18 pounds

11.

$$\begin{array}{r} \$109.56 \\ +\quad 98.90 \\ \hline \end{array}$$

A $208.46
B $198.46
C $207.46
D $308.46
E None of these

12.

$$\begin{array}{r} 99.081 \\ -\ 87.809 \\ \hline \end{array}$$

F 12.272
G   0.11272
H 11.282
J 11.272
K None of these

13.

$5\overline{)192}$

A 39
B 38.4
C 37.4
D   3.84
E None of these

14.

$4.75 \times 10^{3} =$

F   475
G   0.00475
H   0.0475
J 4,750
K None of these

15.

$0.008 \times 0.07 =$

A 0.056
B 0.0056
C 0.00056
D 0.000056
E None of these

16. Which decimals can be added to 0.07 to make a sum that is greater than 1?

F any decimal greater than 0.3
G any decimal greater than 0.03
H any decimal greater than 0.33
J any decimal greater than 0.93

17. At Bob's Burger Barn, it was found that the clerks spent an average of 3.456 minutes with each customer. Bob reported this number as 3.5 minutes. To what place did he round the number?

A ones
B thousandths
C tenths
D fifths

18. What does the 3 in 1.80367 represent?

F 3 hundredths
G 3 thousands
H 3 tenths
J 3 thousandths

19. Which number sentence is true?

A 0.013 < 0.0109
B 0.782 < 0.882
C 1 < 0.789
D 0.45 < 0.097

20. A centimeter equals 0.00001 kilometers. Which of the following shows this measurement in scientific notation?

F 1×10^{5}
G 1×10^{6}
H 1×10^{-5}
J 1×10^{-6}

Fractions

Reviewing the Meaning of Fractions

Knowledge of fractions is important for working in mathematics as well as for carrying out many daily activities. A fraction represents a part of something that has been divided equally. Fractions are written in the form $\frac{a}{b}$, where the **denominator** (bottom number) b is a non-zero number that tells how many equal parts are in a unit or whole, and the **numerator** (top number) a represents how many of those equal parts are being considered.

$$\frac{a}{b} = \frac{\text{numerator}}{\text{denominator}} = \frac{\text{number of equal parts considered}}{\text{number of equal parts in 1 whole unit}}$$

Example Which of these diagrams show $\frac{3}{5}$ of the shape shaded?

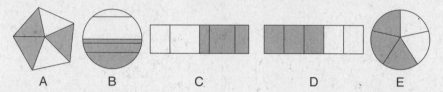

A   B   C   D   E

The fraction $\frac{3}{5}$ tells us something has been divided into **5** equal parts, and we are talking about **3** of those parts. Each figure has **3** of **5** parts shaded, but the parts in some figures are not equal.

Figures A, D, and E each show $\frac{3}{5}$ of the shape shaded.

When each member of the group is considered to be an equal part of the group, a fraction can describe part of that group.

Example The soccer team had **200** T-shirts printed. They sold **100** of the shirts. What fraction of the T-shirts was sold?

Each T-shirt is **1** of 200 shirts in the group.

$$\frac{\text{T-shirts sold}}{\text{total number of T-shirts}} = \frac{100}{200} = \frac{1}{2}$$

$\frac{1}{2}$ of the T-shirts were sold.

PRACTICE

Use the statistics in the table at right.

Write the fraction for 18–24 year olds

1. with less than high school education. _____

2. with high school education or higher. _____

3. with no college. _____

4. with a bachelor's degree. _____

Education Levels of 18 to 24 Year Olds In U.S.
(to the nearest million)

Education Level Attained	Number
Less than high school graduate	7 million
High school graduation (or equivalency)	8 million
Some college or associate degree	10 million
Bachelor's degree or higher	2 million

Source: U.S. Census Bureau

Renaming Mixed Numbers and Improper Fractions

In **proper fractions** such as $\frac{2}{5}$ and $\frac{8}{11}$, the numerator is less than the denominator.

In **improper fractions**, such as $\frac{5}{3}$ and $\frac{15}{14}$, the numerator is greater than the denominator. An improper fraction names an amount greater than 1 whole unit.

A **mixed number** is a combination of a whole number together with a fraction. Examples of mixed numbers are $1\frac{2}{3}$ and $5\frac{7}{10}$.

A mixed number can be renamed as an improper fraction, and an improper fraction can be renamed as a mixed number.

• Multiply to change a mixed number to an improper fraction.

Example   Write $2\frac{2}{3}$ as an improper fraction.

$2\frac{2}{3}$ $3 \times 2 = 6$

• Multiply the whole number by the denominator of the fraction.
• Add the product to the numerator.
• The denominator remains the same.

$$\frac{6+2}{3} = \frac{8}{3}$$

$$2\frac{2}{3} = \frac{8}{3}$$

• Divide to change an improper fraction to a mixed number. Remember that a fraction can be read as a division problem, top divided by bottom—numerator divided by denominator.

Example   Write $\frac{14}{3}$ as a mixed number.

• Divide the numerator by the denominator. $\frac{14}{3} \longrightarrow 3\overline{)14}$
• The quotient becomes the whole number of the mixed number. If there is a remainder, use it as the numerator for the fraction of the mixed number.
• The denominator remains the same.

$$\frac{14}{3} = 4\frac{2}{3}$$

$$\begin{array}{r} 4 \leftarrow \text{whole number} \\ 3\overline{)14} \\ \underline{-12} \\ 2 \leftarrow \text{numerator} \end{array}$$
denominator of fraction — of fraction

PRACTICE

Rename mixed numbers to improper fractions.

1. $1\frac{4}{5} = $ _____ $2\frac{1}{4} = $ _____ $1\frac{1}{8} = $ _____ $3\frac{1}{2} = $ _____

2. $2\frac{1}{9} = $ _____ $1\frac{3}{7} = $ _____ $2\frac{5}{6} = $ _____ $4\frac{1}{10} = $ _____

Rename improper fractions to mixed numbers.

3. $\frac{10}{3} = $ _____ $\frac{19}{8} = $ _____ $\frac{7}{4} = $ _____ $\frac{19}{16} = $ _____

4. $\frac{13}{5} = $ _____ $\frac{17}{12} = $ _____ $\frac{15}{8} = $ _____ $\frac{5}{2} = $ _____

Finding Equivalent Fractions

The same fractional amount can be named in different ways. For example, $\frac{1}{4} = \frac{2}{8} = \frac{3}{12}$, and so on. Such fractions are called **equivalent fractions**.

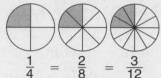

$$\frac{1}{4} = \frac{2}{8} = \frac{3}{12}$$

When a fraction is changed to **higher terms**, the whole unit is divided into a greater number of equal parts. Each part becomes smaller, so more of them are needed. To rename a fraction to higher terms, multiply the numerator and denominator by the same amount. This is the same as multiplying by one; both numbers will become higher.

Example $\qquad \frac{3}{5} = \frac{4 \times 3}{4 \times 5} = \frac{12}{20} \qquad\qquad \frac{3}{5} = \frac{12}{20}$

You can also rename a fraction to **lower terms**. Here, each part is bigger, so fewer of them are needed. The numbers in the numerator and denominator become smaller. This process is called **simplifying** or **reducing** the fraction. To simplify a fraction, divide the numerator and denominator by the same number.

Example $\qquad \frac{8}{12} = \frac{8 \div 4}{12 \div 4} = \frac{2}{3} \qquad\qquad \frac{8}{12} = \frac{2}{3}$

When the only number that can evenly divide both the numerator and denominator is 1, the fraction is in **simplest terms**.

PRACTICE

Write the missing number to name each fraction to higher terms.

1. $\frac{4}{5} = \frac{\square}{15}$ $\qquad\qquad \frac{3}{10} = \frac{9}{\square}$ $\qquad\qquad \frac{5}{6} = \frac{10}{\square}$ $\qquad\qquad \frac{7}{8} = \frac{\square}{24}$

2. $\frac{1}{8} = \frac{5}{\square}$ $\qquad\qquad \frac{4}{7} = \frac{\square}{21}$ $\qquad\qquad \frac{1}{9} = \frac{\square}{36}$ $\qquad\qquad \frac{3}{4} = \frac{\square}{100}$

Write the missing number to name each fraction to lower terms.

3. $\frac{10}{18} = \frac{\square}{9}$ $\qquad\qquad \frac{20}{24} = \frac{5}{\square}$ $\qquad\qquad \frac{12}{16} = \frac{3}{\square}$ $\qquad\qquad \frac{5}{35} = \frac{\square}{7}$

4. $\frac{15}{20} = \frac{\square}{4}$ $\qquad\qquad \frac{8}{10} = \frac{4}{\square}$ $\qquad\qquad \frac{18}{24} = \frac{\square}{8}$ $\qquad\qquad \frac{10}{25} = \frac{2}{\square}$

Write each fraction in simplest terms.

5. $\frac{9}{12} =$ $\qquad\qquad \frac{20}{40} =$ $\qquad\qquad \frac{12}{36} =$ $\qquad\qquad \frac{9}{27} =$

6. $\frac{15}{24} =$ $\qquad\qquad \frac{4}{18} =$ $\qquad\qquad \frac{6}{60} =$ $\qquad\qquad \frac{12}{18} =$

Changing Fractions to Decimals

Fractions and decimals are different ways of naming the same amount. Fractions that have denominators of 10, 100, 1,000, and so on, are easy to rename. As you read the fraction, you name the decimal.

Examples

$\frac{3}{10}$ ⟶ three tenths ⟶ 0.3 $\frac{9}{100}$ ⟶ nine hundredths ⟶ 0.09

PRACTICE

Write each fraction as a decimal.

1. $\frac{12}{100} =$ _____

2. $\frac{7}{10} =$ _____

3. $\frac{3}{1000} -$ _____

4. $2\frac{9}{10} =$ _____

You can use division to find the decimal name for any fraction; divide the numerator by the denominator. In many cases the division will terminate, or end, after a few digits. However, sometimes a repeating pattern occurs.

Examples

$\frac{3}{8}$ ⟶

$$\begin{array}{r} 0.375 \\ 8\overline{)3.000} \\ -24 \\ \hline 60 \\ -56 \\ \hline 40 \\ -40 \\ \hline 0 \end{array}$$

$\frac{7}{15}$ ⟶

$$\begin{array}{r} 0.466 \\ 15\overline{)7.000} \\ -60 \\ \hline 100 \\ -90 \\ \hline 100 \\ -90 \\ \hline 10 \end{array}$$

$\frac{3}{8} = 0.375$ $\frac{7}{15} - 0.466...$ or $0.4\overline{6}$

A digit or set of digits that continually repeats, as does the 6 when you divide 7 by 15, is called a **repeating decimal**. Here are two ways repeating decimals are shown.

0.466...   Write the repeating digit or digits with one repeat followed by three dots.

$0.4\overline{6}$ Place a bar over the digit or digits that repeat.

PRACTICE

Divide to find the decimal equivalent of each fraction.

5. $\frac{1}{3} =$ _____

8. $\frac{7}{12} =$ _____

11. $\frac{4}{9} =$ _____

6. $\frac{4}{5} =$ _____

9. $\frac{3}{4} =$ _____

12. $\frac{1}{6} =$ _____

7. $\frac{1}{11} =$ _____

10. $\frac{1}{4} =$ _____

13. $\frac{5}{8} =$ _____

Changing Decimals to Fractions

To change a decimal to its fraction equivalent, follow these steps:

- Write the digits to the right of the decimal point as the numerator of a fraction. Do not write the decimal point.
- Use the name of the place-value column farthest to the right in the decimal to identify the denominator.

You may be able to simplify the resulting fraction.

Examples

Decimal	Words	Identify Numerator and Denominator	Fraction
0.8	eight tenths	denominator is 10 numerator is 8	$\frac{8}{10} = \frac{4}{5}$
0.25	twenty-five hundredths	denominator is 100 numerator is 25	$\frac{25}{100} = \frac{1}{4}$

When a whole number is followed by a decimal, change the decimal portion to a fraction and write the fraction after the whole number.

Example   Write 1.09 in fraction form.

$$0.09 = \frac{9}{100}, \text{ so } 1.09 = 1\frac{9}{100}$$

PRACTICE

Write each decimal as a fraction. Simplify if the fraction is not in lowest terms.

1. 0.35 = _____

2. 0.015 = _____

3. 0.105 = _____

4. 0.18 = _____

5. 0.6 = _____

6. 1.54 = _____

7. 2.08 = _____

8. 35.20 = _____

9. 0.42 = _____

10. 7.65 = _____

11. 3.120 = _____

12. 0.44 = _____

13. 5.08 = _____

14. 0.012 = _____

Comparing and Ordering Fractions

To compare fractions, first check their denominators. If the denominators are the same, the fraction with the greater number in the numerator is greater.

Example   Compare $\frac{7}{15}$ and $\frac{11}{15}$.

Since both fractions have a denominator of 15, check the numerators. 7 is less than 11.

$$\frac{7}{15} < \frac{11}{15}$$

If the numerators are the same, compare the denominators. The fraction with the lower number in the denominator is greater.

Example   Compare $\frac{5}{11}$ and $\frac{5}{7}$.

Both fractions name 5 parts, but 7ths are bigger than 11ths.

$$\frac{5}{11} < \frac{5}{7}$$

Of course, if both numerators and denominators are the same, the fractions are equal. But when *neither* the denominators *nor* the numerators are the same, rename one or both fractions. One method is to rename to a common denominator. Then compare numerators.

Example   Compare $\frac{3}{4}$ and $\frac{5}{8}$.

Fourths are easily renamed to eighths. $\frac{3}{4} = \frac{2 \times 3}{2 \times 4} = \frac{6}{8}$

$$\frac{6}{8} > \frac{5}{8}, \text{ so } \frac{3}{4} > \frac{5}{8}$$

PRACTICE

Compare. Write $>$, $<$, or $=$ between each pair of fractions.

1. $\frac{5}{7}$ $\frac{11}{14}$

2. $\frac{7}{12}$ $\frac{7}{9}$

3. $\frac{6}{10}$ $\frac{7}{10}$

4. $\frac{1}{5}$ $\frac{4}{20}$

5. $\frac{4}{8}$ $\frac{7}{14}$

6. $\frac{3}{5}$ $\frac{4}{5}$

7. $\frac{5}{12}$ $\frac{8}{24}$

8. $\frac{6}{10}$ $\frac{6}{20}$

Write each set of fractions in order from least to greatest. Rename fractions as needed.

9. $\frac{2}{4}$, $\frac{4}{5}$, $\frac{5}{8}$

10. $\frac{3}{4}$, $\frac{2}{3}$, $\frac{7}{12}$

11. $\frac{4}{7}$, $\frac{1}{2}$, $\frac{9}{14}$

12. $\frac{19}{24}$, $\frac{5}{12}$, $\frac{2}{3}$

Estimating with Fractions

When you round a number, the general rule is that if there is half or more of the unit you are rounding to, you count it as an extra unit and round up. If you have less than half of the unit you are rounding to, the number of units you have does not change—you lose the extra amount.

To estimate fractional amounts, you should be able to easily identify whether a fraction is less than, equal to, or greater than $\frac{1}{2}$.

- A fraction is equal to $\frac{1}{2}$ if, when you double the numerator, you get the denominator. Another way to say this is, if you divide the denominator by 2 and get the numerator, the fraction is equal to $\frac{1}{2}$.

Example $\frac{8}{16} = \frac{1}{2}$ Half of 16 is 8, so $\frac{8}{16} = \frac{1}{2}$.

- A fraction is greater than $\frac{1}{2}$ if the numerator is greater than half of the denominator.

Example $\frac{13}{20} > \frac{1}{2}$ Half of 20 is 10, and 13 is greater than 10, so $\frac{13}{20} > \frac{1}{2}$.

In a common fraction, the closer the amount of the numerator is to the denominator, the closer the fraction is to 1 whole. $\frac{17}{20}$ is closer to one than $\frac{15}{20}$.

- A fraction is less than $\frac{1}{2}$ if the numerator is less than half the denominator.

Example $\frac{3}{10} < \frac{1}{2}$ Half of 10 is 5, and 3 is less than 5, so $\frac{3}{10} < \frac{1}{2}$.

PRACTICE

Compare. Write $>$, $<$, or $=$ between each pair of fractions.

1. $\frac{3}{4}$ $\frac{1}{2}$

2. $\frac{7}{12}$ $\frac{1}{2}$

3. $\frac{5}{16}$ $\frac{1}{2}$

4. $\frac{18}{20}$ $\frac{1}{2}$

5. $\frac{14}{28}$ $\frac{1}{2}$

Circle the letter of the most accurate statement.

6. Three-fifths of the people who were surveyed voted for Candidate A.

   A Over half voted for candidate A.
   B Less than half voted for candidate A.
   C Candidate A got half of the votes.

7. Joe ran $\frac{5}{10}$ of a mile.

   F Joe ran more than $\frac{1}{2}$ of a mile.
   G Joe ran less than $\frac{1}{2}$ of a mile.
   H Joe ran exactly $\frac{1}{2}$ of a mile.

Using Divisibility Rules

Suppose there are 159 boxes that need to be filled and you want to know if the number of boxes can be divided evenly among 3 workers. You can quickly find out if you know the **divisibility rule** for 3. A number is **divisible** (divided with no remainder) by 3 if the sum of its digits is divisible by 3. The sum of the digits of 159 is 15, $(1 + 5 + 9 = 15)$ and 15 is divisible by 3, so 159 is divisible by 3.

Knowing divisibility rules comes in handy when simplifying fractions. Here are some more divisibility rules:

Divisible by	Rule	Examples
2	Even numbers—numbers with 0, 2, 4, 6, or 8 in the ones place—are divisible by 2.	3,976 is an even number. 3,976 is divisible by 2.
4	If the last two digits of the number (the tens and ones digits) are divisible by 4, the number is divisible by 4.	The last two digits of 712 are 12. 12 is divisible by 4. 712 is divisible by 4.
5	Multiples of 5 are 5, 10, 15, 20, 25, and so on. If the number has 0 or 5 in the ones place, it is divisible by 5.	80 has a 0 in the ones place. 345 has a 5 in the ones place. Both 80 and 345 are divisible by 5.
6	If the number is even *and* it is divisible by 3, it is divisible by 6.	72 is an even number. $7 + 2 = 9$, and 9 is divisible by 3. 72 is divisible by 6.
8	If the last three digits of the number are divisible by 8, the number is divisible by 8.	The last three digits of 65,408 are 408. 408 is divisible by 8. 65,408 is divisible by 8.
9	If the sum of the digits is a multiple of 9, the number is divisible by 9.	$24{,}534 \rightarrow 2 + 4 + 5 + 3 + 4 = 18$ 18 is a multiple of 9. 24,534 is divisible by 9.
10	If the number has 0 in the ones place, it is divisible by 10.	3,560 has 0 in the ones place. 3,560 is divisible by 10.

PRACTICE

Circle the correct answers. There is more than one correct answer for each problem.

1. These numbers are divisible by *both* 3 and 9.
   A 732   C 198
   B 2,193   D 41,040

2. These numbers are divisible by 4.
   F 652   • H 421
   G 412   J 96

3. These numbers are divisible by *both* 3 and 4.
   A 162   C 64
   B 232   D 6,324

4. These numbers are divisible by 2, 5, and 10.
   F 750   H 300
   G 30   J 125

Adding and Subtracting Like Fractions

Fractions are "like" if they have the same denominator. They are "unlike" if they have different denominators. To add or subtract like fractions, keep the same denominator and add or subtract the numerators. Simplify the result if it is not in lowest terms.

Examples   Add $\frac{3}{8} + \frac{1}{8}$.

$$\frac{3}{8} + \frac{1}{8} = \frac{3+1}{8} \leftarrow \text{Add the numerators.}$$

$$= \frac{4}{8} = \frac{1}{2}$$

$$\frac{3}{8} + \frac{1}{8} = \frac{1}{2}$$

Subtract $\frac{4}{15}$ from $\frac{9}{15}$.

$$\frac{9}{15} - \frac{4}{15} = \frac{9-4}{15} \leftarrow \begin{array}{l}\text{Subtract the}\\ \text{numerators.}\end{array}$$

$$= \frac{5}{15} = \frac{1}{3}$$

$$\frac{9}{15} - \frac{4}{15} = \frac{1}{3}$$

When working with mixed numbers, first add or subtract the fractions and simplify the sum. Then add or subtract the whole numbers.

Examples   Add $3\frac{3}{4}$ and $2\frac{3}{4}$.

$${}^{1}3\frac{3}{4}$$
$$+ 2\frac{3}{4}$$
$$\overline{\quad 6\frac{1}{2}\quad}$$

• Add the fractions.
$$\frac{3}{4} + \frac{3}{4} = \frac{6}{4} = 1\frac{1}{2}$$

• Write $\frac{1}{2}$ in the answer. Carry the 1.

• Add the whole numbers.
$$1 + 3 + 2 = 6$$

$$3\frac{3}{4} + 2\frac{3}{4} = 6\frac{1}{2}$$

Subtract $3\frac{3}{8}$ from $5\frac{7}{8}$.

$$5\frac{7}{8}$$
$$- 3\frac{3}{8}$$
$$\overline{\quad 2\frac{1}{2}\quad}$$

• Subtract the fractions.
$$\frac{7}{8} - \frac{3}{8} = \frac{4}{8} = \frac{1}{2}$$

• Write $\frac{1}{2}$ in the answer.

• Subtract the whole numbers.
$$5 - 3 = 2$$

$$5\frac{7}{8} - 3\frac{3}{8} = 2\frac{1}{2}$$

PRACTICE

Add or subtract as indicated. Simplify answers. Subtract to check your work on the addition problems. Add to check the subtraction problems.

1. $\frac{3}{4} + \frac{1}{4} =$ _____

2. $\frac{4}{5} + \frac{2}{5} =$ _____

3. $\frac{5}{8} - \frac{4}{8} =$ _____

4. $\frac{7}{12} - \frac{5}{12} =$ _____

5. $4\frac{3}{10} + 1\frac{2}{10} =$ _____

6. $2\frac{12}{15} - 1\frac{2}{15} =$ _____

7. $1\frac{3}{4} - 1\frac{1}{4} =$ _____

8. $6\frac{5}{12} - 3\frac{1}{12} =$ _____

9. $9\frac{5}{7} + \frac{6}{7} =$ _____

10. $2\frac{1}{3} + 3\frac{1}{3} =$ _____

11. $\frac{10}{21} - \frac{2}{21} - \frac{3}{21} =$ _____

12. $\frac{3}{6} + \frac{1}{6} + \frac{4}{6} =$ _____

Regrouping to Subtract Fractions

You may need to regroup before you can subtract. If so, take 1 from the whole number you are subtracting from. Change that 1 to a fraction that is a name for 1 with the denominator you need. If you are regrouping a mixed number, be sure to add the fractional part to the name for 1. Then subtract. Simplify your answer.

Examples

Subtract $\frac{3}{7}$ from 4.

$$4$$
$$-\frac{3}{7}$$

Sevenths are needed to subtract $\frac{3}{7}$.

Take 1 from 4 and change it to $\frac{7}{7}$.

$$3\frac{7}{7}$$
$$\frac{3}{7}$$
$$3\frac{4}{7}$$

$$4 - \frac{3}{7} = 3\frac{4}{7}$$

Subtract $2\frac{5}{6}$ from $4\frac{1}{6}$.

$$4\frac{1}{6}$$
$$-2\frac{5}{6}$$

$\frac{5}{6} > \frac{1}{6}$ There are not enough sixths to subtract.

Take 1 from 4 and change 1 to $\frac{6}{6}$.

Add $\frac{6}{6}$ to $\frac{1}{6}$ to get $\frac{7}{6}$.

$$3\frac{7}{6}$$
$$2\frac{5}{6}$$
$$1\frac{2}{6} = 1\frac{1}{3}$$

$$4\frac{1}{6} - 2\frac{5}{6} = 1\frac{1}{3}$$

PRACTICE

Rename each fraction as indicated.

1. $7 = 6\dfrac{\boxed{}}{5}$

2. $5 = 4\dfrac{8}{\boxed{}}$

3. $8\dfrac{1}{4} = 7\dfrac{\boxed{}}{4}$

4. $5\dfrac{7}{12} = 4\dfrac{\boxed{}}{12}$

5. $2\dfrac{1}{9} = 1\dfrac{10}{\boxed{}}$

Subtract. Regroup as needed. Check your answers with addition.

6. $4\dfrac{5}{8} - 3\dfrac{1}{8} =$ _____

7. $7\dfrac{3}{10} - 4\dfrac{7}{10} =$ _____

8. $12\dfrac{3}{4} - 5\dfrac{3}{4} =$ _____

9. $15\dfrac{1}{7} - 7\dfrac{5}{7} =$ _____

10. $8 - 4\dfrac{7}{9} =$ _____

11. $3\dfrac{1}{4} - \dfrac{3}{4} =$ _____

12. $1\dfrac{5}{9} - \dfrac{7}{9} =$ _____

13. $10 - 9\dfrac{3}{4} =$ _____

14. $8\dfrac{3}{8} - 3\dfrac{5}{8} =$ _____

15. $9\dfrac{1}{3} - 7\dfrac{2}{3} =$ _____

Adding and Subtracting Unlike Fractions

You can only add or subtract like things. To add or subtract fractions, the denominators must be the same. To add or subtract fractions that have different denominators, you will need to rename one or both of the fractions to a **common denominator**.

To find a common denominator, list multiples of each of the denominators. Look for multiples that are the same in each list. Any number that appears in both lists can be a common denominator. The least or lowest number that is the same in the lists is the **least common denominator** (LCD). Renaming the fractions to the LCD is the most efficient way to work.

Example Find a common denominator for $\frac{3}{5}$ and $\frac{2}{3}$.

- List multiples of 5 and of 3. Write a few multiples at a time. Start with the greater number.

- Circle numbers that are common multiples. 15 is the **least common multiple**. Use 15 as the least common denominator.

5   5, 10, 15, 20, 25, 30, 35,...

3   3, 6, 9, 12, 15, 18, 21, 24, 27, 30,...

Rename fractions to a common denominator to add or subtract.

Examples Add $\frac{3}{5}$ and $\frac{2}{3}$.

$$\frac{3}{5} = \frac{3 \times 3}{3 \times 5} = \frac{9}{15}$$
$$+\frac{2}{3} = \frac{5 \times 2}{5 \times 3} = \frac{10}{15}$$
$$\frac{19}{15} = 1\frac{4}{15}$$

$$\frac{3}{5} + \frac{2}{3} = 1\frac{4}{15}$$

Subtract $\frac{3}{5}$ from $\frac{2}{3}$.

$$\frac{2}{3} = \frac{10}{15}$$
$$-\frac{3}{5} = \frac{9}{15}$$
$$\frac{1}{15}$$

$$\frac{2}{3} - \frac{3}{5} = \frac{1}{15}$$

PRACTICE

Find the least common denominator for each pair of fractions.

1. $\frac{1}{4}$ and $\frac{1}{2}$ LCD = ____

2. $\frac{1}{8}$ and $\frac{1}{4}$ LCD = ____

3. $\frac{1}{7}$ and $\frac{1}{3}$ LCD = ____

4. $\frac{1}{5}$ and $\frac{1}{3}$ LCD = ____

5. $\frac{3}{8}$ and $\frac{5}{6}$ LCD = ____

6. $\frac{1}{4}$ and $\frac{1}{5}$ LCD = ____

In each problem below, rewrite the fractions to a common denominator. Then add or subtract as indicated. Be sure to write your answers in simplest terms.

7. $\begin{array}{r} \frac{1}{5} \\ + \frac{1}{4} \\ \hline \end{array}$

9. $\begin{array}{r} \frac{3}{7} \\ - \frac{1}{3} \\ \hline \end{array}$

11. $\begin{array}{r} \frac{1}{3} \\ + \frac{5}{9} \\ \hline \end{array}$

8. $\frac{1}{2} - \frac{1}{10} =$

10. $\frac{5}{12} - \frac{1}{4} =$

12. $\frac{2}{3} - \frac{4}{15} =$

Multiplying Fractions

Multiplying fractions is easy. Multiply numerator times numerator and multiply denominator times denominator. Then simplify your answer.

Example   Multiply $\frac{2}{5} \times \frac{3}{4}$.

- Multiply the numerators and multiply the denominators.

$$\frac{2}{5} \times \frac{3}{4} = \frac{2 \times 3}{5 \times 4} = \frac{6}{20}$$

- Simplify.

$$\frac{6}{20} = \frac{3}{10}$$

$$\frac{2}{5} \times \frac{3}{4} = \frac{3}{10}$$

To multiply a fraction with a whole number, write the whole number as an improper fraction with a denominator of 1. Then multiply the fractions.

Example   Multiply $\frac{2}{3} \times 6$.

- Rewrite 6 as $\frac{6}{1}$.

$$\frac{2}{3} \times 6 = \frac{2}{3} \times \frac{6}{1}$$

- Multiply the fractions.

$$= \frac{2 \times 6}{3 \times 1} = \frac{12}{3}$$

- Simplify.

$$\frac{12}{3} = 4$$

$$\frac{2}{3} \times 6 = 4$$

PRACTICE

Multiply. Simplify answers.

1. $\frac{1}{3} \times \frac{4}{5} =$ _____

2. $\frac{1}{2} \times \frac{5}{8} =$ _____

3. $\frac{2}{5} \times \frac{1}{4} =$ _____

4. $\frac{5}{6} \times 10 =$ _____

5. $12 \times \frac{2}{3} =$ _____

6. $\frac{1}{5} \times 25 =$ _____

7. $\frac{5}{12} \times 12 =$ _____

8. $\frac{3}{8} \times \frac{1}{5} =$ _____

9. $\frac{1}{3} \times \frac{1}{4} \times \frac{2}{3} =$ _____

10. $\frac{3}{4} \times \frac{2}{3} \times \frac{1}{2} =$ _____

Multiplying Mixed Numbers

Write mixed numbers as improper fractions to multiply. (See page 49.)

Example   Find $2\frac{1}{5} \times 1\frac{2}{3}$.

- Rename each mixed number as an improper fraction. $2\frac{1}{5} = \frac{11}{5}$ $1\frac{2}{3} = \frac{5}{3}$

- Use renamed fractions to multiply. $\frac{11}{5} \times \frac{5}{3} = \frac{55}{15}$

- Simplify.

$$2\frac{1}{5} \times 1\frac{2}{3} = 3\frac{2}{3}$$

$$\frac{55}{15} = \frac{11}{3} = 3\frac{2}{3}$$

PRACTICE

Find each product. Simplify answers.

1. $1\frac{2}{8} \times 4 =$ _____

2. $\frac{3}{5} \times 2\frac{1}{5} =$ _____

3. $4\frac{1}{2} \times 1\frac{1}{3} =$ _____

4. $1\frac{3}{4} \times \frac{2}{3} =$ _____

5. $1\frac{1}{7} \times 2\frac{1}{6} =$ _____

6. $1\frac{1}{4} \times \frac{1}{5} =$ _____

7. $3\frac{2}{3} \times 1\frac{1}{2} =$ _____

8. $2\frac{1}{3} \times 2\frac{1}{2} =$ _____

9. $1\frac{1}{3} \times 2\frac{1}{5} =$ _____

10. $7 \times 3\frac{1}{2} =$ _____

Canceling Before You Multiply

Canceling is a shortcut that lets you simplify the fractions *before* you multiply. This allows you to multiply with smaller numbers.

To cancel, divide one number in the numerator and one in the denominator by a common factor. There can be several common factors, so you may find you can divide more than once. For example, $1 \times 6 = 6$ and $2 \times 3 = 6$, so factors of 6 are 1, 2, 3, and 6. A number can be evenly divided by its factors, so 6 can be evenly divided by 1, 2, 3, or 6.

After you finish canceling, multiply as usual. Be sure to use the numbers that result from canceling. If you found all of the common factors, your answer will be in simplest form.

Example   Find $\dfrac{2}{5} \times \dfrac{3}{4} \times \dfrac{1}{6}$.

- 2 is a common factor of 2 in the numerator and 4 in the denominator. Divide both by 2.

$$\dfrac{\overset{1}{2}}{5} \times \dfrac{3}{\underset{2}{4}} \times \dfrac{1}{6}$$

- 3 is a common factor of 3 in the numerator and 6 in the denominator. Divide both by 3.

$$\dfrac{\overset{1}{2}}{5} \times \dfrac{\overset{1}{3}}{\underset{2}{4}} \times \dfrac{1}{\underset{2}{6}}$$

- No more factors can be canceled. Multiply. Be sure to use the numbers that result from canceling.

$$\dfrac{\overset{1}{2}}{5} \times \dfrac{\overset{1}{3}}{\underset{2}{4}} \times \dfrac{1}{\underset{2}{6}} = \dfrac{1 \times 1 \times 1}{5 \times 2 \times 2} = \dfrac{1}{20}$$

$$\dfrac{2}{5} \times \dfrac{3}{4} \times \dfrac{1}{6} = \dfrac{1}{20}$$

PRACTICE

Find each product. Use canceling to simplify before you multiply.

1. $\dfrac{2}{15} \times \dfrac{3}{6} =$ _____

2. $\dfrac{3}{8} \times \dfrac{2}{3} =$ _____

3. $\dfrac{5}{12} \times \dfrac{4}{15} =$ _____

4. $\dfrac{1}{6} \times \dfrac{3}{4} \times \dfrac{2}{9} =$ _____

5. $\dfrac{1}{4} \times \dfrac{2}{3} \times \dfrac{3}{5} =$ _____

6. $3 \times \dfrac{5}{9} =$ _____

7. $\dfrac{4}{7} \times 28 =$ _____

8. $\dfrac{3}{8} \times 1\dfrac{4}{12} =$ _____

9. $2\dfrac{1}{2} \times \dfrac{8}{15} =$ _____

10. $5 \times \dfrac{3}{20} =$ _____

11. $2 \times 1\dfrac{3}{5} \times \dfrac{1}{28} =$ _____

12. $1\dfrac{1}{9} \times 2\dfrac{1}{2} \times 1\dfrac{1}{5} =$ _____

Dividing to Find a Fraction of a Number

You know that in math, the word "of" means multiply, so $\frac{2}{3}$ of 45 is the same as $\frac{2}{3} \times 45$.

$$\frac{2}{3} \times 45 = \frac{2}{3} \times \frac{45}{1} = \frac{90}{3} = 30$$

Another way to find $\frac{2}{3}$ of 45 is to divide 45 into 3 equal parts and take 2 of them. Finding a fraction of an amount is the same as dividing that amount into the number of equal parts named in the denominator of the fraction, and then taking the number of those parts indicated by the numerator.

Example   Find $\frac{2}{3}$ of 45.

• Divide 45 into 3 equal groups.

There are 15 in each group, so $\frac{1}{3}$ of 45 = 15.

• To find $\frac{2}{3}$ of 45, multiply 15 by 2. $2 \times 15 = 30$

$$\frac{2}{3} \text{ of } 45 = 30$$

In division, a remainder represents a fraction of a group. Write a mixed number with the remainder as the numerator of the fraction and the divisor as the denominator.

Example   Find $\frac{3}{5}$ of 57.

• Divide 57 into 5 equal groups.

Each group will contain $11\frac{2}{5}$, so $\frac{1}{5}$ of 57 = $11\frac{2}{5}$

• To find $\frac{3}{5}$ of 57, multiply $11\frac{2}{5}$ by 3.

$$3 \times 11\frac{2}{5} = 33\frac{6}{5} = 34\frac{1}{5}$$

$$\frac{3}{5} \text{ of } 57 = 34\frac{1}{5}$$

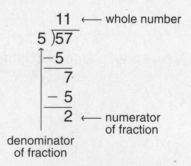

$$57 \div 5 = 11\frac{2}{5}$$

PRACTICE

Use division to find each value.

1. $\frac{1}{4}$ of 300

2. $\frac{2}{4}$ of 300

3. $\frac{1}{5}$ of 245

4. $\frac{3}{4}$ of 420

5. $\frac{5}{6}$ of 126

6. $\frac{7}{12}$ of 180

7. $\frac{5}{8}$ of 44

8. $\frac{2}{3}$ of 49

9. $\frac{5}{9}$ of 50

10. $\frac{5}{8}$ of 100

11. $\frac{3}{7}$ of 51

12. $\frac{1}{2}$ of 17

Dividing Fractions

Before you can divide with fractions, you need to understand **reciprocals**.

To find the reciprocal of a fraction, switch the numerator and denominator.

Examples	Number	$\frac{4}{5}$	$5 = \frac{5}{1}$	$\frac{3}{2}$	$1\frac{3}{7} = \frac{10}{7}$
	Reciprocal	$\frac{5}{4}$	$\frac{1}{5}$	$\frac{2}{3}$	$\frac{7}{10}$

When you multiply a number by its reciprocal, the product equals one.

Examples $\frac{3}{5} \times \frac{5}{3} = \frac{15}{15} = 1$ $\frac{4}{7} \times \frac{7}{4} = \frac{28}{28} = 1$

PRACTICE

Write the reciprocal of each number.

1. $\frac{7}{8}$ _____ $1\frac{1}{3}$ _____ 7 _____ $12\frac{1}{3}$ _____ $2\frac{1}{6}$ _____

To divide fractions, rewrite a division problem as a multiplication problem that uses the reciprocal of the divisor.

Example   Find $\frac{3}{5} \div \frac{9}{10}$.

• Rewrite the problem.

  • Change the division sign to a multiplication sign.
  • Change the divisor (the number to the right of the division sign) to its reciprocal.

$$\frac{3}{5} \div \frac{9}{10} = \frac{3}{5} \times \frac{10}{9}$$

• Multiply. Cancel if you can.

$$\frac{\overset{1}{3}}{\underset{1}{5}} \times \frac{\overset{2}{10}}{\underset{3}{9}} = \frac{2}{3}$$

$$\frac{3}{5} \div \frac{9}{10} = \frac{2}{3}$$

PRACTICE

Rewrite each division as multiplication to find the quotient. Write answers in simplest terms.

2. $\frac{3}{4} \div 3 =$ _____

3. $2\frac{1}{3} \div \frac{1}{3} =$ _____

4. $3\frac{3}{4} \div \frac{3}{4} =$ _____

5. $\frac{1}{5} \div \frac{3}{7} =$ _____

6. $\frac{2}{3} \div \frac{1}{2} =$ _____

7. $\frac{3}{5} \div \frac{1}{5} =$ _____

8. $1\frac{1}{2} \div \frac{3}{8} =$ _____

9. $9 \div \frac{2}{3} =$ _____

10. $2\frac{1}{2} \div 1\frac{1}{4} =$ _____

Using Fractions to Solve Word Problems

Solve each word problem below. Reduce all answers to simplest terms.

1. The Women's Club has sold 180 of the 360 circus tickets they need to sell. What fraction has been sold so far?

    _____

2. Each volume of an encyclopedia is $2\frac{1}{3}$ inches wide. How many volumes will fit on a shelf 18 inches wide?

    _____

3. Damia's kitchen floor measures 240 square feet. If she puts a wood floor over $\frac{2}{5}$ of the floor, how many square feet of wood flooring will she need?

    _____

4. When the Patel family went apple picking, Mr. Patel picked $1\frac{1}{2}$ bushels, Mrs. Patel picked $\frac{3}{4}$ of a bushel, and their three children picked $\frac{1}{4}$ bushel each. How many bushels of apples did the family pick?

    _____

5. One-fifth of the 110 members of Park Street Church are senior citizens. How many senior citizens belong to the church?

    _____

6. It usually takes Derek $2\frac{3}{4}$ hours to drive to Toronto. Today he got caught in a storm and the drive took $5\frac{1}{2}$ hours. How much time did the storm add to Derek's trip?

    _____

7. A sweater marked $65.20 is on sale for $\frac{1}{4}$ off. How much does it cost on sale? (*Hint*: This is a 2-step problem.)

    _____

8. Troy has one $26\frac{1}{2}$-ounce can of chicken stock and three smaller cans, each of which contain $12\frac{1}{2}$ ounces. How many ounces of chicken stock does he have in all?

    _____

9. Tiffany uses $\frac{1}{10}$ of her wages each month to buy company stock. Also, she puts $\frac{1}{20}$ of her wages in a savings account, and $\frac{1}{15}$ into the company pension plan. What fraction of her wages are taken out for these purposes?

    _____

10. Leanne weighs $\frac{2}{3}$ as much as her sister. If her sister weighs 180 pounds, how much does Leanne weigh?

    _____

11. Chuck has $\frac{3}{4}$ of a ton of gravel. He wants to divide it into $\frac{1}{8}$-ton piles. How many piles can he make?

_____

12. Kyle decided to give away his stamp collection. He gave $\frac{1}{3}$ of the stamps to his nephew, $\frac{1}{4}$ to his cousin, and $\frac{1}{8}$ of the stamps to his neighbor's son. What fraction of his stamps are still left to give away?

_____

13. One can contains $1\frac{1}{2}$ cups of beans. If 3 people share the can of beans equally, each will get $\frac{1}{3}$ of the can. What is $\frac{1}{3}$ of $1\frac{1}{2}$ cups?

_____

14. In a poll of 120 members at the Swim Club, $\frac{5}{12}$ of the members said they use the pool every week. One-fifth of that group said they swim at least twice a week. How many of the members polled swim at least twice a week?

_____

15. One-fourth of the 5,248 students at Fairfield Technical School are women. How many women attend Fairfield Technical School?

_____

Use the information below to answer Numbers 16–19.

Last year, Greg's employer rewarded Greg's hard work with a bonus check for $250. Greg put $100 of the bonus into his savings account. He used $75 to buy a new sports jacket and he spent $45 on a gift for his wife.

16. Which fraction represents the amount of Greg's bonus that went into his savings account?

    A $\frac{1}{4}$ C $\frac{2}{3}$

    B $\frac{2}{5}$ D $\frac{1}{2}$

17. What fraction of his bonus did Greg spend on a new sports jacket?

    F $\frac{1}{5}$ H $\frac{3}{10}$

    G $\frac{1}{4}$ J $\frac{3}{8}$

18. The amount spent on his wife's gift is closest to this fraction of Greg's bonus.

    A $\frac{1}{4}$ C $\frac{1}{5}$

    B $\frac{1}{3}$ D $\frac{1}{10}$

19. What fraction of the bonus is not accounted for in the information given?

    F less than half
    G more than half
    H exactly half
    J It is not possible to tell.

Fractions Skills Checkup

Circle the letter for the correct answer to each problem. Write all answers in simplest terms.

1. $\dfrac{5}{6}$

   $-\dfrac{1}{2}$

   A $\dfrac{4}{6}$ C $\dfrac{1}{4}$

   B $\dfrac{1}{3}$ D $\dfrac{1}{12}$

   E None of these

2. $2\dfrac{5}{12}$

   $+\,1\dfrac{2}{3}$

   F $3\dfrac{3}{4}$ H $3\dfrac{7}{15}$

   G $3\dfrac{7}{12}$ J $4\dfrac{1}{12}$

   K None of these

3. $1\dfrac{1}{3} \times \dfrac{2}{5} =$

   A $1\dfrac{2}{15}$ C $\dfrac{8}{15}$

   B $1\dfrac{3}{8}$ D $\dfrac{4}{15}$

   E None of these

4. $2\dfrac{1}{4} \div \dfrac{3}{8} =$

   F 6 H $4\dfrac{2}{3}$

   G $2\dfrac{2}{3}$ J $\dfrac{27}{32}$

   K None of these

5. $\dfrac{4}{5} \div 6 =$

   A $4\dfrac{4}{5}$ C 15

   B $6\dfrac{4}{5}$ D $\dfrac{1}{15}$

   E None of these

6. $\dfrac{3}{5} + \dfrac{3}{20} + \dfrac{1}{2} =$

   F $1\dfrac{1}{5}$ H $\dfrac{7}{20}$

   G $\dfrac{7}{27}$ J $1\dfrac{1}{3}$

   K None of these

7. Which of these would increase $\frac{1}{3}$ to a number greater than 1?

   A Add $\dfrac{1}{2}$.

   B Multiply by 2.

   C Divide by 2.

   D Add $\dfrac{4}{5}$.

8. Which of these fractions is in lowest terms?

   F $\dfrac{3}{15}$

   G $\dfrac{7}{21}$

   H $\dfrac{9}{11}$

   J $\dfrac{4}{30}$

9. Kara spends about $45 a week on groceries. Which choice below shows about how much she spends on groceries per day?

   A $\dfrac{7}{45}$

   B $\dfrac{45}{7}$

   C $\dfrac{1}{7} \div 45$

   D $7 \times \dfrac{1}{45}$

10. One-eighth of the population of Riverview is unemployed. The population is 52,000. How many residents of Riverview are unemployed?

    F   650

    G 1,423

    H 6,500

    J 4,160

11. $1\frac{3}{4}$
    $-\frac{1}{2}$

    A $1\frac{1}{2}$ **C** $\frac{1}{4}$

    B $1\frac{1}{4}$ **D** $1\frac{1}{8}$

    E None of these

12. $6\frac{1}{4} - 2\frac{1}{3} =$

    F $4\frac{1}{4}$ **H** $4\frac{11}{12}$

    G $3\frac{11}{12}$ **J** $4\frac{3}{4}$

    K None of these

13. $5\frac{1}{3} \times 3\frac{3}{4} =$

    A $15\frac{1}{4}$ **C** $18\frac{3}{4}$

    B $15\frac{3}{7}$ **D** 20

    E None of these

14. $\frac{1}{3} \times \frac{3}{5} \times \frac{5}{8} =$

    F $\frac{1}{9}$ **H** $\frac{17}{120}$

    G $\frac{1}{5}$ **J** $1\frac{2}{3}$

    K None of these

15. $9 \div \frac{3}{4} =$

    A 12 **C** $\frac{1}{12}$

    B $\frac{3}{4}$ **D** $6\frac{3}{4}$

    E None of these

16. $6\frac{1}{5} \div 2\frac{2}{5} =$

    F $\frac{12}{31}$ **H** $14\frac{22}{24}$

    G $2\frac{7}{12}$ **J** $3\frac{1}{2}$

    K None of these

17. Which group of fractions is in order from least to greatest?

    A $\frac{1}{3}, \frac{3}{4}, \frac{1}{9}, \frac{5}{8}$

    B $\frac{1}{3}, \frac{1}{9}, \frac{5}{8}, \frac{3}{4}$

    C $\frac{1}{9}, \frac{1}{3}, \frac{5}{8}, \frac{3}{4}$

    D $\frac{1}{3}, \frac{3}{4}, \frac{5}{8}, \frac{1}{9}$

18. One-half of a carrot cake must be divided evenly among 6 children. What fraction of the cake will each child get?

    F $\frac{1}{8}$ **H** $\frac{1}{3}$

    G $\frac{1}{6}$ **J** $\frac{1}{12}$

19. In Springfield, $\frac{3}{5}$ of the adults have children, and $\frac{1}{4}$ of those adults have children under the age of 5. Which of these number sentences could you use to find the fraction of adults in Springfield who have children under 5?

    A $\frac{3}{5} \times \frac{1}{4} = $ _____

    B $\frac{3}{5} \div \frac{1}{4} = $ _____

    C $\frac{3}{5} - \frac{1}{4} = $ _____

    D $\frac{3}{5} + \frac{1}{4} = $ _____

20. Which of these fractions is equal to $\frac{3}{4}$?

    F $\frac{9}{8}$ **H** $\frac{12}{15}$

    G $\frac{5}{6}$ **J** $\frac{15}{20}$

Integers

Reviewing Positive and Negative Numbers

Positive numbers are numbers that are *greater than* zero. Whole numbers such as 1, 2, 3, and so on, and fraction and decimal amounts such as $3\frac{1}{2}$ and 14.05 are positive numbers.

Negative numbers are numbers that are *less than* zero. They are written with a minus sign in front of them. (If there is no sign in front of a number, it is assumed to be positive.) Whole numbers such as −1, −2, −3, and so on, and fraction and decimal amounts such as $-\frac{2}{3}$ and −4.25 are negative numbers. Zero is neither positive nor negative.

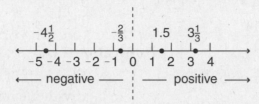

- The farther to the right a number is on the number line, the greater its value.

- The farther to the left a number is on the number line, the less its value.

For example, −12 is farther to the left on the number line than 1, so −12 is less than 1. It might be helpful to think about temperature; it is colder at −12°F than at 1°F, since −12°F is less than 1°F.

Integers are the positive and negative whole numbers, and zero. Fractions and decimals are *not* integers.

PRACTICE

Compare the two numbers. Write >, <, or = between each pair of numbers.

1.	−1	0		7.	35	−52
2.	0	1		8.	−1.3	−0.6
3.	1	−1		9.	−0.03	−0.3
4.	−1	−2		10.	$-\frac{1}{5}$	$-\frac{1}{7}$
5.	−5	−3		11.	−0.2	−2
6.	$-\frac{1}{2}$	$-\frac{1}{4}$		12.	−3.5	−3.50

For Numbers 13–18, write each group of numbers in order from least to greatest.

13. −2, 0, −5, 1

14. 0.25, −0.9, 5, −8.03

15. 22, −33, −4.89, 17

16. 1, $-\frac{1}{2}$, $-\frac{3}{4}$, $\frac{1}{3}$

17. 43, −65, 82, −100

18. 2.5, −8, $\frac{1}{2}$, 0

Working with Absolute Value

Positive and negative numbers can be used to express opposite amounts. Each integer has an opposite.

Examples
   The opposite of spending $10 is earning $10.
   The opposite of gaining 5 pounds is losing 5 pounds.
   The opposite of $^-$3 is +3.

- A number and its opposite are the same distance from zero on the number line. The distance from zero is called the **absolute value** of the number. The symbol for absolute value is | |. You write the absolute value of $^-$6 as |6|.

- Absolute value is always a positive amount.
  Although $^-$2 is less than 2, they are both the same distance from zero, and they both have an absolute value of 2.

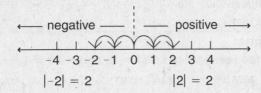

   $|^-2| = 2$ $|2| = 2$

- When you add or subtract absolute values, the result is always a positive amount.

Examples
   $|^-12| = 12$ $|6 - 4| = 2$ $|^-7| + |5| = 7 + 5 = 12$

PRACTICE

For Numbers 1–5, write the absolute value of each number. Then write the opposite of the original integer.

1. 8 _____

2. $^-$40 _____

3. $^-$9 _____

4. 25 _____

5. 17 _____

For Numbers 6–10, find the absolute value of the expression.

6. $|^-35| =$ _____

7. $|62| =$ _____

8. $|12| + |^-10| =$ _____

9. $|^-25| - |^-18| =$ _____

10. $|40| + |10| - |25| =$ _____

Adding Integers

You can use a number line to add integers. Start at zero. To add a positive integer, move to the right. To add a negative integer, move to the left.

Examples

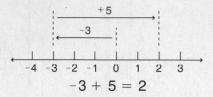

$$-3 + 5 = 2$$

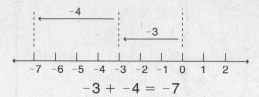

$$-3 + -4 = -7$$

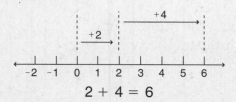

$$2 + 4 = 6$$

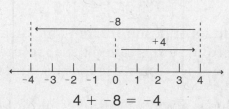

$$4 + -8 = -4$$

You can also use absolute value to add integers.

For addends with the same sign: Find the sum of the absolute values. Give the sum the common sign of the addends.	$5 + 8$ $\lvert 5 \rvert + \lvert 8 \rvert = 5 + 8 = 13$ $5 + 8 = 13$	$-6 + -12$ $\lvert -6 \rvert + \lvert -6 \rvert = 6 + 12 = 18$ $-6 + -12 = -18$
For addends with different signs: Subtract absolute values. Give the result the sign of the number with the *greater* absolute value.	$5 + -7$ $\lvert 5 \rvert = 5$, and $\lvert -7 \rvert = 7$ $7 - 5 = 2$ $\lvert -7 \rvert > \lvert 5 \rvert$, so $5 + -7 = -2$	$-8 + 6$ $\lvert -8 \rvert = 8$, and $\lvert 6 \rvert = 6$ $8 - 6 = 2$ $\lvert -8 \rvert > \lvert 6 \rvert$, so $-8 + 6 = -2$

- A number plus its opposite equals zero. For example, $4 + -4 = 0$, and $7 + -7 = 0$.
- When adding three or more numbers, find the sum of two at a time. You can add in any order.

PRACTICE

Use a number line or the rules above. For Numbers 1–6, write the number that is

1. 9 to the right of zero _____

2. 9 to the left of zero _____

3. 4 to the right of −3 _____

4. 7 to the right of −7 _____

5. 5 to the left of −6 _____

6. 8 to the left of 2 _____

Add.

7. $0 + -6 =$ _____

8. $-10 + -8 =$ _____

9. $17 + -17 =$ _____

10. $-14 + 20 =$ _____

11. $3 + -10 =$ _____

12. $-5 + -7 + 4 =$ _____

13. $6 + -8 + 2 =$ _____

Subtracting Integers

You can use a number line to find the difference between two integers.

Examples

Find $-4 - (-9)$.

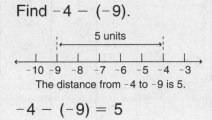

The distance from -4 to -9 is 5.

$$-4 - (-9) = 5$$

Find $4 - (-1)$.

5 units

The distance from 4 to -1 is 5.

$$4 - (-1) = 5$$

You can also use inverses to subtract. Since subtraction is the inverse, or opposite, of addition, you can think of subtraction as adding the opposite of the number being subtracted.

To subtract integers
- Change subtraction to addition.
- Add the opposite of the number being subtracted.

Examples

Subtract	Opposite of number subtracted	Add opposite
$3 - 2 = 1$	-2	$3 + {-2} = 1$
$3 - 1 = 2$	-1	$3 + {-1} = 2$
$3 - 0 = 3$	0	$3 + 0 = 3$
$3 - (-1) = 4$	1	$3 + 1 = 4$

Subtract	Opposite of number subtracted	Add opposite
$-5 - 2 = -7$	2	$-5 + {-2} = -7$
$-5 - 1 = -6$	-1	$-5 + {-1} = -6$
$-5 - 0 = -5$	0	$-5 + 0 = -5$
$-5 - (-1) = -4$	1	$-5 + 1 = -4$

PRACTICE

Solve.

1. $5 - (-4) =$ _____

2. $-6 - 2 =$ _____

3. $-10 - (-5) =$ _____

4. $-1 - (-1) =$ _____

5. $12 - (-5) =$ _____

6. $20 - (-10) =$ _____

7. $-14 - (-12) =$ _____

8. $-5 - 5 =$ _____

9. $0 - (-12) =$ _____

10. $45 - (-45) =$ _____

11. $-30 - (-15) =$ _____

12. $62 - 8 =$ _____

13. $20 - (-40) =$ _____

14. $-50 - 50 =$ _____

15. $-80 - 30 =$ _____

16. $53 - (-17) =$ _____

17. Which of these will take you from -3 to 0?

   A Add -3.
   B Subtract 3.
   C Subtract -3.

18. Which operation has the same effect as the operation "subtract 5"?

   F Add -5.
   G Add 5.
   H Subtract -5.

Multiplying and Dividing Integers

Multiply and divide integers the same way you would whole numbers. Then use the following rules to give the correct sign to the answer.

- If both numbers have the same sign, the answer is positive.
  Multiplication: $(+) \times (+) = (+)$ and $(-) \times (-) = (+)$
  Division: $(+) \div (+) = (+)$ and $(-) \div (-) = (+)$

- If both numbers have different signs, the answer is negative.
  Multiplication: $(+) \times (-) = (-)$ and $(-) \times (+) = (-)$
  Division: $(+) \div (-) = (-)$ and $(-) \div (+) = (-)$

Remember that division can be written in fraction form. Although the form is different, the rules are the same.

- If the numerator and denominator have the same sign, the fraction represents a positive quotient.

Examples $\dfrac{6}{3} = 2$ $\dfrac{-20}{-4} = 5$ $\dfrac{-10}{-20} = \dfrac{1}{2}$

- If the numerator and denominator have different signs, the fraction represents a negative quotient.

Examples $\dfrac{30}{-6} = -5$ $\dfrac{-8}{2} = -4$ $\dfrac{-5}{10} = \dfrac{-1}{2}$

PRACTICE

Solve each problem below.

1. $5 \times -5 =$ _____

2. $-3 \times -2 =$ _____

3. $-4 \times 4 =$ _____

4. $10 \times -3 =$ _____

5. $16 \times -2 =$ _____

6. $-10 \times -10 =$ _____

7. $-8 \times -5 =$ _____

8. $-2 \times 6 =$ _____

9. $10 \times -12 =$ _____

10. $18 \div -9 =$ _____

11. $40 \div -10 =$ _____

12. $-60 \div -3 =$ _____

13. $-75 \div 25 =$ _____

14. $-100 \div -10 =$ _____

15. $240 \div -2 =$ _____

16. $36 \div -3 =$ _____

Simplify each fraction.

17. $\dfrac{-16}{-4} =$ _____

18. $\dfrac{45}{-15} =$ _____

19. $\dfrac{-15}{60} =$ _____

20. $\dfrac{27}{9} =$ _____

21. $\dfrac{-48}{12} =$ _____

Using Integers to Solve Word Problems

The problems below involve addition, subtraction, multiplication, or division of integers. Set up and solve each problem. Be sure to use a negative sign for negative values. *Hint:* Some of these are two-step problems.

This is Dominic's credit card statement for July. Use it to answer Numbers 1–4.

Previous balance	−$62.91
Transactions:	
July 5	−19.50
July 12	−30.10
July 14	+15.00
July 22	−52.87
Total transactions:	−87.47
Fees and/or credits:	−6.75

1. At the beginning of the month, did Dominic owe money or did he have a credit?

   _____

2. On what date, if any, did the credit card company receive a payment from Dominic?

   _____

3. The last entry in the statement is a total of fees and/or credits. Overall, did the company credit money to Dominic or charge him money?

   _____

4. What was Dominic's balance (or total) at the end of July?

   _____

5. The temperature is −2°F. If it drops 1 degree every 10 minutes, what will the temperature be in an hour? (1 hr = 60 minutes)?

   _____

6. The deepest point on earth is 35,802 feet below sea level. The highest point on earth is 29,028 feet above sea level. What is the difference between these elevations?

   _____

7. A scientist drops an instrument into the ocean. It drops 2 feet every second. First express this change as an interger. Then tell how long will it take the instrument to reach a depth of −100 feet.

   _____

8. An elevator is at the 14th floor. It goes up 12 floors and then down 18 floors. How far from the 14th floor is the elevator?

   _____

9. A number multiplied by −11 is 187. What is the number?

   _____

Integers Skills Checkup

Circle the letter for the correct answer to each problem.

1. $\dfrac{-6}{-6} =$
   - A 1
   - B -1
   - C 0
   - D $-\dfrac{1}{6}$
   - E None of these

2. $60 + -15 =$
   - F 75
   - G -75
   - H 45
   - J -45
   - K None of these

3. $-15 \div -5 =$
   - A 3
   - B -3
   - C 75
   - D -75
   - E None of these

4. $-12 \times 3 =$
   - F 36
   - G 4
   - H -36
   - J -4
   - K None of these

5. $10 + -2 + -2 =$
   - A 10
   - B 8
   - C 6
   - D -6
   - E None of these

6. $|2 - (-1)| =$
   - F 3
   - G -3
   - H 1
   - J -1
   - K None of these

7. Which group of numbers is in order from least to greatest?
   - A 0, -1, -2, 5, 9
   - B -1, -2, 0, 5, 9
   - C -2, -1, 0, 5, 9
   - D 0, -2, -1, 5, 9

8. Which of these number sentences is true?
   - F $2 < -3$
   - G $-3 < -2$
   - H $0 < -3$
   - J $-3 < -4$

9. Which of the following choices, if it is added to 5, creates a sum that is less than 0?
   - A any number less than 5
   - B any number less than 0
   - C any number less than -5
   - D None of these

10. The sum of two integers is -2. One of the integers is -7. What is the other integer?
    - F 9
    - G -5
    - H 5
    - J 7

11. Which expression has a negative value?
    - A $|-3| + |-12|$
    - B $|-12| - (-3)$
    - C $-8 + -7$
    - D -5×-3

12. The town of Sedalia is 800 feet below sea level. That is an altitude of −800 feet. There is a quarry just outside of town that is 450 feet deep. What is the altitude at the bottom of the quarry?

    F   350 feet
    G −350 feet
    H 1,250 feet
    J −1,250 feet

13. Which of these expressions has the same value as $-2 - (-4)$?

    A $2 + 4$
    B $-2 + 4$
    C $-2 + -4$
    D $2 + -4$

14. What numbers can be added to −2 to get a number greater than 0?

    F any number less than 2
    G any number less than −2
    H any number greater than 2
    J any number greater than −2

15. Which of these expressions has the same value as -3×-5?

    A $3 \div 5$
    B 3×-5
    C $\dfrac{1}{3} \times \dfrac{1}{5}$
    D 3×5

16. Which of these numbers is between −2 and −8?

    F 0
    G −1
    H 3
    J −5

Use the following information to do Numbers 17–20.

Carlos is a self-employed carpenter. This balance sheet shows his expenses and income for two recent projects.

Hiller House	
Lumber	−$1,800
Hardware	−60
Fee	+2,700
Smith House	
Lumber	−$2,200
Hardware	−260
Crane Rental	−360
Fee	+4,200

17. What were Carlos' total expenses on the Smith house?

    A $2,820   **C** $7,020
    B $2,460   **D** $1,380

18. What is the profit (income − expenses) for the Hiller house?

    F $840   **H** $ 960
    G $900   **J** $4,560

19. Carlos spends $800 a month on insurance. Also, last month he paid an engineer $1,500 for help on a project. How should he enter these figures in his balance sheet?

    A as −$800 and +$1,500
    B as −$800 and −$1,500
    C as −$800 and +$1,500
    D as +$800 and −$1,500

20. Which of these represents the difference in profit between the Smith project and the Hiller project?

    F $1,380   **H** $960
    G $ 840   **J** $540

Ratio, Proportion, and Percent

Writing Ratios

A **ratio** is a comparison between two numbers. Each of the following statements expresses a ratio:

> For each dozen rolls a customer buys, the bakery gives 1 free roll.
> On average, the population of the United States increases by 1 person every 10 seconds.
> Kevin scores 1 free throw out of every 3 he attempts.
> The chocolates cost $10 per pound.

There are three ways to write a ratio.

- using the word *to*   5 to 3
- using a colon $5 : 3$
- as a fraction $\dfrac{5}{3}$

Working with ratios is just like working with fractions, so the fraction is the form most commonly used.

When you are writing a ratio, the order of the numbers is important. The position of the numbers should correspond with the quantities named.

Example: Mike's car gets **18** miles to the gallon.

miles : gallon $\longrightarrow$ 18 : 1   miles to gallon $\longrightarrow$ 18 to 1 $\dfrac{\text{miles}}{\text{gallon}} \longrightarrow \dfrac{18}{1}$

- Ratios should be written in their lowest terms.

- A ratio that is an improper fraction should be left as improper fraction — it *should not* be changed to a mixed number.

PRACTICE

For each relationship, write a ratio in both colon and fraction form. Simplify whenever possible.

1. Zack spent $150 for 3 tickets. What was the ratio of money to tickets? _____

2. In a local election, 1,290 people voted for Beeler and 2,580 people voted for Price. What was the ratio of votes for Beeler to votes for Price? _____

3. There are 24 cans of soup in every carton. Write the ratio of 1 can to the total number of cans in the carton. _____

4. The team won 18 games out of the 27 they played. Write the ratio of wins to losses. _____

5. There are 36 inches for every 3 feet. Write the ratio of inches to feet. _____

Identifying a Proportion

A **proportion** is a statement that two ratios are equal. For example, 2 out of 4, or $\frac{2}{4}$, is equal to 3 out of 6, or $\frac{3}{6}$. Both are equal to $\frac{1}{2}$.

$$\frac{\circ\circ}{\bullet\bullet} = \frac{\circ\circ\circ}{\bullet\bullet\bullet}$$
$$\frac{2}{4} \qquad \frac{3}{6}$$

You can use **cross multiplication** to find out whether two ratios form a proportion.

• Multiply each numerator with the denominator of the other ratio.

• If the **cross products** are equal, the ratios are equal and they form a proportion.

Examples

Do $\frac{2}{4}$ and $\frac{3}{6}$ form a proportion?

$$\frac{2}{4} \overset{?}{=} \frac{3}{6}$$

Cross multiply. $\frac{2}{4} \times \frac{3}{6}$

$2 \times 6 = 12 \quad 4 \times 3 = 12$
$12 = 12$

$$\frac{2}{4} = \frac{3}{6}$$

Yes, $\frac{2}{4}$ and $\frac{3}{6}$ form a proportion.

Do $\frac{5}{12}$ and $\frac{30}{48}$ form a proportion?

$$\frac{5}{12} \overset{?}{=} \frac{30}{48}$$

Cross multiply. $\frac{5}{12} \times \frac{30}{48}$

$5 \times 48 = 240 \quad 12 \times 30 = 360$
$240 \neq 360$

$$\frac{5}{12} \neq \frac{30}{48}$$

No, $\frac{5}{12}$ and $\frac{30}{48}$ do not form a proportion.

PRACTICE

Use cross multiplication to see if each pair of fractions forms a proportion. Remember, in a proportion, cross products are equal. Circle *Y* if the pair is a proportion. Circle *N* if the pair is not a proportion.

1. $\frac{3}{5} \overset{?}{=} \frac{20}{55}$ Y   N

2. $\frac{8}{5} \overset{?}{=} \frac{24}{16}$ Y   N

3. $\frac{8}{7} \overset{?}{=} \frac{56}{49}$ Y   N

4. $\frac{11}{16} \overset{?}{=} \frac{33}{48}$ Y   N

5. $\frac{10}{6} \overset{?}{=} \frac{15}{90}$ Y   N

6. $\frac{4}{3} \overset{?}{=} \frac{32}{24}$ Y   N

7. $\frac{5}{6} \overset{?}{=} \frac{32}{36}$ Y   N

8. $\frac{3}{7} \overset{?}{=} \frac{12}{28}$ Y   N

9. $\frac{4}{6} \overset{?}{=} \frac{15}{22}$ Y   N

10. $\frac{10}{4} \overset{?}{=} \frac{25}{10}$ Y   N

Writing a Proportion

When you write a proportion, it is a good idea to write the names of the things being compared as a ratio in fraction form. The words serve as a guide for placing the numbers to write the proportion.

Each of the numbers in a proportion is called a **term**. To solve many problems, you will need to write a proportion in which one term is missing, and then find the missing term. A letter is usually used to take the place of the missing term.

Example
Yogurt is on sale, 4 cartons for $5. How much will 10 cartons of yogurt cost?

- Write the comparison in words or symbols.

$$\frac{\text{cartons}}{\$}$$

- Write the numbers of the original comparison.

$$\frac{\text{cartons}}{\$} \qquad \frac{4}{5}$$

- Write another ratio to form a proportion. Write a letter in the place of the term you do not know. Here you are looking for cost, so the letter goes in the $ position.

$$\frac{\text{cartons}}{\$} \qquad \frac{4}{5} = \frac{10}{n}$$

The number represented by n is the cost of 10 cartons of yogurt.

PRACTICE

Decide whether the problem can be solved by using a proportion. If it can, write the words as a ratio. Then write a proportion to represent the problem. *It is not necessary to solve.*

1. In a map, 1 centimeter represents 200 miles. How many centimeters represent 1,000 miles?

2. Murray can paint 2 rooms in a day. How many days will it take him to paint 25 rooms?

3. Two cookies have 270 calories. Cara ate 5 cookies. How many calories was that?

4. Jason runs 1 mile in 3 minutes. It takes Maggie 4 minutes to run 1 mile. What is the difference in their speed?

5. It takes Ann 5 minutes to type one page. How long will it take her to type 25 pages?

6. The bookcase is 30 inches wide. Will it fit in a space that is 3 feet wide? (*Hint:* Units must be the same.)

Finding the Missing Term in a Proportion

Once a proportion is set up, you can find the value of a term that is missing. Using cross products is a good way to solve for the missing term.

Examples

Find the missing term. $m : 7 = 9 : 3$

- Cross multiply.

$$\frac{m}{7} \times \frac{9}{3}$$

$$3 \times m = 7 \times 9$$
$$3m = 63$$

- Divide by the number multiplying m. Divide on both sides of the equal sign.

$$\frac{3m}{3} = \frac{\overset{21}{\cancel{63}}}{\cancel{3}}$$
$$m = 21$$

The missing term is 21.

Find the missing term. $\dfrac{15}{n} = \dfrac{70}{42}$

- Cross multiply.

$$\frac{15}{n} \times \frac{70}{42}$$

$$15 \times 42 = 70n$$
$$630 = 70n$$

- Divide by the number multiplying n. Divide on both sides of the equal sign.

$$\frac{630}{70} = \frac{\overset{1}{\cancel{70}}n}{\underset{1}{\cancel{70}}}$$
$$9 = n$$

The missing term is 9.

PRACTICE

Find the missing term in each proportion.

1. $\dfrac{x}{4} = \dfrac{6}{8}$

2. $\dfrac{6}{14} = \dfrac{12}{y}$

3. $\dfrac{14}{n} = \dfrac{42}{15}$

4. $\dfrac{3}{8} = \dfrac{x}{32}$

5. $\dfrac{4}{n} = \dfrac{12}{15}$

6. $\dfrac{10}{4} = \dfrac{25}{x}$

7. $\dfrac{15}{16} = \dfrac{y}{64}$

8. $\dfrac{28}{n} = \dfrac{7}{3}$

9. $\dfrac{x}{24} = \dfrac{2}{5}$

10. $4 : 13 = n : 65$

11. $8 : x = 24 : 45$

12. $y : 39 = 12 : 18$

Finding a Unit Rate

When the two quantities compared in a ratio have different units of measure, the ratio is called a **rate**. Miles to the gallon, dollars per pound, and words per minute are all examples of ratios that are rates. When the denominator of a rate is 1, the rate is called a **unit rate**.

Example   The cruising speed of a jumbo jet is 550 miles per hour.

The rate of speed is $\dfrac{550 \text{ miles}}{1 \text{ hour}}$.

One way to find a unit rate is to simplify the ratio so the number in the denominator is 1. To do that, divide both numerator and denominator by the number in the denominator.

Example   Hank paid $12 for 3 roses. What was the cost of 1 rose?

$$\dfrac{\text{dollars}}{\text{roses}} \dfrac{12}{3} = \dfrac{12 \div 3}{3 \div 3} = \dfrac{4}{1}$$

It cost $4 for 1 rose.

Another way to find a unit rate is to set up a proportion. Write the comparison you know as the first ratio. For the second ratio, write 1 in the denominator, and use a letter to represent the amount you are looking for in the numerator. Then use cross products to solve for the missing term.

Example   The store is selling 10 pens for $5. What is the cost of 1 pen?

- Write the ratio in words and numbers.
  The unit is 1 pen, so put *pens* in the denominator.
- Write the second ratio to create a proportion.
  Write 1 in the denominator. Write n in the numerator.

$\dfrac{\text{dollars}}{\text{pens}}$ $\dfrac{5}{10}$

$\dfrac{\text{dollars}}{\text{pens}}$ $\dfrac{5}{10} = \dfrac{n}{1}$

- Find cross products and solve for n.

One pen costs $0.50 or 50¢.

$\dfrac{5}{10} = \dfrac{10n}{10}$

$n = \dfrac{1}{2}$ (dollar)

PRACTICE

Find the unit rate in each problem. The unit rate will have 1 in the denominator.

1. $93 for 3 hours
   How much for 1 hour?

2. 54 packages for 3 cartons
   How many packages for 1 carton?

3. $160 for 4 sweaters
   How much for 1 sweater?

4. 91 flowers for 13 bouquets
   How many flowers for
   1 bouquet?

5. 9 hot dogs for $22.50
   How much for 1 hot dog?

6. 3 cans for $1.20
   How much for 1 can?

7. 300 miles in 2.5 hours
   How many miles in 1 hour?

8. 30 note cards for $6
   How many note cards for $1?

Using Proportions to Solve Word Problems

Solve each problem. Use words to set up the ratio of the quantities being compared. Make sure to match the placement of numbers to the position of the words, and use a letter such as *n* in place of the term that you do not know. Cross multiply to solve for the value of the letter.

1. One inch equals 2.54 centimeters. How many inches are equal to 30.48 cm?

2. Rasheed drove his new car 255 miles on just 8 gallons of gas. Given similar driving conditions, how far can Rasheed expect to drive on 12 gallons of gas?

3. A blueprint of a house is drawn using a scale of 5 ft to 2 cm. On the blueprint, a room is 5 cm long. What will be the length of the actual room?

4. A map is drawn using a scale of 150 miles to 1 cm. The distance between two cities is 1,200 miles. How many centimeters apart are the two cities on the map?

5. Soup is on sale at 3 cans for $4.20. How much will it cost to buy 8 cans?

6. Henry made a gray paint by mixing 2 parts of black paint with 5 parts of white paint. How many gallons of black paint should be mixed with 24 gallons of white paint to make this gray color?

7. Out of every $150 she earns, Josephine saves $12. At this rate, how much money she will have saved when she has earned $1,350?

8. A recipe for fruit punch calls for 3 parts club soda to 4 parts fruit juice. How much club soda should be added to 6 quarts of fruit juice to make the mixture?

Understanding Percent

The word **percent** means *per hundred*. For example, if 12 out of every 100 cars turned out at the auto factory are red, then 12 percent, or 12%, of the cars turned out are red. Or, if out of every 10 cans of fruit there are 3 cans of peaches, there would be 30 cans of peaches in 100 cans of fruit, so 30% of the cans are peaches.

A percent, like a fraction, is a way to name part of a whole. Every percent can be written as a fraction and as a decimal.

- To write a percent as a fraction, merely remove the percent sign and write the number as the numerator of a fraction with a denominator of 100. Then simplify.

Examples $\quad 25\% = \dfrac{25}{100} = \dfrac{1}{4} \qquad\qquad 80\% = \dfrac{80}{100} = \dfrac{4}{5}$

- To write a percent as a decimal, you can write the percent as a fraction with a denominator of 100, and then write the fraction as a decimal.

Examples $\quad 50\% = \dfrac{50}{100} = 0.50 \qquad\qquad 12\% = \dfrac{12}{100} = 0.12$

Or, you can remove the percent sign and move the decimal point two places *to the left*. Remember, when there is no decimal point, a decimal point can be placed to the right of the ones place.

Examples $\quad 37\% \longrightarrow 37 = 0.37 \qquad\qquad 18\% \longrightarrow 18 = 0.18$

PRACTICE

Complete the table. Write each percent as a fraction with a denominator of 100, as a fraction in simplest terms, and as a decimal.

	Percent	Fraction with Denominator of 100	Fraction in Simplest Terms	Decimal
1.	28%			
2.	75%			
3.	150%			
4.	84%			
5.	12%			
6.	30%			
7.	16%			
8.	200%			
9.	4%			
10.	40%			

Finding a Fraction of a Percent

You have probably seen ads for bank interest rates or mortgage rates that include a fraction of a percent, such as $8\frac{1}{2}\%$ or $4\frac{3}{4}\%$. On occasion the government might announce it is raising the prime rate by $\frac{1}{4}\%$. Since 1% means 1 one-hundredth, $\frac{1}{4}\%$ means $\frac{1}{4}$ of a percent or $\frac{1}{4}$ of 1 one-hundredth.

Study these examples to see how to rename a fraction of a percent.

Examples

Change $\frac{1}{2}\%$ to a decimal and to a fraction.

- Divide numerator by denominator to name the fraction as a decimal.

$$\frac{1}{2} = 1 \div 2 = 0.5 \qquad \frac{1}{2}\% = 0.5\%$$

- Next, remove the % sign and move the decimal point *2 places to the left.*

$$0.5\% = 0.005 = 0.005$$

- Rename the decimal as a fraction in simplest terms.

$$0.005 = \frac{5}{1,000} = \frac{1}{200}$$

$$\frac{1}{2}\% = 0.005 = \frac{1}{200}$$

Change $3\frac{1}{4}\%$ to a decimal and to a fraction.

- Write $\frac{1}{4}$ as a decimal.

$$3\frac{1}{4}\% = 3.25\%$$

- Next, remove the % sign and move the decimal point *2 places to the left*.

$$3.25\% = 0.0325$$

- Rename the decimal as a fraction in simplest terms.

$$0.0325 = \frac{325}{10,000} = \frac{13}{400}$$

$$3\frac{1}{4}\% = 0.0325 = \frac{13}{400}$$

PRACTICE

Write the fraction for each percent.

1. $\frac{3}{5}$ of a percent _____

2. $\frac{1}{8}\%$ _____

3. $2\frac{1}{4}\%$ _____

4. $\frac{3}{10}$ of a percent _____

5. $3\frac{5}{8}\%$ _____

Write the decimal for each percent.

6. $\frac{4}{5}\%$ _____

7. $\frac{3}{8}$ of a percent _____

8. $\frac{1}{10}$ of a percent _____

9. $5\frac{7}{8}\%$ _____

10. 0.3% _____

Changing a Fraction to a Percent

To change a fraction to a percent, remember that percent means *per hundred*. You can rename the fraction to an equal fraction with a denominator of 100 to name it as a percent.

You can set any fraction equal to a fraction with a denominator of 100 and a letter in the numerator. You can then use cross products to find the value of the letter.

Example   Change $\frac{3}{15}$ to a percent.

- Set the fraction equal to a fraction with 100 in the denominator and a letter in the numerator.

$$\frac{3}{15} = \frac{n}{100}$$

- Cross multiply.

$$3 \times 100 = 15 \times n$$
$$300 = 15n$$

- Divide to find the value of n.

$$\frac{300}{15} = \frac{15n}{15} \qquad n = 20$$

- Replace n with the number it equals.

$$\frac{n}{100} = \frac{20}{100}$$

- Write the fraction with a denominator of 100 as a percent.

$$\frac{20}{100} = 20\%$$

$$\frac{3}{15} = 20\%$$

PRACTICE

Write each fraction as a percent.

1. $\frac{1}{4} =$ _____

2. $\frac{2}{5} =$ _____

3. $\frac{3}{8} =$ _____

4. $\frac{5}{6} =$ _____

5. $\frac{1}{2} =$ _____

6. $\frac{5}{8} =$ _____

7. $\frac{7}{10} =$ _____

8. $\frac{1}{3} =$ _____

9. $\frac{3}{4} =$ _____

10. $\frac{7}{8} =$ _____

Changing a Decimal to a Percent

One way to change a decimal to a percent is to write the decimal as a fraction with a denominator of 100.

Examples

    Change 0.125 to a percent.

- Write the decimal as a fraction.

$$0.125 = \frac{125}{1000}$$

- Divide the numerator and the denominator to get an equivalent fraction with a denominator of 100.

$$\frac{125 \div 10}{1000 \div 10} = \frac{1.25}{100}$$

- Write the fraction with a denominator of 100 as a percent.

$$\frac{12.5}{100} = 12.5\%$$

    $0.125 = 12.5\%$

    Change 3.25 to a percent.

- Write the decimal as the numerator of a fraction with a denominator of 100.

$$3.25 \longrightarrow 3\frac{25}{100}$$

- Change the mixed number to an improper fraction.

$$3\frac{25}{100} = \frac{325}{100}$$

- Write the fraction with a denominator of 100 as a percent.

$$\frac{325}{100} = 325\%$$

    $3.25 = 325\%$

Another way to change a decimal to a percent is to move the decimal point.

- Move the decimal point *2 places to the right.* Add zeros as needed.
- Write the percent sign.

    $0.8 \longrightarrow .80 = 80\%$

    $0.04 \longrightarrow 0.04 = 4\%$

    $3.25 \longrightarrow 3.25 = 325\%$

PRACTICE

Write each decimal as a percent.

1. $0.5 =$ _____

2. $0.3 =$ _____

3. $0.25 =$ _____

4. $0.875 =$ _____

5. $0.06 =$ _____

6. $4.4 =$ _____

7. $0.8 =$ _____

8. $3.5 =$ _____

9. $6 =$ _____

10. $0.04 =$ _____

Finding a Percent of a Number

Percent is a way to describe a *part of a whole*. However, while 25% is $\frac{1}{4}$ of the whole, that 25% can represent a different amount depending on the size of the whole. For example, 25% of 100 is 25, but 25% of 1,000 is 250. Remember that the word *of* is a signal to multiply.

To find a percent of a number, first change the percent to either a fraction or a decimal. Then multiply the number by the fraction or the decimal.

Examples   Find 35% of 540 using a fraction.   Find 35% of 540 using a decimal.

- Change the percent to a fraction. $35\% = \frac{\overset{7}{\cancel{35}}}{\underset{20}{\cancel{100}}} = \frac{7}{20}$

- Multiply. $\frac{7}{\cancel{20}_{1}} \times \frac{\overset{27}{\cancel{540}}}{1} = \frac{189}{1} = 189$

$$35\% \text{ of } 540 = 189$$

- Change the percent to a decimal. $35\% = 0.35$

- Multiply. $0.35 \times 540 = 189$

$$35\% \text{ of } 540 = 189$$

PRACTICE

Find the percent of each number.

1. 25% of 400 = _____

2. 15% of 1,000 = _____

3. 6% of 100 = _____

4. 100% of 35 = _____

5. 50% of 150 = _____

6. 10% of 80 = _____

7. 35% of 60 = _____

8. $4\frac{1}{2}$% of 50 = _____

9. 8% of 85 = _____

10. 15% of 70 = _____

Circle the correct answer.

11. What percent of the circles is shaded?

    A $\frac{2}{5}$%   C 25%

    B $\frac{1}{4}$%   D 40%

12. What percent of the square is shaded?

    F 25%   H 68%

    G 75%   J $\frac{3}{4}$%

13. What percent of the shapes are triangles?

    A 20%   C 75%
    B 50%   D 40%

14. What percent of the pitcher is filled?

    F more than 50%
    G less than 50%
    H exactly 50%
    J It is impossible to tell.

Seeing Percent as a Part to Whole Relationship

Percent is a way of describing a part to whole relationship. Suppose 500 people are asked their favorite flavor of ice cream, and 325 name vanilla. All of the people surveyed (500) make up the whole. The number that chose vanilla (325) represents part of the whole. You can say 325 out of 500, which is equal to 65 out of 100, or 65%, chose vanilla.

$$\frac{part}{whole} = \frac{people\ choosing\ vanilla}{people\ surveyed} = \frac{325}{500} = \frac{65}{100} = 65\%$$

To solve a percent problem, you will either have to find the part, the whole, or the percent. In order to find one, you must know the other two, so it is important to be able to identify which is which.

- Generally, the number right after the word *of*, or right after the multiplication sign, is the *whole*.
- Generally, the number right before the word *is*, or right before the equal sign, is the *part*.

Examples

What is 15% of 30?	whole = 30	percent = 15%	part = ?
How much is 3% of 12?	whole = 12	percent = 3%	part = ?
18 is what percent of 75?	whole = 75	percent = ?	part = 18
What percent of 45 is 3?	whole = 45	percent = ?	part = 3
30 is 10% of what number?	whole = ?	percent = 10%	part = 30
25% of what number is 6?	whole = ?	percent = 25%	part = 6

PRACTICE

Identify the percent, the whole, and the part in each statement below.

1. 75 is 20% of 375.

   A percent = _____

   B whole = _____

   C part = _____

2. 80% of 300 is 240.

   D percent = _____

   E whole = _____

   F part = _____

3. 7 is 2% percent of 35.

   A percent = _____

   B whole = _____

   C part = _____

4. 50% of 90 is 45.

   D percent = _____

   E whole = _____

   F part = _____

5. $36 is 20% of $180.

   A percent = _____

   B whole = _____

   C part = _____

6. 45 is 25% of 180.

   D percent = _____

   E whole = _____

   F part = _____

Solving Three Types of Percent Problems

A percent problem involves three numbers: the percent, the whole, and the part. If you know two of these numbers, you can find the third. One way to solve a percent problem is to set up a proportion with equal ratios that name the part to whole relationship.
• In one ratio, write the whole amount in the denominator and the part in the numerator.
• The second ratio will represent the percent. In this ratio the denominator is *always* 100.
One of the terms—the part, the whole, or the number above 100—will be the one you are to find. Write a letter to represent that term. Then use cross products to solve for the missing term.

Examples

Finding the Part   600 jackets were sold. (whole)
12% of the jackets sold had hoods. (percent)
How many of the jackets sold had hoods? (part)

• Write the relationship as a proportion. Use a letter to represent the term to find.

$$\frac{\text{part}}{\text{whole}} \longrightarrow \frac{\text{jackets with hoods}}{\text{jackets sold}} \longrightarrow \frac{n}{600} = \frac{12}{100}$$

• Cross multiply and find the value of n.

$$\frac{\overset{1}{\cancel{100}} \times n}{\cancel{100}_1} = \frac{12 \times \overset{6}{\cancel{600}}}{\cancel{100}_1}$$

    72 of the jackets sold had hoods. $n = 72$

Finding the Whole   12% of the jackets sold had hoods. (percent)
72 of the jackets sold had hoods. (part)
How many jackets were sold? (whole)

• Write the relationship as a proportion. Use a letter to represent the term to find.

$$\frac{\text{part}}{\text{whole}} \longrightarrow \frac{\text{jackets with hoods}}{\text{jackets sold}} \longrightarrow \frac{72}{n} = \frac{12}{100}$$

• Cross multiply and find the value of n.

$$\frac{\overset{6}{\cancel{72}} \times 100}{\cancel{12}_1} = \frac{\overset{1}{\cancel{12}} \times n}{\cancel{12}_1}$$

    600 jackets were sold. $n = 600$

Finding the Percent   600 jackets were sold. (whole)
72 of the jackets sold had hoods. (part)
What percent of the jackets sold had hoods? (percent)

• Write the relationship as a proportion. Use a letter to represent the term to find.

$$\frac{\text{part}}{\text{whole}} \longrightarrow \frac{\text{jackets with hoods}}{\text{jackets sold}} \longrightarrow \frac{72}{600} = \frac{n}{100}$$

• Cross multiply and find the value of n.

$$\frac{\overset{12}{\cancel{72}} \times \overset{1}{\cancel{100}}}{\underset{1}{\overset{6}{\cancel{600}}}} = \frac{\overset{1}{\cancel{600}} \times n}{\cancel{600}_1}$$

    12% of the jackets sold had hoods. $n = 12$

Circle *part*, *whole*, or *percent* to tell what you need to find in each problem. Then write a part to whole proportion. Have one ratio of the proportion represent percent with 100 as the denominator. Use a letter to represent the term you need to find. Finally, solve.

1. Randall borrowed $25,000 to remodel his home. So far he has repaid $15,000 of his loan. What percent of the loan has been repaid?

   Find: part   whole   percent

   _____

2. At Ace Products, 265 of the employees travel more than 10 miles to get to work. That is 25% of the total number of workers. How many employees are there at ACE Products?

   Find: part   whole   percent

   _____

3. Nine-tenths of the students in the class passed the math test. What percent of the class passed the test?

   Find: part   whole   percent

   _____

4. Rhoda earns $1,000 a month at a part-time job. She puts 15% of her earnings into a savings account. How much does Rhoda save each month?

   Find: part   whole   percent

   _____

5. Leroy has 30 hours of free time each week. He spends 6 hours of that free time at a gym. What percent of his free time does Leroy spend at the gym?

   Find: part   whole   percent

   _____

6. In a recent survey 5,240 people said they would like to change careers. That number represents 25% of the people questioned. How many people were questioned?

   Find: part   whole   percent

   _____

7. Mitch uses 30% of his monthly salary for rent. Mitch's monthly salary is $2,460. How much of his salary goes for rent?

   Find: part   whole   percent

   _____

8. There are 75 questions on the social studies test. In order to pass, Alicia must get 60 questions right. What percent must she get right?

   Find: part   whole   percent

   _____

9. Julie gets an employee discount at the store where she works. She can use the discount to get $30 off of the price of a $200 coat. What percent is the employee discount?

   Find: part   whole   percent

   _____

10. The total cost for Theodore's new car was $16,400. If he paid a 20% deposit, how much was his deposit?

    Find: part   whole   percent

    _____

Writing a Percent Problem as an Equation

Another way to set up a percent problem is to write an equation. You can translate words into math symbols to write the equation. In math, the word *of* lets you know you should multiply, and the words *is* and *are* mean "is/are equal to." Use a letter to represent the term you do not know. You can then solve the equation.

Examples

Twenty-one of the people in line want to buy tickets for the concert. They represent 60% of the people in the line. How many people are in line?

21 people are 60% of the people in line ⟶ $21 = 60\% \times n$

Out of 50 students, 12 got an A on the exam. What percent of the students got an A?

12 students are what percent of 50 students? ⟶ $12 = n\% \times 50$

An auto mechanic earns 10% of the total labor charges on a repair. If the total labor charges are $975, how much does the mechanic earn?

10% of $975 is how much? ⟶ $10\% \times \$975 = n$

PRACTICE

Write each of the following as an equation.

1. What is 4% of 30?

2. 10 is 2.5% of what number?

3. 16% of what number is 18?

4. How much is 19% of 65?

5. What is 200 percent of 45?

6. What percent of $340 is $30.60?

7. 210 is what percent of 600?

8. 128 is 40% of what number?

Using Percent to Solve Word Problems

Solve each problem below.

1. In a poll, 86 percent of the 2,000 parents questioned said they think their children are "good kids." How many parents gave this answer?

   _____

2. A couch originally marked $750 is on sale for 20% off. How much is the sale price of the couch?

   _____

3. Celine bought a coat for $120 that was originally marked $160. What percent of the original price did she pay?

   _____

4. Ten years ago, an antique Jenny Lynn plate sold for $12. Today it sells for $66. Today's price is what percent of the old price?

   _____

The list below shows the interest rates a bank is offering to people who invest in certificates of deposit (CDs). Use the list to answer Numbers 5–7.

Certificates of Deposit	
1-year CD:	4% yearly interest
2-year CD:	6% yearly interest
3-year CD:	8% yearly interest
$50 penalty for early withdrawal	

5. If you put $2,400 in a 1-year CD, how much money will you have at the end of one year?

   _____

6. If you put that $2,400 in a 2-year CD, how much interest will you make by the time it matures?

   _____

7. Roger put $3,000 in a 2-year CD, but he withdrew it after just one year. How much did he make on his investment?

   _____

Ratio, Proportion, and Percent Skills Checkup

Circle the letter of the correct answer to each problem. Reduce all fractions to simplest terms.

1. 10.5% of $300 =
   - A $31.50
   - B $315
   - C $3.90
   - D $3.50
   - E None of these

2. 135% of □ = 270
   - F 135
   - G 500
   - H 364.5
   - J 200
   - K None of these

3. What percent of 120 is 20?
   - A 67%
   - B 60%
   - C 40%
   - D 21%
   - E None of these

4. $4\frac{1}{2}$% of $5.30 =
   - F $0.24
   - G $0.45
   - H $0.32
   - J $0.12
   - K None of these

5. What percent of 440 is 264?
   - A 50%
   - B 60%
   - C 65%
   - D 70%
   - E None of these

6. Grant bought a computer game for $32 plus 8% tax. How much did he pay?
   - F $37.60
   - G $34.56
   - H $34.50
   - J $35.50

7. Candice just got a 6% salary increase. She was making $28,700 per year. How much will she now make each year?
   - A $30,422
   - B $17,220
   - C $27,220
   - D $19,978

8. Kelly buys a $50 shirt on sale for $45. How much was the shirt marked down?
   - F 5%
   - G 10%
   - H 90%
   - J 15%

9. One yard of fabric sells for $7.95. How many yards of fabric did Carmen buy if the bill was $63.60 before tax?
   - A $3\frac{1}{2}$
   - B 5
   - C 7
   - D 8

10. Of every 250 widgets that are made, 3 are rejected. If 1,000 widgets are made, how many are rejected?
    - F 83
    - G 75
    - H 25
    - J 12

11. Which of the following is equal to 60%?

A $\dfrac{2}{3}$ C $\dfrac{3}{5}$

B 0.06 D $\dfrac{6}{100}$

12. Ronnie buys a blouse for $65 plus 8% tax. She uses this number sentence to figure out how much she owes.

$$\$65 \times 0.08 = \underline{\qquad}$$

What does the answer to the number sentence represent?

F the price of the blouse before tax
G the cost of the blouse, including tax
H what percentage $65 is of the final cost
J how much tax she will pay

13. Which of these number sentences could you use to solve the following proportion?

$$\dfrac{35}{125} = \dfrac{90}{n}$$

A $35 \times 90 = 125 \times n$
B $35 \times n = 125 \times 90$
C $125 \times 35 = 90 \times n$
D Any of these number sentences would work.

14. Mark earns $1,000 a month plus a 6% commission on all his sales. In August, his sales were a total of $12,000. How much money did he earn altogether that month?

F $720
G $780
H $1,720
J $8,200

15. If one dozen eggs cost $0.90, how much will 20 eggs cost?

A $1.20
B $1.50
C $1.00
D $1.30

16. Akiko paid $325 for a chair that was originally marked $500. By what percent was the chair marked down?

F 35%
G 65%
H 0.35%
J 28%

17. Tuition at the Performers' Dance School is $150 per 20-week semester. When Rosa started class, there were only 8 weeks left in the winter semester. Which of these proportions could she use to figure out how much tuition she owes?

A $\dfrac{\$150}{20} = \dfrac{8}{x}$

B $\dfrac{20}{\$150} = \dfrac{x}{8}$

C $\dfrac{\$150}{20} = \dfrac{x}{8}$

D Any of these proportions would work.

18. The Jay family makes $720 a week. If they spend $180 each week on food, what percent of their income is spent on food?

F 15%
G 20%
H 25%
J 30%

Probability, Statistics, and Data Analysis

Investigating Probability

Probability is the study of how likely it is for an **event** to occur. The different results that can occur are called **outcomes**.

The probability of an event is often expressed with words such as *likely*, *very likely*, or *not likely*. When the chances for a particular outcome are good, the probability is favorable. If the outcome is sure to happen, we say it is certain; but if there is no chance for the outcome to occur, we say it is impossible.

Probability can also be described as a number. The number is found by comparing the number of ways that are favorable for an event to occur with all of the outcomes that are possible.

$$\text{probability} = \frac{\text{number of favorable outcomes}}{\text{total number of outcomes}}$$

The number that represents a probability can be expressed using words, as a fraction, as a decimal, or as a percent.

Example

Art, Etan, José, Ryan, and Dwight each write their names on separate slips of paper and put the papers in a box. One name will be drawn to win a prize. Each has an equal chance of winning. What is the probability that Ryan's name will be drawn?

There are 5 different names that can be drawn. Only 1 name is Ryan's.

$$\text{probability (of Ryan's name being drawn)} = \frac{\text{favorable outcomes}}{\text{possible outcomes}} = \frac{1}{5} = 0.2 = 20\%$$

The probability that Ryan's name will be drawn is $\frac{1}{5}$, 0.2, or 20%.

Ryan's chances are 1 out of 5, or 20%.

- If there is no chance that an event can happen, the probability is 0.
  The probability of a banana turning into an apple is 0.

- If an event is certain to happen, its probability is 1, or 100%.
  The probability that you will get wet if you stand in the rain without a raincoat or an umbrella is 1, or 100%.

- The greater the probability that an event will occur, the closer the number will be to 1 or 100%; the less the probability, the closer the number will be to 0.

Circle the correct answer.

1. A box contains 7 green and 5 blue counters. What is the probability that Craig reaches into the box without looking and picks a blue counter?

   A $\dfrac{1}{5}$ C $\dfrac{1}{12}$

   B $\dfrac{5}{7}$ D $\dfrac{5}{12}$

2. What is the probability that if you ask someone to pick a number from 1 through 10, the number picked will be less than 5?

   F $\dfrac{2}{5}$ H $\dfrac{2}{3}$

   G $\dfrac{1}{2}$ J $\dfrac{1}{4}$

3. When the club voted for a new president, Orlando got 12 votes, Isiah got 14 votes, and Jacques got 10 votes. If a person in the class is selected at random, what is the probability that he or she voted for Orlando?

   A $\dfrac{1}{3}$ C $\dfrac{5}{18}$

   B $\dfrac{1}{12}$ D $\dfrac{5}{13}$

4. What is the probability that a letter picked at random from the first 10 letters of the alphabet will not be a consonant?

   F $\dfrac{3}{10}$ H $\dfrac{4}{7}$

   G $\dfrac{2}{5}$ J $\dfrac{3}{5}$

5. What is the probability of a person being born in a month beginning with the letter "A"?

   A $\dfrac{1}{12}$ C $\dfrac{1}{2}$

   B $\dfrac{1}{3}$ D $\dfrac{1}{6}$

6. What is the probability of tossing an even number with a number cube numbered 1 through 6?

   F $\dfrac{4}{6}$ H $\dfrac{1}{3}$

   G $\dfrac{2}{3}$ J $\dfrac{1}{2}$

Use the diagram of the lettered discs to answer Numbers 7 and 8.

7. If you reach into the bag without looking and take out a disc, what is the probability it will be a "B"?

   A 25%   C 10%
   B 30%   D 2%

8. What is the probability you will pick the letter "D"?

   F 100%   H 50%
   G 25%   J 0%

9. What is the probability that if you drop something, it will fall down rather than up?

   A $\dfrac{1}{2}$ C 3:4

   B 0.25   D 100%

Finding Mean, Median, and Mode

When a set of data is collected, the least value is called the **minimum**. The greatest value is the **maximum**. The difference between the minimum and the maximum values is called the **range**.

Example   These were Rob's scores the last 10 times he bowled:
152, 167, 139, 151, 163, 169, 201, 171, 168, 169

The data is the set of Rob's bowling scores.
The minimum of the data is 139.
The maximum is 201.
The range of the data is the difference between 201 and 139, or 62.

There are different ways to find a typical value to represent the data. They include finding the mean, the median, and the mode.

Mean
The **mean,** or **average,** is the number you would have if all the values in the set of data were the same. To find an average, add all of the numbers in the set of data. Then divide that sum by the total number of values.
To find the mean, or average, of Rob's scores:
- Add all 10 scores. The sum of the scores is 1,650.
- Then divide the sum by the number of scores. $1,650 \div 10 = 165$

        Rob's mean, or average, score is 165.

Median
The **median** is the value that is in the middle of the list when the values have been arranged in order from least to greatest. To find the median, write the values in order. If there is an odd number of values, the median will be the one in the middle of the list. If the list has an even number of values, there will be two middle values. Find the average of the two middle values.
To find Rob's median score:
- Arrange the scores in order from least to greatest.
  139, 151, 152, 163, 167, 168, 169, 169, 171, 201
- Find the value in the middle. There is an even number of scores. Find the average of the two middle scores. $167 + 168 = 335$ $335 \div 2 = 167\frac{1}{2}$

        Rob's median score is $167\frac{1}{2}$.

Mode
The **mode** is the value that appears most often in a set of numbers. It is possible for a set of data to have more than one mode. If no number appears more often than any other, then the set of values has *no mode*.
To find the mode of Rob's scores:
- Find the score that appears more often than any other.
  Rob scored 169 twice.
- No other score appears more than one time.

        The mode of Rob's scores is 169.

Circle the correct answer.

Use the following information to answer Numbers 1–3.

Five of the houses in the neighborhood where the Gordons live were sold recently. The houses sold for $175,000, $183,000, $182,300, $177,000, and $184,700.

1. What was the mean (average) selling price of the houses?

    A $182,300
    B $180,100
    C $180,400
    D $177,000

2. What was the median selling price of the houses?

    F $182,300
    G $175,000
    H $183,000
    J $184,700

3. What was the range of the sale prices of the houses?

    A $359,700
    B $175,300
    C $ 18,400
    D $ 9,700

4. Glenn shipped 10 boxes; 5 weighed 12 pounds, 4 weighed 15 pounds, and 1 weighed 20 pounds. What was the average weight of the boxes Glenn shipped?

    F 12 pounds
    G 14 pounds
    H 16 pounds
    J 18 pounds

5. On his last 4 Spanish quizzes, David had scores of 85, 93, 82, and 96. What is David's average so far?

    A 80
    B 83
    C 85
    D 89

6. To get an A in Spanish, David must have an average of 90 or better. Which of these scores on his next 2 quizzes will *not* be enough for David to earn an A?

    F 88 and 94
    G 97 and 84
    H 85 and 90
    J 90 and 92

7. When Jolene shopped for a coffee maker, she found a range of $23 in the price for the same item at different stores. If the least expensive price she found was $49.99, what was the most expensive?

    A $69
    B $98
    C $83.99
    D $72.99

8. Coretta bought 5 gifts for friends. The gifts cost $46.50, $38.75, $42.25, $51, and $36.50. What was the average amount Coretta spent on a gift?

    F $37.50
    G $41
    H $43
    J $45.25

Gathering Data for a Survey

When a company or an organization wants to find out what people think, it can conduct a **survey** and ask questions to gather information, or **data**. The data are usually gathered from a **sample group**, which is a small part of the population the organization wants to know about.

- The **population** consists of people or objects that the survey is about. In a survey to find out how many people living in particular city plan to vote for Candidate A, the population is all of the registered voters in that city.

- The sample group should be members of the population.

- The sample group should represent a **random sample**. That means every member of the group has an equal chance of being selected. The survey of voters should include people from different walks of life throughout the entire city rather than from only one group or one neighborhood.

It is important that survey questions are **unbiased**; they should not influence the answers. Look at these two questions designed to find what kind of food people like:

What kind of pizza do you like?

What is your favorite food?

The first question limits the answers because it assumes a person would select pizza as a favorite food, while the second question leaves the choice open to any type of food.

PRACTICE

Circle the correct answer.

1. The local coffee shop plans to add items to its lunch menu. Which of these sample groups would give the best data about what items to add?

    A people who buy coffee only in the morning

    B all customers of the store

    C the people who work in the shop

2. Herman is writing a questionnaire for a survey to find out what brand of dish detergent people prefer. Which of these questions would produce the most unbiased results?

    F Do you prefer Brand A or Brand B for washing dishes?

    G Do you like Brand Y because it is gentle to your hands or because it has a nice fragrance?

    H Which brand of dish detergent do you normally buy?

3. Which question would get the most unbiased results about a person's reaction to a movie?

    A What did you think of the movie?

    B What was your favorite part of the movie?

    C Weren't the special effects great?

4. The high school drama club is planning to put on a play. They want to find out what type of play most people would prefer to see. Which of these would make up the best sample group?

    F the members of the drama club

    G a random sampling of the students, parents, and faculty

    H a random sampling of the faculty

Reading a Table

Tables and graphs are useful ways to organize information and make it easier to read. To understand what a table shows, read the title and the headings of the rows and the columns. They explain the relationships of the information shown.

The title of the table below tells us that the table contains information about the schedule for people who work at a restaurant.

The rows of the table represent the different jobs the people have; cook, bus staff, and so on.

The columns represent the days of the week the restaurant is open.

The boxes within the table show the names of people scheduled for each job on each day. The shaded box shows the names of waiters scheduled to work on Tuesday.

Morning Work Schedule at Petra's Cafe

	Sun.	Tues.	Wed.	Thurs.	Fri.	Sat.
Cook	Marcus Allen	Marcus	Allen	Marcus	Marcus Allen	Allen
Bus staff	Stan			Stan	Stan	Stan
Waiters	Alicia Adolfo Connie Greta	Adolfo Lana Alicia	Adolfo Allen Lana	Alicia Greta Lana	Alicia Adolfo Connie	Connie Adolfo
Host	Lana				Lana	Lana

PRACTICE

Use the table above to answer each question.

1. Who will be cooking Thursday morning? _____

2. Who will be busing tables Saturday morning? _____

3. What job will Allen be doing Friday morning? _____

4. How many people will be working at the restaurant Wednesday morning? _____

5. On which morning will the greatest number of people be working? _____

6. How many days will Connie work this week? _____

7. What day will the restaurant be closed? _____

8. On what day will both Greta and Allen be working? _____

Reading a Complex Table or Chart

A chart or a table may have several sections. To find information in this type of chart, read all of the labels carefully to make sure you know what each section represents.

PRACTICE

Use the table below to answer Numbers 1–5. Find the information you need in the table and check that it is correct *before* you do any figuring.

Work Schedule at Petra's Cafe for the Week of May 6–12

MORNING SHIFT	Sun.	Tues.	Wed.	Thurs.	Fri.	Sat.
Cook	Marcus Allen	Marcus	Allen	Marcus	Marcus Allen	Allen
Bus Staff	Stan			Stan	Stan	Stan
Waiters	Alicia Adolfo Connie Greta	Adolfo Lana Alicia	Adolfo Allen Lana	Alicia Greta Lana	Alicia Adolfo Connie	Connie Adolfo
Host	Lana				Lana	Lana

DAY SHIFT	Sun.	Tues.	Wed.	Thurs.	Fri.	Sat.
Cook	Gail Tomas	Gail	Roger	Gail	Gail Tomas	Roger
Bus Staff	Roger			Roger	Roger	
Waiters	Wendy Mo	Sandy Wei	Sandy Wei	Wendy Mo Wei	Wendy Sandy Shawn	Shawn
Host	Wei				Wei	

EVENING SHIFT	Sun.	Tues.	Wed.	Thurs.	Fri.	Sat.
Cook	Dan S.	Dan S.	Bailey	Dan S.	Dan S.	Bailey
Bus Staff						
Waiters	Ali Juana	Juana Maria	Juana Maria	Ali Mary	Ali Juana	Dick Dan R.
Host	Maria				Maria	Maria

1. How many people will work the evening shift on Tuesday? _____

2. How many cooks does this restaurant employ? _____

3. What day and shift have the smallest staff? _____

4. Waiters make $3.50 an hour, and each shift is 8 hours long. How much will the day shift waiters be paid for their work on Thursday? _____

5. Cooks receive $72 per shift. How much will the restaurant pay its cooks for the work they do this week? _____

Reading a Bar Graph

Bar graphs can use either vertical (up and down) or horizontal (side to side) bars to show data. One side, or axis, is labeled with numbers. The categories are listed along the other axis.

The length of the bar for each category corresponds to its number. If the end of a bar falls between two numbers, estimate where it lies between the two numbers.

Example   What is the minimum cost to purchase a Supercuts franchise?

In the graph shown at right, the top of the bar for Supercuts is a little higher than the $100,000 mark. It is about $\frac{1}{5}$ the distance between 100 and 150 or about $\frac{1}{5}$ of 50, which would be 10. You might estimate Supercuts at 100 plus 10, or 110, which would be $110,000.

The minimum cost of a Supercuts franchise is about $110,000.

PRACTICE

Estimate the minimum start-up cost for opening each franchise to answer each question.

1. Which of the franchises shown requires the least amount of money?

   _____

2. What is the minimum cost of a franchise for a Martinizing Dry-Cleaning store?

   _____

3. How much more money is needed to get a franchise for an Oil Express than for a UPS Store?

   _____

4. Which of the franchises shown can be acquired for less than $100,000?

   _____

5. Ramon wants to open an Oil Express. He has $120,000 to put towards that franchise. How much more money does he need?

   _____

6. What is the minimum cost of a franchise for a Subway?

   _____

Reading a Double Bar Graph

To show similar information about two or more things, you can use a double bar graph. The graph at right shows money earned in sales at the two locations of Herman's Gift Shop during the last six months of the year.

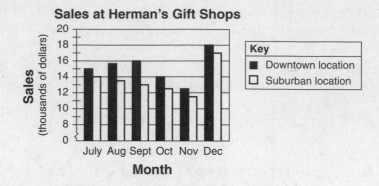

Sales at Herman's Gift Shops

Key
■ Downtown location
□ Suburban location

PRACTICE

Use the graph above to answer these questions.

1. During how many months were the sales at either location $13,000 or less?

   A 2 months
   B 3 months
   C 4 months
   D 5 months

2. During which two months did Herman's Gift Shops earn the least amount?

   F August and September
   G July and December
   H October and November
   J September and December

3. In which month did the downtown store earn about $3,000 more than the suburban store?

   A July
   B August
   C September
   D October

4. During which month were the combined sales at both stores more than $30,000?

   F July
   G August
   H September
   J December

5. In which month did the suburban store earn between $12,000 and $13,000?

   A August
   B September
   C October
   D November

6. Based on the graph, which of the following can you conclude?

   F The suburban store has better sales people.
   G The downtown store earns less money than the suburban store.
   H The downtown store earns more money than the suburban store.
   J People like the downtown store more.

Reading a Line Graph

A **line graph** is often used to show a change over time. The units of time are usually shown along the horizontal axis. Each piece of data is shown by a point on the grid, and the points are then connected.

A **double line graph** allows you to compare the data for two things over the same period of time. This graph shows the average temperatures in Shellville for the months of January and June from 1990 through 2004. In January of 1990, the temperature was about 54° F, while in June of that same year, the temperature was about 85° F.

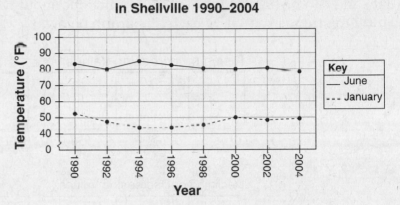

PRACTICE

Use the data in the graph above to estimate the answers for these questions.

1. What was the temperature in June of 2004?

   A about 70°F
   B about 80°F
   C about 53°F
   D about 48°F

2. Between which years was there the least change in the average temperature for the month of January?

   F 1990 and 1994
   G 1998 and 2002
   H 1994 and 1998
   J It is impossible to tell.

3. In which year did Shellville have the greatest difference between the average temperature for June and January?

   A 1990
   B 1994
   C 1998
   D 2002

4. In which year did Shellville have the least difference between the average temperature for June and January?

   F 1990   H 2000
   G 1996   J 2002

5. In which year were the average temperatures for both January and June lower than the previously reported year?

   A 1990   C 1994
   B 1992   D 2000

6. Based on the graph, which of the following can you conclude?

   F Shellville is a good place to live.
   G In Shellville, the difference between the temperature in January and June tends to be about 30°.
   H If the pattern shown continues, Shellville can expect the average temperature for the month of June to be 90°F by 2006.
   J You cannot draw any conclusions from this graph.

Identifying Trends and Making Predictions

A **trend** is a pattern of change that occurs in a particular direction over time. For example, with advanced technology, there has been a trend for people to purchase digital cameras rather than conventional cameras. Identifying a trend gives general information about the data and can be helpful for making predictions about what will happen in the future. Study the trends shown by each line graph below.

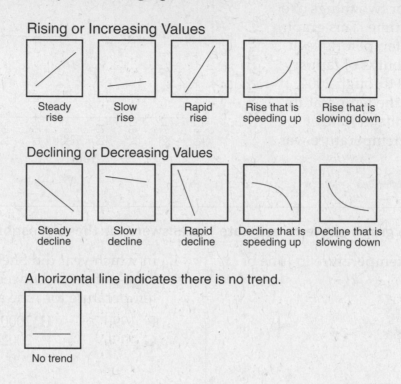

Rising or Increasing Values

Steady rise | Slow rise | Rapid rise | Rise that is speeding up | Rise that is slowing down

Declining or Decreasing Values

Steady decline | Slow decline | Rapid decline | Decline that is speeding up | Decline that is slowing down

A horizontal line indicates there is no trend.

No trend

PRACTICE

Identify the trend, if any, that is shown in each graph. Then use the graphs to answer Questions 1–4.

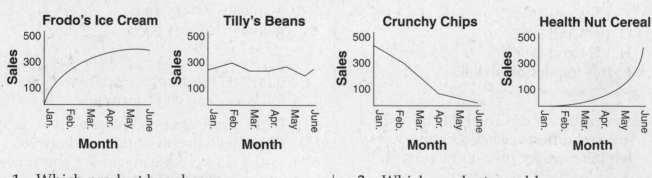

Frodo's Ice Cream | Tilly's Beans | Crunchy Chips | Health Nut Cereal

1. Which product has shown a rapid decline in sales? _____

2. Which product had a rapid rise in sales followed by a leveling-off period? _____

3. Which product would you predict will have the greatest sales in July? _____

4. For which product would you predict the number of sales for July to be a little less than 300? _____

Reading a Circle Graph

In a circle graph, a circle is divided into wedges. Each wedge or section represents a fraction of the total—the larger the section, the greater the fraction of the whole represented. This type of graph allows the viewer to compare the sizes of the parts more easily. Circle graphs are often called pie charts.

The sections in a circle graph are usually labeled with fractions or with percents. To find the actual number represented by a section, multiply the total amount represented in the graph by the fraction or percent.

Example
The circle graph at right represents people who immigrated to the United States from other countries in North America in 2001. About how many of those people immigrated to the United States from Canada?

- Approximately 5% of the 408,000 came from Canada.
- Find 5% of 408,000. Multiply 0.05 × 408,000.
  0.05 × 408,000 = 24,000

Approximately 24,000 of the people came from Canada.

North America Immigrants to U.S. in 2001 by Country of Origin
(to nearest thousand)

Graph represents 408,000 people
Source: U.S. Census

PRACTICE

Use the graph above to answer Numbers 1–3.

1. The greatest number of immigrants came from which location?

   A Caribbean countries
   B Central America
   C Mexico
   D Canada

2. Approximately how many people came from Central America?

   F 78,000   H 94,000
   G 100,000   J 87,000

3. About how many times as many people came from Caribbean countries as from Canada?

   A 2 times as many
   B 3 times as many
   C 4 times as many
   D 5 times as many

Use this graph to answer Numbers 4–6.

The Condition of the Water in the 2,111 U.S. Watersheds

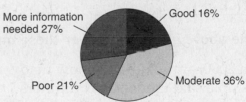

4. Which fraction best describes how many U.S. watersheds have poor water?

   F $\frac{1}{4}$ H $\frac{1}{20}$

   G $\frac{1}{5}$ J $\frac{1}{8}$

5. To the nearest whole number, how many U.S. watersheds are known to have good water? _____

6. To the nearest whole number, how many U.S. watersheds are known to have poor water? _____

Finding Percent of Change in a Graph

The information in a graph can be used to find the percent by which a value has increased or decreased. Divide the starting amount by the **amount of change**, and then express the result as a percent.

Example
What was the percent of increase from 2000 to 2004 in computer use for word processing among people 18 to 24 years old?

- Find the difference between the numbers for each year. The difference is the amount of change.
$$10.0 - 5.3 = 4.7$$
- Use number for the earlier year as the starting amount. Divide the amount of change by the starting amount.
$$4.7 \div 5.3 = 0.8867 \approx 89\%$$
- From 2000 to 2004 the amount increased, so 89% represents a percent of increase.

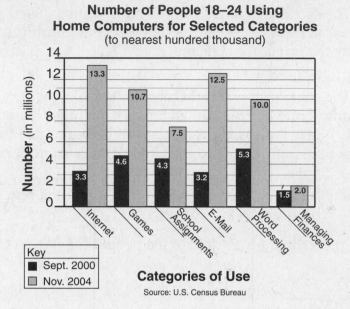

Number of People 18–24 Using Home Computers for Selected Categories
(to nearest hundred thousand)

Key
■ Sept. 2000
▨ Nov. 2004

Categories of Use
Source: U.S. Census Bureau

From 2000 to 2004, there was approximately an 89% increase in the number of people from 18 to 24 using the computer for word processing.

PRACTICE

Use the above graph to answer these questions.

1. In 2000, approximately how many people said they used computers for school assignments? _____

2. About how many times as many people reported using their computers for games in 2004 as did in 2000? _____

3. From 2000 to 2004, what was the percent of increase in using computers for games? _____

4. What was the percent of increase in using the computer for managing finances? _____

5. Based on the graph, which of the following conclusions can be made about people 18–24? (*Hint:* There is more than one correct answer.)

   A The number using home computers has greatly increased.

   B The greatest number used their computers for school assignments.

   C There was an increase of about 300% in the number using the Internet.

   D About 3 million more reported using computers for school assignments in 2004 than in 2000.

Recognizing Appropriate Display of Data in Graphs

Since graphs offer information in a visual way to make it easy for the viewer to understand, it is important that the "picture" matches the data. You can often tell whether a graph is reasonably accurate by using logical thinking.

Example

In a survey of 100 people to find whether red, yellow, or blue was their preferred color, 35 said red, 45 said blue, and 20 chose yellow. Which graph shows these results?

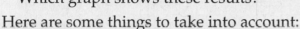

Here are some things to take into account:
- Yellow got the fewest votes, so the section for yellow should be smallest.
- The red section should be smaller than the blue section.
  The red section should be almost twice as big as the yellow section.
- Blue got the greatest number of votes, so the blue section should be largest.
  Since 45 out of 100, or a little less than $\frac{1}{2}$, chose blue, a little less than half of the graph should be blue.

The graph in the middle appears to match the data.

PRACTICE

Circle the correct graph.

Favorite Type of Movie

	Drama	Adventure
Men	35	15
Women	15	35

1. Fifty men and 50 women were asked to choose either drama or adventure as their favorite type of movie. The results of the survey are shown in the above table. Which graph correctly shows the results of the survey?

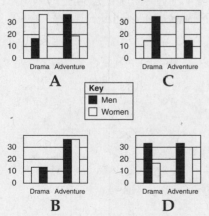

Survey for Merging Towns

	Residents of Marshville	Residents of Braeside
Yes	600	500
No	400	750

2. The above table shows the number of residents in neighboring towns who voted for or against a proposal to join and become one town. Which graph shows how the residents of Marshville voted?

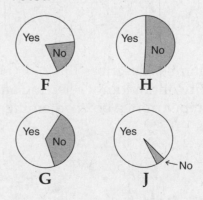

Probability, Statistics, and Data Analysis Skills Checkup

Circle the correct answer.

1. In Cicily's sweater drawer, there are 4 red sweaters, 2 green sweaters, 1 brown sweater, and 3 blue sweaters. If she selects a sweater from the drawer at random, what is the probability it will be green?

   A $\dfrac{1}{5}$ **C** $\dfrac{5}{6}$

   B $\dfrac{3}{4}$ **D** $\dfrac{2}{3}$

   E None of these

2. Sam's scores on 5 math quizzes were 82, 94, 78, 86, and 90. What number represents the range of Sam's scores?

   F 12   **H** 18
   G 15   **J** 20
   K None of these

3. What is Sam's mean (average) score?

   A 82   **C** 88
   B 86   **D** 90
   E None of these

4. The price for the same item found at 4 different stores was $19.95, $23.59, $22.99, and $24.89. What is the median of the prices found?

   F $22.99   **H** $23.29
   G $22.61   **J** $23.75
   K None of these

5. Which number describes the probability of randomly selecting an even number from a box containing the numbers 1–15?

   A $\dfrac{1}{2}$ **C** $\dfrac{7}{15}$

   B $\dfrac{2}{3}$ **D** $\dfrac{1}{5}$

   E None of these

6. Which line graph shows a trend of slowly rising values?

   F   H

   G   J

7. Two hundred children had their choice of either a hot dog or a hamburger for lunch. One hundred fifteen chose hot dogs. The rest chose hamburgers. Which graph shows the results of their choices?

   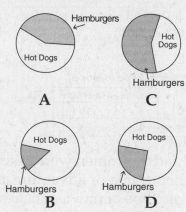

8. Janice bought a bathing suit for $38.80 that originally sold for $48.50. What was the percent of decrease?

   F 30%
   G 25%
   H 20%
   J 15%

These tables show a simplified version of the state income tax rates for one state.
Study the tables. Then do Numbers 9–12.

State Income Tax Rates

Single		
Tax Rate	Taxable Income	
15%	$0	to	$24,650
28%	$24,651	to	$59,750
31%	$59,751	to	$124,650
36%	$124,651	to	$271,050
39.6%	more than $271,050	

Married Filing Jointly or Qualifying Widow(er)		
Tax Rate	Taxable Income	
15%	$0	to	$41,200
28%	$41,201	to	$99,600
31%	$99,601	to	$151,750
36%	$151,751	to	$271,050
39.6%	more than $271,050	

Married Filing Separately		
Tax Rate	Taxable Income	
15%	$0	to	$20,600
28%	$20,601	to	$49,800
31%	$49,801	to	$75,875
36%	$75,876	to	$135,525
39.6%	more than $135,525	

Head of Household		
Tax Rate	Taxable Income	
15%	$0	to	$33,050
28%	$33,051	to	$85,350
31%	$85,351	to	$138,200
36%	$138,201	to	$271,050
39.6%	more than $271,050	

9. Between which two income levels does the greatest increase in the tax rate occur?

   A the first and second: 15% to 28%
   B the second and third: 28% to 31%
   C the third and fourth: 31% to 36%
   D the fourth and fifth: 36% to 39.6%

10. Rochelle is married, but she and her husband file separately. Rochelle earns $62,000 per year. According to these tables, how much must Rochelle pay in taxes?

   F $ 9,300
   G $19,220
   H $17,360
   J $22,320

11. Who will pay the greatest amount in taxes on earnings of $140,000 a year?

   A a single person
   B a married person filing separately
   C a married couple filing jointly
   D a head of household

12. Last year Ron, a single man, made $22,000. This year he made $25,000. If the tax rates have not changed, how much more will Ron pay in taxes this year?

   F $ 450
   G $3,300
   H $3,700
   J $ 840

Algebra

Identifying Patterns

An important part of solving problems is recognizing patterns. The study of algebra includes describing, extending, and making generalizations about geometric and numeric patterns.

PRACTICE

Circle the letter of the correct answer.

1. How many bricks are needed for the next figure in the sequence below?

   A 9   C 15
   B 12   D 18

2. Which describes the pattern below?

   F thick, thin, thick, thin
   G thick, thick, thick, thick
   H thick, thick, thin, thick, thick, thin
   J   thick, thin, thin, thick, thin, thin

3. In this sequence each number is the last number multiplied by 3.
   5, 15, 45, 135, 405, 1215, …

   If the sequence is continued, which number will *not* appear in the list?

   A 3,645   C 32,855
   B 10,935   D 98,415

4. In this sequence each new number is the last number multiplied by 2.
   1, 2, 4, 8, 16, 32, …

   If continued, which number will eventually appear in the list?

   F 54   H 99
   G 63   J 128

Write the correct answer to each question.

5. What are the next two numbers in this sequence?
   1, 2, 4, 7, 11, 16, …

   _____

6. What number is missing from this sequence?
   1, 5, 3, 7, 5, 9, ___, 11, 9…

   _____

7. What should be the next letter in this sequence?
   A, E, I, M, Q, U, ___, …

   _____

8. What will be the first shape in Row 5?

Row 1	□	○	△	⬡	☆
Row 2	○	△	⬡	☆	□
Row 3	△	⬡	☆	□	○
Row 4	⬡	☆	□	○	△

   _____

Analyzing Relationships in Number Sentences

In math, you may add to, subtract from, multiply, or divide a starting amount to find the result. However, sometimes you will know the starting amount and the result, and you have to find what was done to get from one number to the other.

Example   What operation sign is missing in the number sentence $2^5 \bigcirc 4 = 8$?

- First find the value of 2^5. $2^5 = 2 \times 2 \times 2 \times 2 \times 2 = 32$
- Examine the relationships in the number sentence.
  Since the result of 8 is less than the starting number, 32, the number 4 was either subtracted from 32, or 32 was divided by 4. $32 - 4 \neq 8$, but $32 \div 4 = 8$.

  A division sign is missing. The complete sentence is $32 \div 4 = 8$.

PRACTICE

Write +, −, ×, or ÷ to complete each number sentence.

1. $100 \bigcirc 10 = 10$

2. $67 \bigcirc 67 = 0$

3. $(3 + 3) \bigcirc 2 = 12$

4. $2 \times (3 \bigcirc 3) = 18$

5. $105 \bigcirc 25 = 80$

6. $920 \bigcirc 0 = 920$

7. $4 \times (568 \bigcirc 568) = 4$

8. $3 \times (17 \bigcirc 14) = 9$

9. $1.9 \bigcirc 100 = 190$

10. $0.4124 \bigcirc 2.1 = 2.5124$

11. $20 \bigcirc 0.5 = 10$

12. $20 \bigcirc 0.5 = 40$

13. $\dfrac{1}{5} \bigcirc \dfrac{1}{5} = \dfrac{1}{25}$

14. $\dfrac{3}{10} \bigcirc \dfrac{1}{10} = \dfrac{2}{5}$

15. $12 \bigcirc \dfrac{1}{3} = 11\dfrac{2}{3}$

16. $5 \bigcirc \dfrac{1}{5} = 25$

17. $-12 \bigcirc 8 = -20$

18. $4 \bigcirc -9 = -5$

19. $-2 \bigcirc -3 = -5$

20. $-10 \bigcirc -10 = 1$

21. $-4 \bigcirc -4 = 0$

22. $3.102 \bigcirc 10^5 = 310,200$

23. $560 \bigcirc 10^2 = 5.6$

24. $7.19 \bigcirc 10^{-3} = 0.00719$

Working with Functions

A rule that changes one value to another value is called a **function**. The starting number is called the **input**, the result is called the **output**. You can examine a set of input/output numbers for a pattern to find out what the rule, or function, is.

Examples

Rule: Subtract 3, then multiply by 5.

Input	4	5	6	20
Output	5	10	15	85

What is the rule?

Input	2	8	10
Output	4	64	100

Rule: Square the number.

PRACTICE

For Numbers 1–4, use the rule to find the missing numbers.

1. Triple the number.

Input	3	5	11	20
Output	9			

2. Mutiply by 4, then subtract 1.

Input	2	6	9	25
Output	7			

3. Subtract 3, then multiply by 2.

Input	1	3	4.5	$\frac{3}{4}$
Output	−4			

4. Divide by 4.

Input	100	64	88	20
Output	25			

For Numbers 5 and 6, circle the letter of the phrase that describes the function.

5.

Input (x)	1	2	3	4
Output (y)	4	7	10	13

  A Add 10 to x, then divide by 2.
  B Multiply x by 3, then add 1.
  C Divide x by 2, then multiply by 5.

6.

Input (x)	10	25	16	37
Output (y)	90	75	84	63

  F Multiply x by 9.
  G Multiply x by 4, then add 35.
  H Subtract x from 100.

For Numbers 7–10, write the rule.

7.

Input	15	20	35	72
Output	15	20	35	72

Rule: _____

8.

Input	80	74	90	56
Output	40	37	45	28

Rule: _____

9.

Input	5	10	15	20
Output	13	23	33	43

Rule: _____

10.

Input	4	12	9	1
Output	28	84	63	7

Rule: _____

Using Inverse Operations

Inverse means opposite. Addition and subtraction are **inverse operations**; the inverse of adding 3 is subtracting 3. Multiplication and division are also inverse operations; the inverse of multiplying by 6 is dividing by 6.

One way to find a missing number in a math sentence is to rewrite the number sentence using the inverse operation. The same numbers are used in each sentence.

Examples

- Subtract what was added to get the starting number.
  $9 + 3 = 12$, so $12 - 3 = 9$ $\Box + 3 = 12$, so $12 - 3 = \Box$

- Divide by the multiplier to get the number that was multiplied.
  $7 \times 8 = 56$, so $56 \div 7 = 8$ $7 \times \Box = 56$, so $56 \div 7 = \Box$

Sometimes you can rewrite the sentence to the related sentence with the same operation.

Examples

- Subtract one amount from the total to find the other.
  $350 - 182 = 168$, so $350 - 168 = 182$ $350 - \Box = 168$, so $350 - 168 = \Box$

- Divide the quotient by one factor to find the other.
  $63 \div 9 = 7$, so $63 \div 7 = 9$ $63 \div \Box = 7$, so $63 \div 7 = \Box$

After you find the missing number, check your answer. Replace the missing number in the equation with the value you have found. The result should be a true sentence.

Example   In $145 + \Box = 235$, what number in the box will make the sentence true?

$145 + \Box = 235$, so $235 - 145 = \Box$, and $\Box = 90$

$145 + 90 = 235$, so the solution is correct.

PRACTICE

Write the number that belongs in the space to make the number sentence true.

1. $105 + \underline{\hspace{1cm}} = 199$

2. $3.3 \times \underline{\hspace{1cm}} = 0.099$

3. $\underline{\hspace{1cm}} + 89 = 113$

4. $\dfrac{1}{5} + \underline{\hspace{1cm}} = \dfrac{9}{25}$

5. $0.33 + \underline{\hspace{1cm}} = 1.6$

6. $\underline{\hspace{1cm}} + {-12} = -40$

7. $0 + \underline{\hspace{1cm}} = -17$

8. $\underline{\hspace{1cm}} - 16 = 42$

9. $\underline{\hspace{1cm}} \div 8 = 35$

10. $96 \div \underline{\hspace{1cm}} = 16$

11. $2 - \underline{\hspace{1cm}} = \dfrac{3}{4}$

12. $\underline{\hspace{1cm}} - \dfrac{1}{4} = \dfrac{1}{3}$

13. $\underline{\hspace{1cm}} - 2.01 = 9.99$

14. $\underline{\hspace{1cm}} \div 12 = 15$

15. $4\dfrac{4}{5} - \underline{\hspace{1cm}} = \dfrac{1}{10}$

16. $2.1 - \underline{\hspace{1cm}} = 0.08$

17. $\underline{\hspace{1cm}} \times 35 = 280$

18. $4 \times 3 \times \underline{\hspace{1cm}} = 60$

Using Variables in Algebraic Expressions

In algebra, letters or **variables**, also called **unknowns**, are used to represent numbers.

An **algebraic expression** is part of a math sentence. Variables and numbers can be combined with operation signs to create algebraic expressions. The variable in an expression can represent different values, so the value of an expression can change depending on the value assigned to the variable. (See page 116.)

Here are some things to keep in mind when writing algebraic expressions:
* Addition and subtraction are shown with plus ($+$) or minus ($-$) signs.

* Multiplication can be shown in different ways. A multiplication sign is generally *not* used.
    * A dot between numbers means multiply.
    $4 \cdot 5$ means "4×5."
    * A number in front of a variable signals multiplication.
    $4x$ means "4 times x."
    * Letters written together signal multiplication.
    xy means "x times y."
    * A number or a variable in front of parentheses signals multiplication.
    $3(y + 2)$ means "3 times the sum of y and 2."
    $p(4 + z)$ means "p times the sum of 4 and z."

* Division is usually shown in fraction form.
    $\frac{m}{4}$ means "divide m by 4."

Review the words and phrases that signal addition, subtraction, multiplication, and division.

Addition	Subtraction	Multiplication	Division
plus	minus	times	divided by
sum	difference	multiplied by	apiece
total	take away	product	each
added to	subtract	twice, three times, and so on	per
all together	left over	apiece	quotient
in all	how much change	each	how many equal groups
combined	more than		shared equally
increased by	less than		separated into equal groups
	decreased by		

Follow the order of the words when writing an algebraic expression.

Examples
The difference between a number and 12 $\longrightarrow$ $n - 12$.
The difference between 12 and a number $\longrightarrow$ $12 - n$.
Eight added to a number $\longrightarrow$ $n + 8$.
A number added to 8 $\longrightarrow$ $8 + n$.

Circle the algebraic expression that matches the words.

1. a number increased by 7

   A $7n$

   B $\dfrac{7}{n}$

   C $n - 7$

   D $n + 7$

2. six less than m

   F $m - 6$

   G $6 - m$

   H $6m$

   J $\dfrac{6}{m}$

3. 45 divided by y

   A $\dfrac{45}{y}$ C $\dfrac{y}{45}$

   B $45y$ D $45 - y$

4. one-fourth of g

   F $\dfrac{1}{4} \div g$ H $\dfrac{1}{4}g$

   G $g - \dfrac{1}{4}$ J $g + \dfrac{1}{4}$

5. three times h, decreased by 4

   A $3h + 4$

   B $3(h + 4)$

   C $3h - 4$

   D $3(h - 4)$

6. the product of 5, and a number y increased by 2

   F $5y + 2$

   G $5y - 2$

   H $5(y - 2)$

   J $5(y + 2)$

Write an algebraic expression for each phrase below. Use the variable n to represent the unknown.

7. a number divided by 14 _____

8. a number increased by 2 _____

9. a number squared _____

10. half of a number _____

11. a number tripled _____

12. seven more than three times a number _____

13. the difference between a number and 75 _____

14. negative six divided by a number minus 2 _____

15. negative six divided by a number, minus 2 _____

16. the product of ⁻4 and a number _____

17. two-fifths of a number _____

18. thirteen divided by a number _____

19. six less than five times a number _____

20. two more than 12 times a number _____

Evaluating Algebraic Expressions

The value of an algebraic expression depends on the value given to the variable it contains. To **evaluate**, or find the value of the expression, replace the variable with its number value.

Examples

Find the value of $m + 7$.
- Let $m = 4$.
  $m + 7 = 4 + 7 = 11$
  $m + 7 = 11$

- Let $m = -3$.
  $m + 7 = -3 + 7 = 4$
  $m + 7 = 4$

Find the value of $\frac{a}{12} + 2$.
- Let $a = 7$.
  $\frac{a}{12} + 2 = \frac{7}{12} + 2 = 2\frac{7}{12}$
  $\frac{a}{12} + 2 = 2\frac{7}{12}$

- Let $a = 24$.
  $\frac{a}{12} + 2 = \frac{24}{12} + 2 = 4$
  $\frac{a}{12} + 2 = 4$

PRACTICE

Evaluate each expression using the values shown below.

$$n = 3 \qquad x = 2 \qquad y = 5 \qquad m = 10$$

1. $3y =$ _____

2. $m + 5 =$ _____

3. $y - (-7) =$ _____

4. $n^2 =$ _____

5. $0.25m =$ _____

6. $3n + 4 =$ _____

7. $4y - 8.24 =$ _____

8. $30 - nx =$ _____

9. $\dfrac{m}{y} + 3\dfrac{1}{8} =$ _____

10. $-5n =$ _____

11. $x(n + y) =$ _____

12. $\dfrac{3}{5}m =$ _____

13. $15 - ny =$ _____

14. $\dfrac{8m}{-5} =$ _____

15. $\dfrac{x^3 + y^2}{m + 1} =$ _____

16. $0.5y(\dfrac{m^2}{2}) =$ _____

Writing Algebraic Equations and Inequalities

An **equation** is a mathematical sentence stating that two expressions are equal. An equation contains an equal sign and may contain one or more variables. These sentences are examples of equations:

$$n = 4 \qquad 3 + 8 = 11 \qquad m - \frac{3}{y} = 5a$$

An **inequality** is a mathematical sentence stating that two expressions are *not equal*. An inequality can use > (greater than), < (less than), ≥ (greater than or equal to), ≤ (less than or equal to), or ≠ (not equal to). These sentences are examples of inequalities:

$$0 > -7 \qquad 2x - 5 < 27 \qquad 4 \times 8 \neq 5 \times 7$$

PRACTICE

Circle the letter of the sentence that matches the words. Do not solve.

1. Add ten to the product of 5 and n. The result is less than or equal to 75.

   A $5 + 10n \leq 75$
   B $5n + 10 \leq 75$
   C $5 + 10n = 75$
   D $5n + 10 < 75$

2. When you subtract 15 from the sum of n and y^2, the result is not equal to 24.

   F $(15 - n) + y^2 \neq 24$
   G $n + (y^2 - 15) \neq 24$
   H $(n + y^2) - 15 \neq 24$
   J $15 - (n + y^2) \neq 24$

3. Multiply negative 12 by the sum of n plus 5. The product is greater than 47.

   A $-12n + 5 > 47$
   B $-12(n + 5) > 47$
   C $-12 + 5n > 47$
   D $-12 + (5 + n) > 47$

4. The sum of 15 and $\frac{2}{3}$ of x is equal to $y - 5$.

   F $15 + \frac{2}{3} + x = y - 5$
   G $x(15 + \frac{2}{3}) = y - 5$
   H $\frac{2}{3}x + 15 = y - 5$
   J $15(\frac{2}{3} + x) - y - 5$

Write an equation or an inequality for each of the following.

5. 15 less than a number w equals 12 _____

6. 45 is more than a number n _____

7. 87 is equal to 3 times a number n _____

8. 14 is less than 6 times a number y _____

9. a number r divided by 4 equals 18 _____

10. 7 times a number n is equal to 224 _____

11. 96 minus a number r equals 28 _____

12. a number n plus a number p is equal to 35 _____

13. 4 times a number x is greater than 18 _____

14. a number n divided by 15 is greater than 16 _____

Solving Equations

An equation is solved when you have the variable alone on one side of the equal sign and a number alone on the other side. Inverse operations are used in solving equations.

Inverse operations undo one another, so, for example, if an amount has been added to the variable, you can subtract that amount to have only the variable. If the variable was multiplied by an amount, you can divide by that amount, and so on.

An equation is a balanced sentence. Whatever you do on one side of the equal sign must also be done on the other side of the equal sign to keep the balance.

Example Undo addition with subtraction.

$$
\begin{aligned}
x + 12 &= 43 \\
-12 &= -12 \\
\hline
x + 0 &= 31 \\
x &= 31
\end{aligned}
$$

12 has been added to x. Subtract 12.
To keep the balance, subtract 12 from both sides of the equation.

Adding zero to a number does not change its value.

Check: Replace x with 31 in the equation. $31 + 12 = 43$, so the solution is correct.

Example Undo subtraction with addition.

$$
\begin{aligned}
n - 7 &= 22 \\
+7 &= +7 \\
\hline
n &= 29
\end{aligned}
$$

Here 7 has been subtracted from n. Add 7.
To keep the balance, add 7 on both sides of the equation.

Check: $29 - 7 = 22$, so the solution is correct.

Example Undo subtraction of the variable.

$$
\begin{aligned}
35 - n &= 19 \\
+n &= \quad +n \\
\hline
35 &= 19 + n \\
-19 &= -19 \\
\hline
16 &= n
\end{aligned}
$$

The variable has been subtracted. Add it back before you continue.

In this equation, 19 has been added to n. Subtract 19.
Subtract 19 from both sides of the equation.

Check: $35 - 16 = 19$, so the solution is correct.

Example Undo multiplication with division.

$$
\begin{aligned}
3y &= 108 \\
3y \div 3 &= 108 \div 3 \\
\hline
y &= 36
\end{aligned}
$$

Here y has been multiplied by 3.
Divide by 3 on both sides of the equation.

Check: $3 \times 36 = 108$ is true. The solution is correct.

Example Undo division with multiplication.

$$w \div 6 = 9$$ Here w has been divided by 6.

$$\underline{6 \times w \div 6 = 6 \times 9}$$ Multiply by 6 on both sides of the equal sign.

$$w = 54$$

Check: $54 \div 6 = 9$, so the solution is correct.

PRACTICE

Find the value of x in each equation.

1. $x + 95 = 270$

   $x =$ _____

2. $x + 113 = 605$

   $x =$ _____

3. $x - 93 = 25$

   $x =$ _____

4. $x - 2.5 = 10.2$

   $x =$ _____

5. $17 = x + 9$

   $x =$ _____

6. $16 + x = 12$

   $x =$ _____

7. $39 - x = 0$

   $x =$ _____

8. $23x = 46$

   $x =$ _____

9. $105 = 5x$

   $x =$ _____

10. $\dfrac{x}{6} = 36$

    $x =$ _____

11. $\dfrac{156}{x} = 12$

    $x =$ _____

12. $-16x = 80$

    $x =$ _____

13. $\dfrac{15.3}{x} = 3$

    $x =$ _____

14. $\dfrac{7}{3}x = 2$

    $x =$ _____

15. $7.81 - x = 2.95$

    $x =$ _____

Combining Terms

Parts of an expression that are separated by a plus or minus sign are called **terms**. For example, $2x^2$, yz, and 3 are the terms in the expression $2x^2 - yz + 3$.

Like terms are made up of the same variables and/or exponents. For example, $3xm^2$ and xm^2 are like terms—both are amounts of xm^2. You can combine like terms by adding or subtracting.

Examples

$$2a + 3a = 5a \qquad 5x^2 - x^2 = 4x^2 \qquad x^2y^3 + 2x^2y^3 = 3x^2y^3$$

Unlike terms cannot be added or subtracted. For example, you cannot add xy and x^2 since the terms xy and x^2 are not the same.

Examples

$$6b + 5ab = 6b + 5ab \qquad 5n^2 - n = 5n^2 - n$$

However, unlike terms can be multiplied or divided. Remember than multiplication is commutative, so you can change the order of the factors and the product will be the same.

Examples

$$3y \times 5m = 3 \times y \times 5 \times m = 3 \times 5 \times y \times m = 15ym$$

$$3b^2 \times 4b^2 = 3 \times b \times b \times 4 \times b \times b = 3 \times 4 \times b \times b \times b \times b = 12b^4$$

$$\frac{10\,x^2yz^3}{2xz^2} = \frac{\overset{5}{\cancel{10}} \cdot \overset{1}{\cancel{x}} \cdot x \cdot y \cdot z \cdot \overset{1}{\cancel{z}} \cdot \overset{1}{\cancel{z}}}{\underset{1}{\cancel{2}} \cdot \underset{1}{\cancel{x}} \cdot \underset{1}{\cancel{z}} \cdot \underset{1}{\cancel{z}}} = 5xyz$$

When you add, subtract, multiply, and divide terms in an expression, you are **simplifying the expression**.

PRACTICE

Simplify each expression if possible. If the terms cannot be combined, write "Cannot be combined."

1. $5ab + 2ab$

2. $3a + 4b$

3. $4x(3x)$

4. $-2a(3a)$

5. $6x - 2x^2$

6. $-4n(-4a)$

7. $5b^2(2b^5)$

8. $\dfrac{2a}{a}$

9. $\dfrac{x^2}{x}$

10. $\dfrac{4t^2s}{ts}$

11. $3ab + 5b$

12. $\dfrac{4x^3y^2}{4x^2y}$

13. $3ab(a^2)$

14. $\dfrac{16u^3q^2}{2u^2q^2}$

15. $\dfrac{8xy^2}{2x}$

16. $3y - 4b$

Solving Equations with More than One Step

Some equations require more than one step to solve.

Example $x + 3x + 5 = x - 4$

$$
\begin{array}{rl}
x + 3x + 5 = & x - 4 \\
4x + 5 = & x - 4 \\
\underline{ - 5 = - 5} \\
4x = & x - 9 \\
\underline{x = x} \\
3x = & -9 \\
\end{array}
$$

- First simplify by combining terms.
- Next, undo addition with subtraction.

$$\frac{3x}{3} = \frac{-9}{3}$$

- Then undo multiplication with division.

$$x = -3$$

Check.
$$
\begin{array}{rl}
x + 3x + 5 = x - 4 \\
-3 + (3)(-3) + 5 = -3 - 4 \\
-3 + -9 + 5 = -3 - 4 \\
-12 + 5 = -7 \\
-7 = -7
\end{array}
$$

PRACTICE

Solve each equation. Check your answer.

1. $3y - 10 = 47$ $y =$ _____

2. $\dfrac{m}{15} + 62 = 23$ $m =$ _____

3. $37 - p = 28 + 4p$ $p =$ _____

4. $\dfrac{b}{3} + 6 = 82$ $b =$ _____

5. $6y - 2y = 84$ $y =$ _____

6. $9r + 17 = 6r + 32$ $r =$ _____

Simplifying Equations that Contain Fractions

A fraction can have more than one term in the numerator. When this happens, you can write each term as a separate fraction over the same denominator without changing the value of the expression. You can then simplify each term to solve the equation.

Example   Find the value of x in $\dfrac{4 + 6x}{2} = 42$.

- Write each term in the numerator as a separate fraction with the same denominator.

Place the sign between the terms between the fractions.

- Simplify.

- Solve.

$$x = 13\tfrac{1}{3}$$

$$\frac{4}{2} + \frac{6x}{2} = 42$$

$$2 + 3x = 42$$
$$\underline{-2 \qquad\quad -2}$$
$$3x = 40$$

$$x = \frac{40}{3} = 13\tfrac{1}{3}$$

PRACTICE

Simplify by separating the fraction in each equation below. Then solve the equation.

1. $\dfrac{10 + 5x}{5} = 12$ _____

2. $\dfrac{4 + 4x}{4} = 9$ _____

3. $\dfrac{10 + 2x}{2} + 5 = 20$ _____

4. $\dfrac{2(x + 4)}{4} = 5$ _____

5. $\dfrac{2x - 6}{12} = 0$ _____

6. $\dfrac{5x + 10}{5} = 1$ _____

You can cancel variables the same way you cancel numbers.

Example   Find the y in $\dfrac{2xy + x}{x} = 5$.

- Write terms as separate fractions.
- Cancel like terms to simplify.
- Solve.

$$y = 2$$

$$\frac{2x^1 y}{x_1} + \frac{x^1}{x_1} = 5$$

$$2y + 1 = 5$$

$$\frac{2^1 y}{2_1} = \frac{4}{2} = 2$$

PRACTICE

Simplify each expression below.

7. $\dfrac{3x - x^2}{x}$ _____

8. $\dfrac{5xy + y}{xy}$ _____

9. $\dfrac{2xy - x^2 y}{xy}$ _____

10. $\dfrac{2x - 4x^2}{2x}$ _____

11. $\dfrac{x + x^2}{x} + 14$ _____

12. $\dfrac{3x^3 + 9x^2}{x^2}$ _____

Using the Distributive Property to Solve Equations

The **distributive property of multiplication over addition** says that when you multiply the sum of the addends, the result is the same as when you multiply each addend separately and then find the sum of the products. The distributive property looks like this:

using numbers

using variables

$5(1 + 2) = (5 \times 1) + (5 \times 2)$

$a(b + c) = (a \times b) + (a \times c)$

You can use the distributive property to make it easier to compute mentally. The distributive property can also help you solve equations.

Examples

$$12(4 + 10) = (12 \times 4) + (12 \times 10)$$
$$12(14) = 48 + 120$$
$$168 = 168$$

$$8(13 + y) = (8 \times 13) + (8 \times y)$$
$$104 + 8y = 104 + 8y$$

You can also distribute multiplication over subtraction.

$$8(70 - 8) = (8 \times 70) - (8 \times 8)$$

$$a(b - c) = (a \times b) - (a \times c)$$

Examples

$$5(17 - 6) = (5 \times 17) - (5 \times 6)$$
$$5(11) = 85 - 30$$
$$55 = 55$$

$$3(y - 4) = 3(y) - (3 \times 4)$$
$$3y - 12 = 3y - 12$$

PRACTICE

Use the distributive property to solve each equation.

1. $5(x + 2) = 510$ $x =$ _____

2. $4(2c + 5) = 28$ $c =$ _____

3. $3(x - 5) = 30$ $x =$ _____

4. $84 = n(3 + 4)$ $n =$ __12__

5. $10 = 5(b - 3)$ $b =$ __5__

6. $1.5(2y + 5) = 16.5$ $y =$ __3__

$$3y + 7.5 = 16.5$$
$$3y = 9$$
$$y = 3$$

For problems 7–10, distribute the multiplication over the addition or the subtraction. Do not try to solve.

7. $3x(x + 5)$

_____

8. $4c(11 - c^2)$

_____

9. $2ab(a + b)$

_____

10. $3yz(y + z^2)$

_____

Using Equations to Solve Word Problems

You can write an equation that describes a situation in a word problem to help you solve the problem.

Example
    Each person on the sales staff of the local paper earns $4 per hour plus a $0.75 commission for each newspaper he/she sells. Last week Len worked 32 hours and made a total of $203. How much did Len earn in commissions last week?

Here is one way to solve this problem.

We know that Len's pay plus his commission totaled $203. Write an equation.

- Let p represent pay and c represent commission. $p + c = \$203$

- $p = \$4 \times 32$ hours worked $= \$128$
  Replace p with $128.

$$\$128 + c = \quad \$203$$

- Subtract to find c.

$$\$128 + c = \quad \$203$$
$$\underline{- \$128 \qquad = - \$128}$$
$$c = \quad \$75$$

    Len made $75 in commissions last week.

PRACTICE

Circle the correct equation to use to solve each problem. Then solve. Check your answers.

1. Jay bought a speaker for his stereo. The price was $40 less than twice the price it had been last year. Last year the speaker cost $100. What is the price this year?

    A $2(100 - 40) = p$
    B $2(100) - 40 = p$
    C $100 - (2 \times 40) = p$ _____

2. Lila has two jobs. One pays $5 more than twice the other. If her total pay is $245, how much does she earn from each job?

    F $5 + 2p = 245$
    G $p + (2p + 5) = 245$
    H $p + 2(p + 5) = 245$ _____

3. Manny worked a 40-hour week and was paid $250. This amount included a $50 bonus. What is Manny's pay per hour?

    A $250 = 40h + 50$
    B $250 + 50 = 40h$
    C $250 = 40h - 50$ _____

4. A truck weighs 4,347 pounds. The body of the truck weighs 6 times as much as the engine. How much does the engine weigh?

    F $4,347 + 6x = x$
    G $6x = 4,347 \div x$
    H $7x = 4,347$ _____

Using Formulas

When money is borrowed, the amount that is borrowed is called the **principal** (*p*). The principal is borrowed at certain **rate** (*r*), or percent. The lender charges the borrower a fee for borrowing the money; this fee is the **interest** (*i*). To find the amount of the interest, you can use the formula $i = prt$; the interest equals the principal multiplied by the rate and the amount of **time** (*t*) of the loan.

A **formula** is an equation that states the relationship between quantities in algebraic form. You can use a formula to find one amount when all of the other amounts are known. When you use a formula, you substitute known values for letters in the formula. You can then solve the equation to find the value of the unknown.

Example
Brian borrowed $2,000 and paid it back 2 years later with $200 interest. What was the rate of interest Brian paid on the loan?

- Use the formula $i = prt$.
  Identify the values that are known.
  $i = \$200 \quad p = \$2,000 \quad t = 2 \text{ years} \quad r = ?$

  $i = prt$

- Substitute known values into the formula.

  $200 = 2,000 \times r \times 2$

- Solve to find the unknown.

  $\dfrac{200}{4,000} = \dfrac{4,000 \times r}{4,000}$

- Change the fraction to a percent

  $r = \dfrac{1}{20} = 0.05 = 5\%$

  The rate of interest was 5%.

PRACTICE

Solve each problem using the given formula.

1. Josh puts $1,500 into an account that earns 6% interest each year. How many years will it take him to earn $450 in interest? (Use $i = prt$.)

2. A turtle crawls at an average rate (*r*) of speed of 2 feet a minute. At that rate, what distance (*d*) will it travel in a time (*t*) of 10 minutes? (Use $d = rt$.)

3. If Sonia hikes at an average speed of 2 miles an hour, how many hours will it take her to hike 7.4 miles? (Use $d = rt$.)

4. A grocer buys 104 flats of strawberries at a rate of $14 per flat. How much does he pay? (Use $c = rn$, where *c* is the total cost, *r* is the unit rate, and *n* is the number of units.)

Solving Inequalities

An **inequality** is a statement that two expressions are *not* equal. (See page 117.) In an equation, a variable has one value, but in an inequality, a variable can have many values. A number line helps us see this.

Examples

What values make $x < 5$ true?
Some solutions include 4.5, $2\frac{1}{3}$, 0, and -56.
However, since x can be any number less than
5, it would not be possible to list them all. To show all the values that are less than 5 but not including 5, place an open circle on 5 and shade the number line to the left of 5.

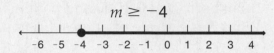

$x < 5$

What values make $m \geq -4$ true?
To show all the values that are equal to or greater than -4, place a filled circle on -4, and shade the number line to the right of -4.

$m \geq -4$

You can create equivalent inequalities the same way you create equivalent equations.

Examples   Start with $6 > 2$ and perform each operation.

Add 5	Subtract -4	Multiply by 3	Divide by 2
$6 > 2$	$6 > 2$	$6 > 2$	$6 > 2$
$6 + 5 > 2 + 5$	$6 - {-4} > 2 - {-4}$	$6 \times 3 > 2 \times 3$	$6 \div 2 > 2 \div 2$
$11 > 7$	$10 > 6$	$18 > 6$	$3 > 1$

However, notice what happens when you multiply or divide by a negative number.

Multiply by -3   Divide by -1
$6 > 2$ $6 > 2$
$6 \times {-3} \ ?? \ 2 \times {-3}$ $6 \div {-1} \ ?? \ 2 \div {-1}$
$-18 < -6$ $-1 < -2$

Note: When you multiply or divide both sides of an inequality by a negative number, the inequality sign is reversed.

To solve an inequality, work the same way you do with an equation.

Example   Solve $-3m - 5 \geq 16$ for m.

$$
\begin{aligned}
-3m - 5 &\geq 16 \\
+5 \quad &\quad +5 \\
\hline
-3m &\geq 21 \\
\frac{-3m}{-3} &\leq \frac{21}{-3} \\
m &\leq -7
\end{aligned}
$$

- Undo subtraction of 5. Add 5 on both sides.

- Undo multiplication by -3. Divide by -3 on both sides. Remember, when you multiply or divide by a negative number, reverse the inequality sign.

Circle the letter that shows all of the values for x that will make the inequality true.

Solve each inequality below. Reduce all fractions to simplest terms.

1. $x - 3 < 7$

   A $x < 20$
   B $x < 15$
   C $x < 10$
   D $x < 5$

2. $x + 8 > 3$

   F $x > 5$
   G $x > -5$
   H $x > 11$
   J $x > -11$

3. $2x \geq 8$

   A $x \geq 16$
   B $x \geq 10$
   C $x \geq 6$
   D $x \geq 4$

4. $-6x \leq 18$

   F $x \leq 3$
   G $x \geq -3$
   H $x \geq 3$
   J $x \leq -3$

5. $\dfrac{x}{5} < -20$

   A $x < -4$
   B $x > 100$
   C $x > 4$
   D $x < -100$

6. $2x + 4 \geq 14$

   F $x \geq 5$
   G $x \geq 9$
   H $x \leq 5$
   J $x \leq 9$

7. $a - 5 > 22$

   _____

8. $b + 15 < -10$

   _____

9. $4x > 15$

   _____

10. $3u + 5 \geq 17$

   _____

11. $8y < 18 - y$

   _____

12. $\dfrac{1}{2}n + 17 \leq 25$

   _____

13. $\dfrac{a - 5}{10} < 20$

   _____

14. $\dfrac{2}{3}y < 36$

   _____

15. $x^2 - 5 < 11$

   _____

16. $5a - 3a + 3 > 17$

   _____

17. $5y + y \leq 20$

   _____

18. $8 - y > 5$

   _____

Algebra Skills Checkup

Simplify.

1. $7x + x =$

    A $7x^2$ **C** $8x$

    B $7x$ **D** 7

    E None of these

2. $3(-x + 2y) - 15 =$

    F $3x + 6y - 15$

    G $-3x + 5y - 15$

    H $-3x + 6y - 15$

    J $-3x + 2y - 15$

    K None of these

3. $\dfrac{3ab - 2ab}{ab} =$

    A $3b - 2$ **C** $\dfrac{3}{b}$

    B 1 **D** $3ab^2 - 2$

    E None of these

4. $5y^2 - 3y^2 + 2y^2 =$

    F 0 **H** y

    G $5y^2$ **J** $5y^5 - 5y^0$

    K None of these

5. $-x(3x - 3m) =$

    A $3x^2 + 3mx$

    B $-3x^2 + 3mx$

    C $-3x^2 - 3mx$

    D mx^3

    E None of these

Circle the correct answer.

6. A class of 28 students has 3 times as many boys as girls. Which of these equations could you use to find the number of girls (g) in the class?

    F $\dfrac{28}{4} = g$ **H** $\dfrac{3}{4}g = 28$

    G $3g = 28$ **J** $\dfrac{1}{4}g = 28$

7. Hector spent $36 for a tool on sale. The regular price is 1.25 times that amount. How much did Hector save?

    A $(1.25 \times 36) - 36 = n$

    B $n \times 36 = 1.25$

    C $36n - 1.25 = n$

    D $36 - (1.25 \times 36) = n$

8. Which of these equations represents the relationship that 10 times the sum of a number n plus 12 is 240?

    F $10n + 12 = 240$

    G $10(n + 12) = 240$

    H $n + 12 = 10(240)$

    J $10(n - 12) = 240$

9. Daryl spent $5.75 for lunch and had $2.15 left over. Which equation can be used to find the amount (m) Daryl had before lunch?

    A $m - \$5.75 = \$2.15$

    B $m + \$5.75 = \$2.15$

    C $m + \$2.15 = \$5.75$

    D $\$5.75 - m = \$2.15$

10. If you multiply a number (n) by 14, the product is 168. Which is the value of n?

    F 16 **H** 12

    G 14 **J** 10

Circle the value of x that makes the statement true.

11. $28 = 2(x + 7)$

  A $x = 6$ **C** $x = 7$

  B $x = 3\dfrac{1}{2}$ **D** $x = 10.5$

  E None of these

12. $2x - 13 = 3x$

  F $x = 13$ **H** $x = 26$

  G $x = 5\dfrac{3}{5}$ **J** $x = 20$

  K None of these

13. $9x - 11 < 16$

  A $x < 9$ **C** $x < 3$

  B $x > 4$ **D** $x > 4$

  E None of these

14. $4x \le -8$

  F $x \le 2$ **H** $x \le 32$

  G $x \le \dfrac{1}{2}$ **J** $x \le -\dfrac{1}{2}$

  K None of these

15. $3(x - 10) = 12$

  A $x = \dfrac{2}{3}$ **C** $x = 7\dfrac{1}{3}$

  B $x = 14$ **D** $x = 9$

  E None of these

16. $-3x = 96 \div x$

  F $x = 24$ **H** $x = -32$

  G $x = -24$ **J** $x = 32$

  K None of these

Circle the correct answer.

17. What rule is applied to the input number to produce the output number?

Input (x)	1	2	3	4
Output (y)	1	8	27	64

  A Multiply x by 5, then subtract 4.
  B Multiply x by 0.5, then round to the nearest whole number.
  C Multiply x to the 3rd power
  D Multiply x by 6, then divide by 2.

18. Which answer choice shows how to find the next number in this pattern?

  $$1, 1, 2, 6, 24, \underline{\quad}$$

  F $24 + 18 = \underline{\quad}$
  G $24 \times 4 = \underline{\quad}$
  H $24 + (6 \times 4) = \underline{\quad}$
  J $24 \times 5 = \underline{\quad}$

19. In a sale at a local store, the shirts are $16.95 each and sweaters are selling for $25 each. Sammy has $85. Which inequality represents the amount (A) Sammy has to spend on shirts if he buys two sweaters?

  A $A \le \$85 - (2 \times \$16.95)$
  B $A \le \$85 - (2 \times \$25)$
  C $A \ge \$80 - (2 \times \$25)$
  D $A \ge \$85 + (2 \times \$16.95)$

20. Which of these equations represents the relationship that $\frac{1}{3}$ of a number n minus 6 equals 42?

  F $\dfrac{n - 6}{3} = 42$ **H** $\dfrac{n}{3} - 6 = 42$

  G $n - 6 = \dfrac{42}{3}$ **J** $n - \dfrac{6}{3} = 42$

Geometry

Reviewing Basic Geometry Terms

Geometry deals with lines, points, angles, surfaces, and solids, and with relationships among these things. The chart contains some basic terms used in geometry.

Term	Definition	Symbol
point	a location on an object or a position in space	A point is shown by a capital letter. •A
line	a connected set of points extending forever in both directions	A line is named by two points on the line. $\overleftrightarrow{AB}$ (or $\overleftrightarrow{BA}$)
line segment	two points (endpoints) and the straight path between them	A line segment is named by its endpoints. $\overline{ST}$ (or $\overline{TS}$)
ray	part of a line that extends in one direction	Ray WX is written $\overrightarrow{WX}$. The endpoint is always named first.
angle	a figure formed by two rays or line segments that have a common endpoint	$\angle ABC$ or $\angle CBA$
vertex	common point of two rays of an angle, common point of two sides of a polygon, or three or more faces of a solid	vertex
plane	a flat region that extends forever in each direction	Three letters, such as A, B, and C that represent points, and do not form a straight line.

PRACTICE

Circle the correct name for each.

1.

A line   C angle
B point   D plane

2.

F line
G line segment
H angle
J plane

Draw and label each figure.

3. point E

4. line segment BC

5. line VW

6. angle DFG

Classifying Angles

Two rays that have a common endpoint, or vertex, form an **angle**. An angle can be named with an angle sign followed by the letter of the vertex, for example, $\angle B$. However, if 2 or more angles share the same vertex, each angle must be named using 3 letters. The order of the letters may be reversed, but the letter that identifies the vertex should be in the middle. For example, $\angle ABC$ and $\angle CBA$ can name the same angle.

Example

In the diagram at right, 6 different angles share the vertex P.
They are $\angle APB$, $\angle APC$, $\angle APD$, $\angle BPC$, $\angle BPD$, and $\angle CPD$.

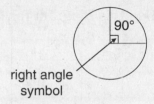

Angles are classified by the number of degrees they contain. Angle measurements are based on the number of degrees in a full circle, which is 360º.

- A **straight angle** is a straight line. It is half of a circle, or 180º.

- A **right angle** is $\frac{1}{4}$ of a circle. It measures 90°. A right angle looks like a square corner.

right angle symbol

- An **acute angle** is an angle that is less than 90º.

An acute angle is less than 90°.

- An **obtuse angle** is an angle that is greater than 90°, but less than 180°.

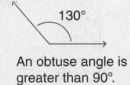

An obtuse angle is greater than 90°.

An instrument called a protractor is used to find how many degrees are in the angle.

PRACTICE

Classify each angle as acute, right, obtuse, or straight. Then circle the best estimate of its measure. If you have a protractor, use it to find the actual measure of the angle.

1.   _____

   A 120º
   B 90°
   C 35°

2.   _____

   F 100°
   G 150°
   H 50°

3.   _____

   A 75°
   B 50°
   C 25°

4.   _____

   F 80°
   G 130°
   H 90°

Recognizing Relationships Between Lines

Intersecting lines are two lines that cross or that will cross if they are extended.

Intersecting Lines

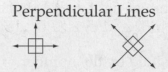

Parallel lines are lines that lie on the same plane and are always the same distance apart. Parallel lines will never meet. The symbol for parallel is ‖.

Parallel Lines

Perpendicular lines are lines that meet at 90° angles. The symbol for perpendicular is ⊥.

Perpendicular Lines

PRACTICE

Use this diagram for Numbers 1–4.

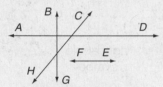

1. This line is parallel to $\overleftrightarrow{AD}$.
    A $\overleftrightarrow{BG}$
    B $\overleftrightarrow{FE}$
    C $\overleftrightarrow{CH}$

2. These lines are perpendicular.
    F $\overleftrightarrow{AD}$ and $\overleftrightarrow{HC}$
    G $\overleftrightarrow{BG}$ and $\overleftrightarrow{HC}$
    H $\overleftrightarrow{AD}$ and $\overleftrightarrow{BG}$

3. Which most accurately describes the relationship of $\overleftrightarrow{BG}$ and $\overleftrightarrow{HC}$?
    A parallel
    B perpendicular
    C intersecting

4. This line intersects with $\overleftrightarrow{AD}$ and $\overleftrightarrow{BG}$.
    F $\overleftrightarrow{AD}$
    G $\overleftrightarrow{FE}$
    H $\overleftrightarrow{CH}$

Use this map to answer Numbers 5–7.

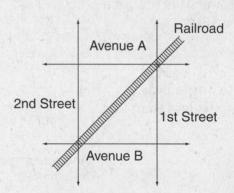

5. Which street is parallel to 1st Street?

    _____

6. Name two perpendicular streets.

    _____

7. Which most accurately describes the relationship of the railroad tracks with Avenue A?
    A parallel
    B perpendicular
    C intersecting

Recognizing Corresponding Angles

When a line intersects a pair of parallel lines, 8 angles are formed. Angles that are in the same position relative to the intersecting line are called **corresponding angles**.

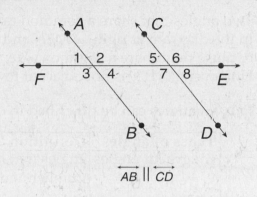

In the diagram at right, angles 2 and 6 are corresponding angles because both are on the right side of a parallel line and are above the intersecting line. Angles 1 and 5, angles 8 and 4, and angles 3 and 7 are also pairs of corresponding angles.

Corresponding angles are **congruent**, which means the angles are equal in measure. So ∠2 is congruent to ∠6, ∠1 is equal to ∠5, ∠8 is equal to ∠4, and ∠3 is equal to ∠7.

PRACTICE

Use the diagram to name angles for Questions 1–6.

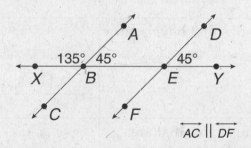

1. Name an angle that is congruent to ∠CBX. _____

2. What is the measure of ∠FEY? _____

3. What is the measure of ∠BEF? _____

4. What angle corresponds to ∠CBE? _____

5. What angle is vertical to ∠ABE? _____

6. What is the measure of ∠ABC? _____

Using Angle Relationships

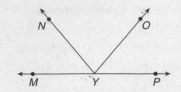

Two angles that share a common ray are **adjacent angles**.
In the diagram at right, $\angle MYN$ and $\angle NYO$ are adjacent
because they share a common side, the ray YN.
However, $\angle MYN$ is not adjacent to $\angle OYP$.

Pairs of angles can be described in different ways.

Types of angles	Definition	Example
congruent angles	angles that have the same number of degrees	50° 50°
complementary angles	two angles that have a sum of 90°	20° 70° 60° 30°
supplementary angles	two angles that have a sum of 180°	120° 60° 80° 100°
vertical angles	opposite angles that are congruent—formed when two lines cross each other	

When you know the measure of one angle that fits a relationship described above,
you can find the measure of the other.

Example   How many degrees are in the complement
of an angle that measures 32°?

Since you know that complementary angles together measure 90°, you can find the
complement of a 32° angle by subtracting.
90° − 32° = 58°.

There are 58° in the complement of an angle that measures 32°.

PRACTICE

Identify the relationship of each pair of angles. Then find the measure of the unmarked angle(s).

1.

_____

∠1 = _____

2.

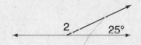

_____

∠2 = _____

3.

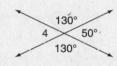

_____

∠4 = _____

4.

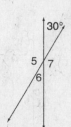

_____

∠5 = _____

∠6 = _____

∠7 = _____

Use the figure below to complete Numbers 5–8.

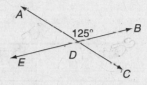

5. What is the measure of the supplement to ∠CDE? _____

6. Name an angle vertical to ∠BDC? _____

7. What is the measure of ∠BDC? _____

8. What is the measure of ∠CDE? _____

Figure ABCD is a rectangle. Use the figure to answer Numbers 9–12.

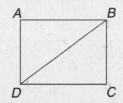

9. What is the measure of ∠BCD? _____

10. Name an angle that is a complement to ∠CBD. _____

11. Name an angle that is congruent to ∠DAB. _____

12. Which angle is a supplement to ∠BCD?

   A ∠CDB
   B ∠BDA
   C ∠CDA

Identifying Polygons

A **polygon** is a 2-dimensional shape that is closed and has straight sides. Polygons are classified by the number of sides they have.

Some Common Polygons

Name	Examples	Number of Sides	Number of Angles
triangle		3	3
quadrilateral		4	4
pentagon		5	5
hexagon		6	6
octagon		8	8
decagon		10	10

To name a polygon, list the letters of the vertices in order. For example, you can name the figure at the right *ABCE, BCEA,* or *CBAE,* but *not ACBE.*

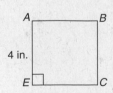

In a **regular polygon,** all sides are the same length and all angles are congruent. A square is a regular quadrilateral; it has four sides that are the same length, and each of its four angles measures 90°.

There are several special quadrilaterals that are identified by the relationship of their sides and by their angles. The sum of the four angles in any quadrilateral is 360°.

Quadrilaterals	Definition	Examples
parallelogram	opposite sides are parallel, and opposite sides and opposite angles are equal	
rhombus	a parallelogram with four equal sides	
rectangle	a parallelogram with four right angles	
square	a rectangle with four equal sides	
trapezoid	a quadrilateral with exactly one pair of parallel sides	

PRACTICE

Write the letter of each figure described by the term.

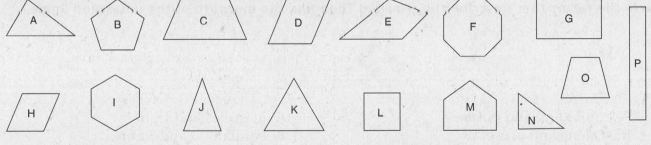

1. parallelogram _____	6. rectangle _____
2. quadrilateral _____	7. pentagon _____
3. triangle _____	8. square _____
4. trapezoid _____	9. regular polygon _____
5. hexagon _____	10. octagon _____

Recognizing Types of Triangles

There are several things that make triangles an interesting group of polygons.

- The sum of any two sides of a triangle must be greater than the third side.

- The sum of the three angles of any triangle is always 180º.

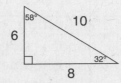

6 + 8 is greater than 10.
6 + 10 is greater than 8.
8 + 10 is greater than 6.

32° + 58° + 90° = 180°.

Triangles are classified by the lengths of their sides and by the measures of their angles.

By sides

equilateral triangle—three equal sides (and three equal angles)

isosceles triangle—at least two equal sides (and two equal angles)

scalene triangle—no equal sides (and no equal angles)

By angles

acute triangle—three acute angles

right triangle—exactly one right (90º) angle

obtuse triangle—exactly one obtuse angle

Examples

Types of Triangles

By sides	scalene	isoceles	equilateral
By angles	right	obtuse	acute
Sum of angles	90°+54°+36°=180°	136°+22°+22°=180°	60°+60°+60°=180°

PRACTICE

Circle the terms that describe the triangle. Then find the measure of the unlabeled angle.

1.

   A equilateral and obtuse
   B scalene and acute
   C isosceles and acute
   measure of unlabeled angle _____

2.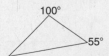

   F equilateral and right
   G scalene and obtuse
   H scalene and right
   measure of unlabeled angle _____

3.

   A isosceles and right
   B equilateral and right
   C scalene and right
   measure of unlabeled angle _____

4.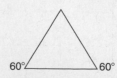

   F equilateral and acute
   G isosceles and right
   H scalene and acute
   measure of unlabeled angle _____

Using the Pythagorean Theorem

In a right triangle, the side opposite the right angle is called the **hypotenuse**. The other two sides are called **legs**. The hypotenuse of a right triangle is generally identified with the letter c and the legs with the letters a and b.

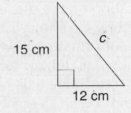

The **Pythagorean Theorem** defines a special relationship between the lengths of the legs and the hypotenuse of any right triangle. It states that if you square the length of each leg and add the squares together, the sum will equal the square of the hypotenuse. Written in algebraic notation, the Pythagorean Theorem is $a^2 + b^2 = c^2$.

Example

Find the hypotenuse of the triangle. Round the answer to the nearest tenth of a centimeter.

$a^2 + b^2 = c^2$ $a = 12$, so $a^2 = 12 \times 12 = 144$
$b = 15$, so $b^2 = 15 \times 15 = 225$
$144 + 225 = c^2$
$c^2 = 369$

$c = \sqrt{369} = 19.2 \ cm$

The hypotenuse of the triangle is 19.2 cm.

PRACTICE

Name the right triangles in each window pane below. If there are no right triangles, write "None."

1.
   _____

2.
   _____

3.
   _____

Find the length of the hypotenuse in each right triangle below. Round each answer to the tenths place.

4.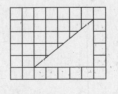

   _____

5.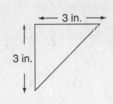

   _____

6.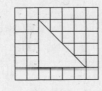

7. This diagram shows a pole leaning against a wall.

   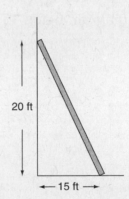

   How long is the pole?

   _____

Working with the Coordinate Grid

When you cross a horizontal and a vertical number line, the result is a two-dimensional **coordinate grid** with four regions called **quadrants**. Each quadrant on the plane is named with a Roman numeral as shown in the diagram.

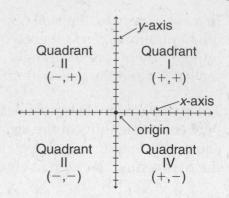

The point at which the number lines intersect is called the **origin**. The number lines are called **axes**; the horizontal line is the **x-axis** and the vertical line is **y-axis**.

Each location on the plane is identified by an **ordered pair**, two coordinates that are separated by a comma. The coordinates for the origin are (0, 0).
- The x-coordinate is always the first number of the pair; it tells how far right or left of the origin the point lies.
- The y-coordinate tells how far above or below the origin the point lies.
- The order of the numbers in a coordinate pair is important. In the grid at right, Point A, (3, 5) names a different location on the plane than Point B (5, 3).

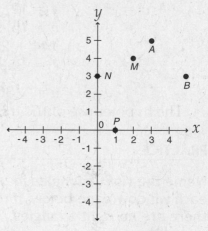

PRACTICE

Use the diagram below to find the correct answer for Numbers 1– 5.

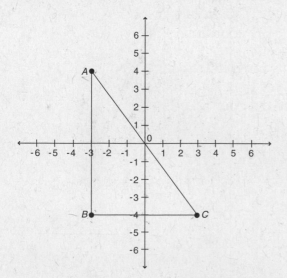

1. For triangle ABC, what is the length of side AB?

   A 6 units   C 8 units
   B 7 units   D 9 units

2. Which coordinates name point A?

   F (–3, 4)   H (4, –3)
   G (–3, –4)   J (–4, –3)

3. What is the difference in the lengths of sides AB and BC?

   A 0 units   C 2 units
   B 1 unit   D 3 units

4. What is the length of side AC?
   (*Hint*: Use the Pythagorean Theorem.)

   _____

5. What is the sum of the 3 sides of triangle ABC?

   F 48 units   H 24 units
   G 18 units   J 36 units

Understanding Transformations

A **transformation** is a process that changes the shape or position of a geometric figure. Three different types of transformations are reflections (or flips), translations (or slides), and rotations (or turns).

Reflections

A **reflection** (flip) is a mirror image of a point or shape. The reflection lies on the other side of a line of symmetry. Corresponding points are the same distance from the line of symmetry.

Examples

Point P' (read P prime) is the reflection of point P across line l. P' is called the **image** of P.

Triangle XYZ is reflected on the other side of line m. The image of XYZ is $X'Y'Z'$.

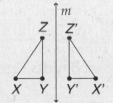

To place the image of a shape, select key points on the shape. Measure the distance of each point from the line symmetry. Corresponding points of the image should be the same distance from the line of symmetry, but should be on the opposite side of the line.

PRACTICE

Use the diagram to complete Numbers 1–4.

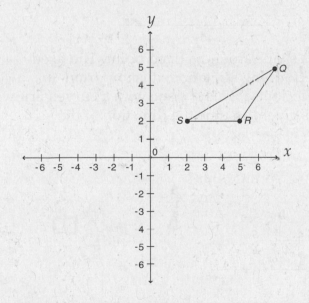

1. What are the coordinates for point R? _____

2. If triangle QRS is reflected over the x-axis, what will be the coordinates of R'? _____

3. If triangle QRS is reflected over the y-axis, what will be the coordinates of Q'? _____

4. If triangle QRS is reflected over the origin, what will be the coordinates of S'? _____

Understanding Transformations (continued)

Translations

A **translation** (slide) is the result of sliding a point, line, or figure to a new position without turning it.

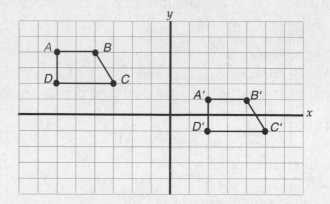

Example

Trapezoid $A'B'C'D'$ is the image of trapezoid $ABCD$. Point B' has been moved **8** units to the right and **3** units down from point B. All of the other points of the trapezoid have also moved **8** units right and **3** units down.

PRACTICE

Decide whether the pair of figures represents a translation. If so, write "yes" and then describe the translation. If not, write "no".

5.

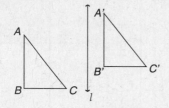

_____

6.

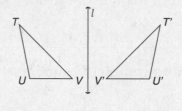

_____

Rotations

A **rotation** is a transformation that turns a line or a shape around a fixed point. The fixed point is called the **center of the rotation**. When performing a rotation, it is important to indicate whether the turn is clockwise or counterclockwise. This is done with a curved arrow showing the direction of the turn. If no direction is given, assume the direction of the rotation is counterclockwise.

Examples

Parallelogram $QRST$ has been rotated **110°** counterclockwise around point T.

The letter B has been rotated **90°** clockwise around point R.

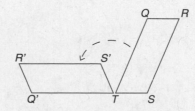

PRACTICE

Tell the direction and the number of degrees of each rotation.

7.

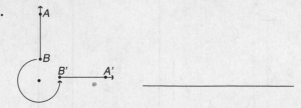

_____

8.

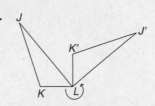

_____

Geometry Skills Checkup

Use the figures on the coordinate plane to answer Numbers 1–8.

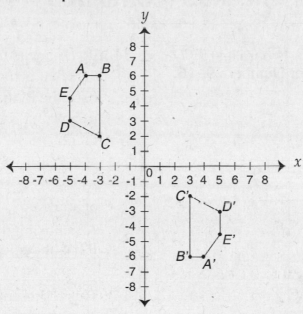

1. What is the shape of figure *ABCDE*?

   A hexagon   **C** trapezoid
   B pentagon   **D** quadrilateral

2. What are the coordinates of point *A*?

   F (−5, 3)   **H** (−6, 5)
   G (4, −6)   **J** (−4, 6)

3. If figure *ABCDE* were flipped over the *y*-axis, which pair of coordinates would name *B'*?

   A (3, 6)   **C** (6, 3)
   B (4, 6)   **D** (6, 4)

4. If figure *ABCDE* were slid right 3 and down 2, which coordinates would name *C'*?

   F (−3, 0)   **H** (0, 0)
   G (−2, 0)   **J** (1, 0)

5. Which of these names a pair of lines in figure *ABCDE* that are parallel?

   A $\overline{AB}$ and $\overline{DC}$ **C** $\overline{AB}$ and $\overline{BC}$
   B $\overline{AB}$ and $\overline{ED}$ **D** $\overline{ED}$ and $\overline{BC}$

6. Which of these names a pair of lines in figure *ABCDE* that are perpendicular?

   F $\overline{AB}$ and $\overline{DC}$ **II** $\overline{AB}$ and $\overline{BC}$
   G $\overline{AB}$ and $\overline{ED}$ **J** $\overline{ED}$ and $\overline{BC}$

7. Which of these is an acute angle?

   A $\angle ABC$ **C** $\angle CDE$
   B $\angle BCD$ **D** $\angle EAB$

8. Which describes the translation of figure *ABCDE* to *A'B'C'D'E'*?

   F a slide right 4 and down 3
   G a flip over the *y*-axis
   H a clockwise rotation of 90º around the origin
   J a counterclockwise rotation of 180º around the origin

Geometry Skills Checkup (continued)

In the diagram below, $\overleftrightarrow{AB}$ is parallel to $\overleftrightarrow{CD}$. Use the diagram to answer Numbers 9–16.

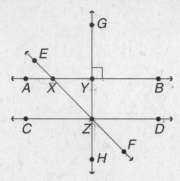

9. Which angle is vertical to $\angle GYB$?

   A $\angle GYX$ **C** $\angle XYZ$
   B $\angle YZD$ **D** $\angle HZD$

10. Which angle is a complement for $\angle FZD$?

    F $\angle HZF$ **H** $\angle CZH$
    G $\angle YZD$ **J** $\angle HZD$

11. Which names a pair of corresponding angles?

    A $\angle XYZ$ and $\angle GYB$
    B $\angle HZD$ and $\angle GYB$
    C $\angle GYB$ and $\angle YZD$
    D $\angle ZYB$ and $\angle ZYX$

12. This figure is formed by the lines that connect points X, Y and Z.

    F an acute triangle
    G an obtuse triangle
    H an equilateral triangle
    J a right triangle

13. Which names a pair of supplementary angles?

    A $\angle CZH$ and $\angle GYB$
    B $\angle HZD$ and $\angle HZF$
    C $\angle GYB$ and $\angle YZX$
    D $\angle ZYB$ and $\angle DZF$

14. If $\overleftrightarrow{XY}$ measures 6″ and $\overleftrightarrow{YZ}$ measures 8″, what is the measure of $\overleftrightarrow{XZ}$? (Use the Pythagorean Theorem.)

    F 10″   **H** 14″
    G 12″   **J** 15″

15. Angle AXZ is an example of this type of angle.

    A acute angle   **C** obtuse angle
    B right angle   **D** straight angle

16. This represents an acute angle.

    F $\angle HZC$ **H** $\angle XZH$
    G $\angle DZC$ **J** $\angle HZF$

The circle in the diagram has a radius of 5 units. Two verticies of the triangle are points on the circumference. Use the diagram to answer Questions 17 and 18.

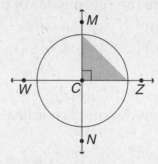

17. Which describes the triangle shown?

    A acute and isosceles
    B right and isosceles
    C acute and scalene
    D right and scalene

18. Which would be the best estimate of the length of the hypotenuse of the triangle? (Use the Pythagorean Theorem.)

    F 6 units   **H** 8 units
    G 7 units   **I** 9 units

Measurement

Reading a Scale

A number line on a measurement tool is called a **scale**. **Tick marks** mark off equal distances called **intervals**.

The amount represented by an interval can vary from one scale to another. To find the value represented by each tick mark, first find the difference between two consecutive numbers on the scale. Then divide that difference by the number of tick marks from one number to the next, including the end mark. If there are no tick marks between the numbers, estimate the reading.

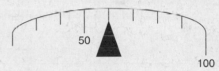

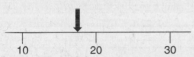

On this scale there are 5 tick marks from 50 to 100.
$100 - 50 = 50$, and $50 \div 5 = 10$
The distance from one tick mark to the next is 10 units. The pointer is at **60** units.

This pointer is about $\frac{4}{5}$ of the way between 10 and 20.
$20 - 10 = 10$, and $\frac{4}{5}$ of 10 is 8. Add 8 to 10.
The reading on the scale is about **18** units.

PRACTICE

Identify the number of units for each measurement.

1. The pointer on a scale is $\frac{3}{5}$ of the way from 15 to 20.

   _____

2. The pointer is about $\frac{2}{3}$ of the way from 0 to 100.

   _____

3. The pointer is about $\frac{1}{5}$ of the way from 60 to 80.

   _____

4. The pointer is about $\frac{1}{4}$ of the way from 30 to 40.

   _____

5.

   _____

6.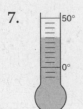

   _____

7. (thermometer 0° to 50°)

8.

   _____

9. (protractor scale 0 to 140)

   _____

10.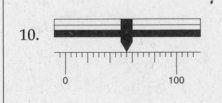

Using a Ruler

Rulers, meter sticks, yardsticks, and tape measures use scales to measure length.

Inches are used in the customary system. The space between each inch (in.) may be divided into halves, fourths, eighths, or sixteenths. The longest tick marks will be for inches; $\frac{1}{2}$-inch marks are a little shorter, $\frac{1}{4}$-inch marks shorter still, and so on. The ruler below has marks that represent inch, $\frac{1}{2}$-inch, and $\frac{1}{4}$-inch units.

Metric rulers use centimeters. The space between each centimeter (cm) is divided into 10 equal spaces. The tick marks between centimeters represents millimeters (mm).

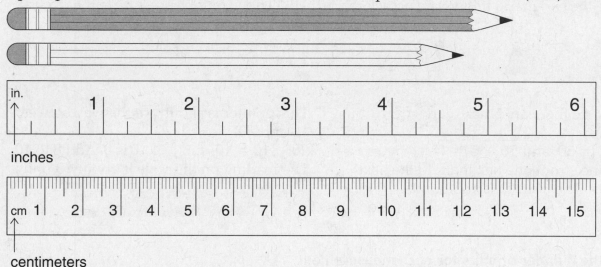

PRACTICE

Use the rulers above to answer each of the following questions.

1. Which represents the greater length?
   A 2 in. **B** 4 cm

2. About how many centimeters are equal to 1 inch?
   G 2 **H** $2\frac{1}{2}$

3. What is the smallest unit of measure marked on the inch ruler above?
   A $\frac{1}{8}$ in. **C** $\frac{1}{4}$ in.
   B $\frac{1}{2}$ in. **D** 1 in.

4. What is the length of the longer pencil?
   F $3\frac{3}{4}$ in. **H** $5\frac{1}{4}$ in.
   G $4\frac{2}{4}$ in. **J** $4\frac{3}{4}$ in.

5. What is the length of the shorter pencil?
   A $3\frac{1}{2}$ cm **C** $4\frac{3}{4}$ cm
   B 9 cm **D** 12 cm

6. Which best describes the difference in length between the two pencils?
   F between $\frac{1}{4}$ in. and $\frac{3}{4}$ in.
   G between $\frac{1}{2}$ in. and 1 in.
   H between 1 in. and $1\frac{1}{2}$ in.
   J between $1\frac{1}{2}$ in. and 2 in.

Reviewing Customary Units of Measure

The **customary system** of measurement is used in the United States.

Customary Units of Measure

Temperature degrees Fahrenheit (°F)	Normal body temperature is 98.6°F. Water boils at 212°F. Water freezes at 32°F.

Length
    12 inches (in.) = 1 foot (ft)
    3 feet = 1 yard (yd)
    5,280 feet = 1 mile (mi)
	An inch is about the length of a straight pin.
	A foot is about the length of a man's foot.
	A yard is about the length of your arm.
	A mile is 8 to 10 city blocks.

Weight
    1 pound (lb) = 16 ounces (oz)
    1 ton (T) = 2,000 lb
	A pencil weighs about 1 ounce.
	An eggplant weighs about 1 pound.
	A car weighs about 1 ton.

Capacity
    1 pint = 2 cups
    1 quart = 4 cups (or 2 pints)
    1 gallon = 4 quarts (or 16 cups)
	An ice cream dish holds about 1 cup.
	A mug holds about 1 pint.
	A narrow milk carton holds 1 quart.
	A large plastic milk jug holds 1 gallon.

Time
1 minute (min) = 60 seconds (sec) 1 hour (hr) = 60 min 1 day = 24 hr

PRACTICE

Circle the letter for the best estimate for each measurement.

1. the temperature of frozen ice cream

   A 70°F
   B 30°F
   C 48°F

2. the length of a shoelace

   F 3 inches
   G 3 feet
   H 14 inches

3. the weight of an audio tape

   A $\frac{1}{2}$ pound
   B $\frac{1}{3}$ ounce
   C 3 ounces

4. the capacity of a bathtub

   F 30 cups
   G 30 gallon
   H 30 quarts

Circle the *greater* measurement in each pair.

5. 8 inches   1 foot

6. 5 feet   1 yard

7. 10 ounces   1 pound

8. 10 ounces $\frac{1}{2}$ pound

9. $\frac{1}{2}$ cup   1 pint

10. 10 cups   1 gallon

11. 1 gallon   2 quarts

Converting Units Within the Customary System

In order to convert from one unit of measurement to another, you need to know the exchange rate. For example, in changing from feet to inches, you need to know that 1 foot = 12 inches. You can use the table on page 147 as a reference.

One way to convert between units is to set up a proportion. Be sure to place like units in the numerator and like units in the denominator.

Example   Change 50 feet to inches.
To make this conversion, you need to know that 1 foot = 12 inches.

- Set up a proportion. $\dfrac{\text{feet}}{\text{inches}}$ $\dfrac{1}{12} = \dfrac{50}{n}$
- Cross multiply. $n = 600$

$$50 \text{ feet} = 600 \text{ inches}$$

Another way to convert between units is to use multiplication or division.
- Multiply to change from larger units to smaller units.

Examples   To change feet to inches, think: *For every foot there are 12 inches.*
Multiply the number of feet by 12.

To change pounds to ounces, think: *For every pound there are 16 ounces.*
Multiply the number of pounds by 16.

- Divide to change from smaller units to larger units.

Examples   To change feet to yards, think: *It takes 3 feet to equal 1 yard.*
Divide the number of feet by 3.

To change pounds to tons, think: *It takes 2,000 pounds to equal 1 ton.*
Divide the number of pounds by 2,000.

PRACTICE

Convert each measurement below to the given unit.

1. 9 feet = _____ yd

2. 2.5 feet = _____ in.

3. 54 in. = _____ ft

4. $\frac{1}{4}$ ft = _____ in.

5. $\frac{1}{4}$ lb = _____ oz

6. $\frac{3}{4}$ foot = _____ in.

7. 1 hr 10 min = _____ min

8. 3 yd 2 ft = _____ ft

9. 12 ft 3 in. = _____ in.

10. 1 gal 2 qt = _____ qt

11. 15 in. = _____ ft, _____ in.

12. 35 oz = _____ lb, _____ oz

13. How many cups fill an 8-gallon water cooler?

_____

14. Rina walks 4.3 miles. How many feet is that?

_____

15. The electric company promises to restore power within 48 hours. How many days is that?

_____

Reviewing the Metric System

The **metric system of measurement** uses **metric units**. Most countries around the world use the metric system.

Metric Units of Measure

Temperature degrees Celsius (°C)	Water boils at 100°C. Water freezes at 0°C. Normal body temperature is 37°C.
Length – basic unit is the meter 1 meter (m) = 1,000 millimeters (mm) = 100 centimeters (cm) 1 cm = 10 mm 1 kilometer (km) = 1,000 m	A needle is about 1 millimeter wide. Your little finger is about 1 centimeter wide. A kindergarten student is about 1 meter tall.
Mass (weight) – basic unit is the gram 1 gram (g) = 1,000 milligrams (mg) 1 kilogram (kg) = 1,000 g	The mass of a needle is about 1 milligram. The mass of a peanut is about 1 gram. The mass of a city telephone directory is about 1 kilogram.
Capacity – basic unit is the liter 1 liter (L) = 1,000 milliliters (mL) 1 kiloliter (kL) = 1,000 L	A large plastic soda bottle holds 2 liters. A dose of cough medicine is about 1 milliliter. A septic tank holds about 2 kiloliters.

PRACTICE

Fill in each blank.

1. A cherry weighs about 1 _____.

2. A bottle of glue holds about 200 _____.

3. The mass of a magazine is about $\frac{1}{5}$ _____.

4. The mass of a potato is about 20 _____.

5. $\frac{1}{2}$ gram = _____ mg

6. 2 cm = _____ mm

7. 4,200 mg = _____ g

8. $\frac{1}{4}$ meter = _____ cm

9. 500 mm = _____ m

10. 10,000 mm = _____ cm

11. $\frac{3}{4}$ kL = _____ L

12. 15,000 mL = _____ L

13. $2\frac{1}{2}$ meters = _____ cm

14. 5.3 kL = _____ L

15. 2L, 150 mL = _____ mL

16. 12g, 700 mg = _____ mg

Converting Units Within the Metric System

In the metric system, prefixes are used to identify amounts greater than or less than the basic units. Notice that the values of the columns for the metric units are the same as those in our decimal place-value system. This makes it easy to convert metric units.

1,000	100	10	1	0.1 or $\frac{1}{10}$	0.01 or $\frac{1}{100}$	0.001 or $\frac{1}{1000}$
kilo (k)	hecto (h)	deka (dk)	basic unit	deci (d)	centi (c)	milli (m)
km	hm	dkm	meter (m)	dm	cm	mm
kL	hL	dkL	liter (L)	dL	cL	mL
kg	hg	dkg	gram (g)	dg	cg	mg

As with customary units, you can use a proportion to convert between units within the metric system. Converted units should be expressed as decimals.

Example   24 cg = _____ g

- Set up a proportion.

$$\frac{cg}{g} \quad \frac{100}{1} = \frac{24}{n}$$

- Cross multiply.

$$100 \times n = 24 \times 1 \qquad 100n = 24$$

- Solve. Write the answer as a decimal.

$$\frac{100n}{100} = \frac{24}{100} \qquad n = \frac{24}{100} = 0.24$$

$$24 \text{ cg} = 0.24 \text{ g}$$

You can also use multiplication or division to convert units.

- Multiply to convert larger units to smaller units.
  The place-value chart can help you. When the unit you are moving *to* is right of the unit you are moving *from*, the number will become greater and the decimal point will move to the *right*. For each column moved, multiply by 1 power of 10. For example, if the move is 1 column, multiply by 10^1 or 10. The decimal point will move 1 place to the right. If the move is 2 columns, multiply by 10^2 or 100. The decimal point will move 2 places to the right. Write zeros after the number as needed.

Example   5 hm = _____ dm

		multiply →				
km	hm	dkm	meter (m)	dm	cm	mm

Since **dm** are 3 columns to the right of **hm**, multiply the number of hm by 10^3 or 1,000. The decimal point moves 3 places to the right.
5 × 1,000 = 5,000

$$5 \text{ hm} = 5,000 \text{ dm}$$

- Divide to convert smaller units to larger units.
  When the unit you are moving *to* is left of the unit you are moving *from*, the number will be decreased and the decimal point will move to the *left*. For each column moved, divide by 1 power of 10. For example, if the move is 1 column, divide by 10^1 or 10. The decimal point will move 1 place to the left. If the move is 2 columns, divide by 10^2 or 100. The decimal point will move 2 places to the left. Write zeros in front of the number as needed.

Example   14 L = _____ kL

← divide

kL	hL	dkL	liter	dL	cL	mL

Since **kL** are 3 columns to the left of **L**, divide the number of **L** by 10^3 or 1,000.
The decimal point moves 3 places to the left.
$14 \div 1,000 = 0.014$

14 L = 0.014 kL

PRACTICE

State whether the decimal point should be moved left or right. Then state the number of places to move the decimal point. The first one has been done for you.

1. m to km   _____left 3 places_____

2. km to cm   _____

3. L to mL   _____

4. g to mg   _____

5. m to dm   _____

6. mm to cm   _____

Convert each measure to the unit indicated.

7. 153 dm = _____ m

8. 1.4 hm = _____ m

9. 35 km = _____ hm

10. 24 L = _____ mL

11. 10 cg = _____ dg

12. 6.4 L = _____ cL

13. 0.5 hm = _____ m

14. 6,290 g = _____ kg

15. 3.5 m = _____ km

Converting Between Customary and Metric Units

Sometimes a measurement is given in the metric units, but you need to know what that measurement equals in customary units, or vice versa. Some common exchange rates are show in the table below. These exchange rates have been rounded, so the symbol ≈, which means approximately equal to, is used to show the relationship between the measurements.

Length	Mass/Weight	Capacity
1 in. ≈ 2.5 cm	1 kg ≈ 2.2 lb	1 L ≈ 1.1 qt
1 m ≈ 1.1 yd	1 oz ≈ 28 g	1 kL ≈ 275 gal
1 km ≈ 0.6 mi		1 pt ≈ 0.5 L

On previous pages you used ratios to convert measurements within the same system. You can use that same procedure to convert measures between the two systems.

Example   40 cm ≈ _____ in.

- Set up a proportion. $\dfrac{\text{in.}}{\text{cm}} \quad \dfrac{1}{2.5} = \dfrac{n}{40}$

- Cross multiply. $2.5 \times n = 1 \times 40$

- Solve. $\dfrac{2.5 \times n}{2.5} = \dfrac{40}{2.5}$

     $n = 16$

     40 cm ≈ 16 in.

PRACTICE

Circle the larger measurement in each pair.

1. 1 meter   1 inch

2. 1 yard   1 meter

3. 1 gallon   1 liter

4. 1 kilometer 1 mile

5. 1 ounce   1 gram

6. 1 inch   1 centimeter

7. 1 kiloliter 1 gallon

8. 1 liter   1 quart

9. 1 kilogram 1 pound

Fill in each blank. Round all answers to the nearest tenth.

10. 18 yd ≈ _____ m

11. 23 g ≈ _____ oz

12. 12 mi ≈ _____ km

13. 6 kg ≈ _____ lb

14. 10 qt ≈ _____ L

15. 2 yd ≈ _____ m

16. 8 lb ≈ _____ kg

17. 25 cm ≈ _____ in.

18. 1,000 m ≈ _____ yd

19. 3 pt ≈ _____ L

Finding Perimeter

Perimeter (*P*) is the distance around the outside of a closed figure. You can find the perimeter of a polygon by adding the lengths of its sides.

Examples

What is the perimeter of a rectangle that is 3 ft long and 2 ft wide?

A rectangle has 4 sides, with opposite sides that are equal. There are 2 sides that measure 3 ft, and 2 sides that measure 2 ft.
Add. $3 + 3 + 2 + 2 = 10$

$P = 10$ ft

Find the perimeter of the figure.

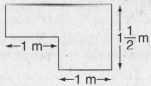

The two "bottoms" total 2 meters.
The top is 2 meters.
The right side is $1\frac{1}{2}$ meters. The two left sides combined are $1\frac{1}{2}$ meters.

Add. $2 + 2 + 1\frac{1}{2} + 1\frac{1}{2} = 7$

$P = 7$ meters

PRACTICE

Find the perimeter of each shape.
Hint: **The symbol " is an abbreviation for inches. The symbol ' is an abbreviation for feet.**

1.

   10' 3"
   17' 8"

   $P = $ _____

2.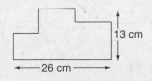

   13 cm
   26 cm

   $P = $ _____

3.
   20 in.
   7 in.
   13 in.

   $P = $ _____

4.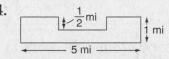

   $\frac{1}{2}$ mi
   1 mi
   5 mi

   $P = $ _____

5.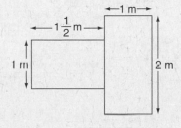

   1 m
   $1\frac{1}{2}$ m
   1 m
   2 m

   $P = $ _____

6.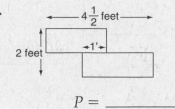

   $4\frac{1}{2}$ feet
   1'
   2 feet

   $P = $ _____

7. This figure is made up of three squares, each with sides 3 mm long.

   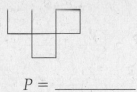

   $P = $ _____

8. A rectangular room is 21 feet long by 11 ft, 2 in. wide.

   $P = $ _____

9. One side of a regular hexagon measures 2 feet.

   $P = $ _____

Finding Circumference

Circumference is the distance around a circle. A circle's circumference is approximately 3 times the length of its diameter. For example, the circumference of a circle with a diameter of 10 ft would be about 3 × 10, or about 30 feet. Since the circumference is about 3 diameters, the diameter is about $\frac{1}{3}$ of the circle's circumference.

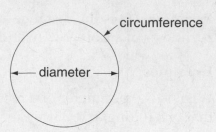

The formula for finding a more exact measurement of circumference is $C = \pi d$, where C stands for circumference, $\pi = 3.14$ or $\frac{22}{7}$, and d is the diameter of the circle. You can double the radius to find the diameter.

Both diameter and circumference are measures of length. When you find the number, be sure to include the units the number represents.

Examples

Find the circumference of the circle shown. (Use $\pi = 3.14$.)

$r = 3$ yd, so $d = 6$ yd

$C = \pi d$
$C = 3.14 \times 6 = 18.84$

$C = 18.84$ yd

Find the diameter of a circle with a circumference of 15.7 meters. (Use $\pi = 3.14$.)

$C = \pi d$
$15.7 = 3.14 \times d$
$\dfrac{15.7}{3.14} = \dfrac{3.14}{3.14} \times d$
$d = 5$ m

PRACTICE

Find each circumference. Use $\pi = 3.14$. Round answers to the hundredths place.

1.
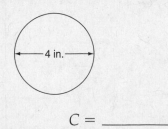
(4 in.)

$C = \underline{\hspace{3cm}}$

2.
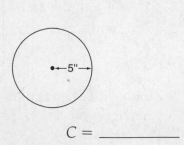
(5")

$C = \underline{\hspace{3cm}}$

3.
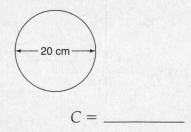
(20 cm)

$C = \underline{\hspace{3cm}}$

4.
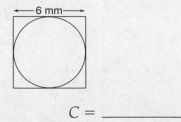
(6 mm)

$C = \underline{\hspace{3cm}}$

5. The curve below is one quarter of a circle.

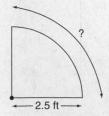
(2.5 ft)

What is the length of the curve? $\underline{\hspace{2cm}}$

6. What is the diameter of a circle with a circumference of 62.8 inches?

$\underline{\hspace{4cm}}$

Finding Area

Area (*A*) is the measure of the surface within a given boundary. Area is generally reported by the number of squares needed to cover that surface. A square yard (yd^2) is a square that measures 1 yard on each side; a square foot (ft^2) is a square that measures 1 foot on each side, and so on. The size of the squares used, for example sq ft or ft^2, or square units or $units^2$, must be included with the number.

Formulas for finding the area for several different figures are shown in the table below. To find the area of a figure, substitute values for the letters in its formula.

Figure	Formula	Example
rectangle	$A = lw$ l = length w = width	2 m, 3 m $A = lw$ $l = 3$ m, $w = 2$ m $A = 3$ m $\times$ 2 m $= 3 \times$ m $\times 2 \times$ m $A = 6$ m²
square	$A = s^2$ s = length of a side	4 ft $A = s^2$ $s = 4$ ft $A = 4$ ft $\times$ 4 ft $A = 16$ ft²
triangle	$A = \frac{1}{2}bh$ b = base h = height	6 ft, 10 ft $A = \frac{1}{2}bh$ $b = 10$ ft, $h = 6$ ft $A = \frac{1}{2} \times 10$ ft $\times$ 6 ft $A = 30$ ft²
circle	$A = \pi r^2$ $\pi = 3.14$ or $\frac{22}{7}$ r = radius r^2 = radius $\times$ radius	2 in. $A = \pi r^2$ $\pi = 3.14$, $r = 2$ in., $r^2 = 4$ in.² $A = 3.14 \times 4$ in.² $A = 12.56$ in.²

PRACTICE

Find each area. Use this diagram for Numbers 1–3.

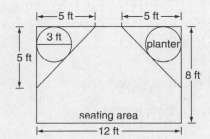

Use this diagram of the plans for a window box for Numbers 4–6.

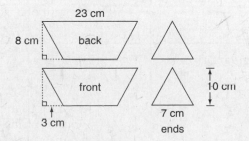

1. the area of each circular planter (Round your answer to the nearest whole number.) _____

2. the total area of the deck _____

3. the area of the seating area of the deck _____

4. the area of the front _____

5. the area of each end _____

6. What is the total area of the outside of this box? _____

Finding Volume

Volume (*V*) is the amount of space contained in a solid figure. The volume of an object is the number of cubes that fill the space, so the size of the **cubic units** (units³) that are used must be included with the number. A cubic yard (yd³) is a cube that measures 1 yard on each side; a cubic foot (ft³) is a cube that measures 1 foot on each side, and so on.

- A **prism** is a solid that has two congruent faces called **bases**. These faces are parallel to each other. The distance between the bases is the **altitude** or **height** of the figure. The faces that separate the bases are called **lateral faces**.

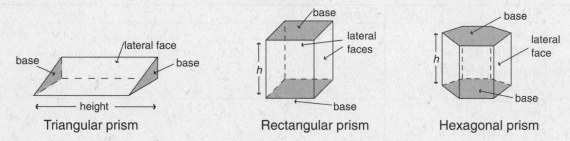

| Triangular prism | Rectangular prism | Hexagonal prism |

- A **cylinder** is a solid with circular bases that are parallel. The distance between the two circular bases is the height.

Formulas for finding the volume for several different figures are shown in the table below. To use the formula, replace variables with the values they represent and then solve.

Figure	Formula	Example
rectangle prism	$V = l \times w \times h$ l = length w = width h = height	$V = l \times w \times h$ l = 4 m, w = 6 m, h = 4 m V = 4 m × 6 m × 4 m V = 4 × 6 × 4 × m × m × m V = 96 m³
cube	$V = s^3$ s = length of a side	$V = s^3$ s = 4 cm V = 4 cm × 4 cm × 4 cm V = 64 cm³
triangular prism	$V = \frac{1}{2}\, l\, w\, h$ l = length of triangle w = width of triangle h = height	$V = \frac{1}{2}\, l\, w\, h$ l = 4 yd, w = 2 ft, h = 6 yd $V = \frac{1}{2} \times$ 4 yd × 2 yd × 6 yd V = 24 yd³
cylinder	$V = \pi r^2 h$ π = 3.14 or $\frac{22}{7}$ r = radius h = height	$V = \pi r^2 h$ π = 3.14 r = 3 in., r^2 = 9 in.², h = 6 in V = 3.14 × 9 in.² × 6 in. V = 169.56 in.³

Find the volume of each figure. Round answers to the nearest hundredth.

1.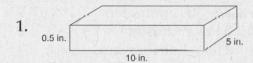

   0.5 in.   5 in.

   10 in.

   _____

2.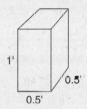

   1'

   0.5'

   0.5'

   _____

3.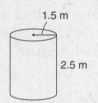

   1.5 m

   2.5 m

   _____

4.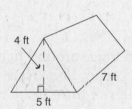

   4 ft

   7 ft

   5 ft

   _____

5.

   8 m

   8 m

   8 m

   _____

6. A sugar cube is 2 cm on each side. What is its volume?   _____

7. A cylindrical pail is 12 inches wide (*r* = 6 in.) and 10 inches tall. How many times would you have to fill the pail to move 5,600 cubic inches of dirt?   _____

8. A cube has a volume of 125 ft³. What is the area of its base?   _____

9. A full crate holds 24 boxes. If the volume of the crate is 144 cubic feet, what is the volume of one box?   _____

10. How much greater is the volume of the cube than that of the cylinder?   _____

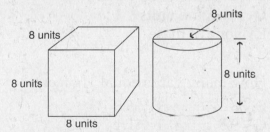

8 units

8 units

8 units

8 units

8 units

8 units

Measurement Skills Checkup

Circle the letter for the correct answer to each problem.

1. Which of these is about the same amount as $5\frac{1}{2}$ gallons of apple cider?

   (1 gallon $\approx$ 3.785 liters)

   A 20.8 liters   C   2.08 liters
   B   1.4 liters   D 14 liters
   E None of these

2. What is the area of a circle with a radius of 8 meters? (Use π = 3.14)

   F   50.24 ft²   H 200.96 ft²
   G 25.12 ft²   J   48.32 ft²
   K None of these

3. What is the area of this figure?

   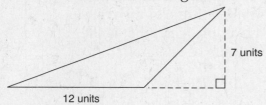

   A 84 square units
   B 48 square units
   C 42 square units
   D 36 square units
   E None of these

4. How many yards equal 114 feet?

   F 38   H 36.8
   G 9.5   J 11.4
   K None of these

5. What is the area of this figure?

   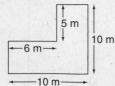

   A 100 m²   C   70 m²
   B 130 m²   D 20 m²
   E None of these

6. This vase is 30 centimeters tall and has a radius of 3 centimeters. Latrice wants to buy colored sand to fill the vase $\frac{1}{3}$ full. About how many cubic centimeters of sand does she need?

   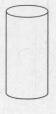

   F   60 cm³
   G   90 cm³
   H 180 cm³
   J   270 cm³

7. A box 10 cm wide, 12 cm tall, and 20 cm long is filled with a product that weighs 13 grams per cubic centimeter. What is the weight of the product inside the box?

   A   31 kilograms, 200 grams
   B   2 kilograms, 400 grams
   C 184 kilograms
   D 312 grams

8. Rita wants to put a fence around her circular garden to keep rabbits from eating the vegetables. If the garden has a radius of 6 feet, how many yards of fencing does she need? (Use π = 3.14)

   F 10.85 yd   H   12.56 yd
   G 37.68 yd   J   113.04 yd

9. How many square inches are in one square foot?

   A 12   C 144
   B 24   D   9

10. About how many inches are there in 10 centimeters?

    F   2   H   4
    G 10   J   15

Use the following information for Questions 11 and 12.

Jordan is recovering his kitchen floor. The floor is 15 feet wide and 22 feet long. The tiles are 6 inches by 6 inches.

11. In which of these number sentences is x the number of tiles Jordan needs?

    A $\dfrac{(15 \times 12)(22 \times 12)}{6 \times 6} = x$

    B $\dfrac{15 \times 22}{6 \times 6} = x$

    C $\dfrac{15 \times 12}{6} = x$

    D $15 \times 22 = x$

12. One can of tile adhesive covers 100 square feet. How many cans does Jordan need?

    F 1   H 3
    G 2   J 4

13. Viola bought 400 quilting squares. Each square is 4-inches by 4-inches. Viola plans to sew all the squares into a square quilt. How large will the quilt be?

    A 1,600 in.²   C   10,400 in.²
    B 6,400 in.²   D 160,000 in.²

14. Viola wants to finish off the edges of the quilt with ribbon. The ribbon is sold by the yard. How many yards of ribbon are needed?

    F 2.22 yd   H 4.75 yd
    G 6.67 yd   J 8.88 yd

15. A contractor needs to build the ramp shown in the diagram from the street to the front door of the garage. How many cubic yards of fill will be needed for the ramp?

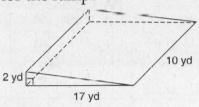

    A 130 yd³   C 170 yd³
    B 150 yd³   D 240 yd³

16. How many square 7 cm tiles will Kevin need to cover a rectangular tray that is 42 cm by 56 cm?

    F 24   H   96
    G 48   J 235

17. Which of these is a measure of area?

    A 25 inches   C 2.5 kg
    B 33 yd³   D 18 meters
    E 12 square feet

18. Sylvia paid $288 for 16 square yards of carpet. How much did the carpet cost per yard?

    F $12 per yard
    G $15.50 per yard
    H $17.50 per yard
    J $18 per yard

19. Which is the correct area for the figure shown?
    (Use $\pi = \frac{22}{7}$)

    A 15 units²
    B 38.5 units²
    C 11 units²
    D 2.75 units²

7 units

Skills Inventory Posttest

Part A: Computation

Circle the letter for the correct answer to each problem.

1.

$9.802 + 0.08 =$

    A 10.602
    B   9.81
    C   9.882
    D   9.722
    E None of these

2.

$59.2 - 5.8 =$

    F   1.2
    G 54.4
    H 53.4
    J   66
    K None of these

3.

What is 60% of 115?

    A 69
    B 52.2
    C 19.2
    D 73
    E None of these

4.

$16 \times (-4) =$

    F   4
    G −4
    H 64
    J −64
    K None of these

5.

$$\frac{2}{3}$$
$$-\frac{1}{6}$$

    A $\frac{1}{6}$ C $\frac{1}{3}$
    B $\frac{1}{2}$ D $\frac{1}{9}$
    E None of these

6.

$0.072 \div 6 =$

    F 12
    G 0.12
    H 0.012
    J 0.0012
    K None of these

7.

$5\overline{)1.75}$

    A 0.31
    B 3.1
    C 0.41
    D 3.5
    E None of these

8.

$3\frac{1}{5} \times \frac{2}{3} =$

    F $2\frac{2}{15}$ H $\frac{2}{3}$
    G $3\frac{2}{15}$ J $\frac{8}{15}$
    K None of these

9.

$-15 + (-2) =$

    A 13
    B −13
    C −17
    D 17
    E None of these

10.

$3^2 \times 10^4 =$

    F 30^6
    G 90,000
    H 300,000
    J 30^8
    K None of these

11.

$20 + 20 \div 4 - 4$

    A 6
    B 21
    C −40
    D −24
    E None of these

12.

$$\begin{array}{r} 90.15 \\ \times\ \ 6 \\ \hline \end{array}$$

    F 540.9
    G 540.6
    H 54.9
    J 5.409
    K None of these

13.

$3x(x^2 + xy^2) =$

   A $4x^2 + 3x^2y^2$
   B $3x^3 + 3xy^2$
   C $3x^3 + 3x^2y^2$
   D $3x^4y^2$
   E None of these

14. What is 125% of 42?

   F 300   H 33.6
   G 52.5 J 525
   K None of these

15. What percent of $15 is 60¢?

   A 4%   C 2.5%
   B 25% D 40%
   E None of these

16.

$9\frac{1}{4} - 2\frac{1}{2} =$

   F 7   H $6\frac{1}{2}$
   G $6\frac{3}{4}$ J $13\frac{1}{2}$
   K None of these

17.

$\dfrac{-15}{-5} =$

   A -5 C 3
   B 5   D -3
   E None of these

18.

320% of $\square = 96$

   F 307.2 H 30
   G $33\frac{1}{3}$ J 300
   K None of these

19. $2x + x(3 + xy + y^2) =$

   A $5x^2 + x^2y + xy^2$
   B $6x + x^2y + xy^2$
   C $5x + x^3y^3$
   D $5x + x^2y + xy^2$
   E None of these

20.

$xy + x + x =$

   F $3xy$
   G $2xy$
   H x^3y
   J $xy + 2x$
   K None of these

21.

30% of $\square = 21$

   A 70
   B 63
   C 14.2
   D 76
   E None of these

22.

$\dfrac{1}{2} + \dfrac{3}{4} + \dfrac{1}{12} =$

   F $1\frac{1}{4}$ H $\frac{1}{3}$
   G $\frac{1}{4}$ J $1\frac{1}{3}$
   K None of these

23.

$5\frac{1}{4} \div 2\frac{1}{3} =$

   A $10\frac{1}{12}$ C $12\frac{1}{4}$
   B $2\frac{1}{4}$ D $5\frac{1}{4}$
   E None of these

24.

$-2 - (-7) =$

   F 5
   G -5
   H -9
   J 9
   K None of these

25.

$6 + (-8) =$

   A -14
   B 14
   C 2
   D -2
   E None of these

Part B: Applied Mathematics

1. You are estimating by rounding to the nearest whole number. What numbers should you use to estimate the product of 8.02 and 1.87?

   A 8 and 1
   B 8 and 2
   C 8.0 and 1.9
   D 8.0 and 1.8

2. By how much does the value of the number 234,679 increase if you change the 3 to a 4?

   F one
   G one thousand
   H ten thousand
   J one hundred thousand

3. $\sqrt{64} + \sqrt{9} =$

   A $\sqrt{73}$
   B 11
   C 36.5
   D $\sqrt{20}$

4. One serving of ice cream is $\frac{1}{2}$ cup. How many servings of ice cream are there in $\frac{1}{2}$ gallon?

   F 8
   G 5
   H 16
   J 32

5. Which of these statements is true?

   A $-4 > -2$
   B $-4 > 3$
   C $-4 > 0$
   D $-4 > -5$

6. Between what two whole numbers is $\sqrt{15}$?

   F 14 and 15
   G 2 and 3
   H 3 and 4
   J 4 and 5

7. Which of these numbers, when added to 0.09, produces a sum greater than 1?

   A 0.1
   B 0.02
   C 0.12
   D 0.92

8. Which of these fractions is greater than $\frac{1}{2}$?

   F $\frac{3}{7}$
   G $\frac{2}{5}$
   H $\frac{5}{6}$
   J $\frac{4}{9}$

9. On a buying trip, Kurt buys 50 sweaters for $9.50 each. He then sells them for $50 each at a craft fair. Which of these number sentences can Kurt use to figure out how much money he made?

   A $50(\$50) - 50(\$9.50) = \square$
   B $50(\$50) \times 50(\$9.50) = \square$
   C $50(\$50) = \square$
   D $50(\$50) - \$9.50 = \square$

10. For which of these situations could you use an estimate?

    F writing checks
    G reporting finishing times in a race
    H finding the distance between two towns
    J making out time cards

11. Which of these equations represents the relationship that 2 times the difference between 10 and a number is 40?

    A $2n - 10 = 40$
    B $2(10 - n) = 40$
    C $2(10) - n = 40$
    D $2(40) = 10 - n$

12. Which of these numbers has a value between -2 and -6?

    F -7
    G 0
    H -1
    J -3

This table gives parents an idea of how much money they can expect to spend raising their children. It shows the average amount that experts predict middle-class parents will spend each year per child. Use the table for Numbers 13–17.

Estimated Yearly Costs of Raising a Child Born in 2000

Child's Age	Yearly Costs	Child's Age	Yearly Costs
under 1	$ 8,740	9	$12,520
1	9,070	10	13,000
2	9,420	11	13,490
3	10,040	12	15,160
4	10,420	13	15,740
5	10,820	14	16,330
6	11,240	15	17,250
7	11,670	16	17,910
8	12,120	17	18,590
		Total	**$233,530**

Source: 2000 Annual Report, U.S. Department of Agriculture

13. According to the table, approximately what percent of the total cost of raising a child born in 2000 will be spent when the child is under 1 year old? (Round to the nearest percent.)

    A 2%   C 4%
    B 3%   D 5%

14. If 18% of the estimated cost for raising the child when he/she is 5 years old is spent on food, about how much will be spent on food?

    F $1,000   H $3,000
    G $2,000   J $4,000

15. Sending a child to college increases the cost of raising the child by about 50%. About how much can a middle-class parent who sends a child to college expect to spend altogether on the child?

    A $ 200,000   C $400,000
    B $1,200,000   D $350,000

16. According to the table, what is the median yearly cost for a middle-class family to raise a child born in 2000 through the age of 17?

    F $12,120   H $12,520
    G $12,320   J $12,975

17. Two parents decide to make a graph showing how much they can expect to pay each year of their child's life. Which of these graphs shows the general relationship between the child's age and the yearly expense of raising the child?

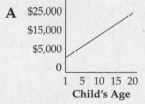

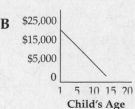

This graph shows one state's income for a year. Study the graph. Then use it to answer Questions 18–21.

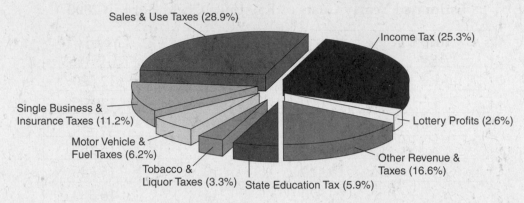

Total of State Revenues: $21,000,000,000

Sales & Use Taxes (28.9%)

Income Tax (25.3%)

Single Business & Insurance Taxes (11.2%)

Lottery Profits (2.6%)

Motor Vehicle & Fuel Taxes (6.2%)

Other Revenue & Taxes (16.6%)

Tobacco & Liquor Taxes (3.3%) State Education Tax (5.9%)

18. What fraction of the state's income came from income taxes?

F about $\frac{1}{2}$ **H** about $\frac{1}{4}$

G about $\frac{1}{3}$ **J** about $\frac{1}{5}$

19. How much were the lottery profits for the year shown?

A $5,460 million
B $5.46 million
C $54.6 million
D $546 million

20. What percentage of the state's income came from a combination of lottery profits, motor vehicle and fuel taxes, and single business and insurance taxes?

F 15%   **H** 25%
G 20%   **J** 30%

21. How much more did the state make through sales and use taxes than it made through income taxes?

A $ 3.6 million
B $756 million
C $606 million
D $360 million

22. Jerold needs to set his ladder to reach a window that is 12 feet above the ground. His ladder is 13 feet long. How far from the wall should he place the base of the ladder?

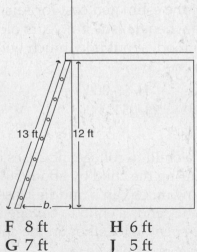

13 ft   12 ft

b.

F 8 ft   **H** 6 ft
G 7 ft   **J** 5 ft

23. How much farther do you run on a circular course by running 1 complete lap in the lane that is 21 feet from the center than the lane that is 14 feet from the center? (Use $\pi = \frac{22}{7}$)

A 22 ft   C 66 ft
B 44 ft   D 88 ft

24. A guard on duty walks around a building that is 120 feet long and 42 feet wide. If each step he takes averages 30 inches, about how many steps does he take with each trip around the building?

F 323   H 973
G 130   J 420

25. An airplane travels due west 65 km and then 72 km due north. How many kilometers is the plane from its starting point? (Use the Pythagorean Theorem)

A 85 km   C 137 km
B 68.5 km   D 97 km

26. Mr. Tang uses a whirling sprinkler to water his lawn. The sprinkler waters a circle with a radius of 3 meters. What is the area of the lawn watered by the sprinkler as it whirls?

F 18.84 sq meters
G 24.62 sq meters
H 28.26 sq meters
J 30.5 sq meters

27. What is the probability of randomly choosing an even multiple of 3 from a bag of disks numbered 1 through 25?

A $\frac{4}{25}$ C $\frac{7}{25}$

B $\frac{1}{4}$ D $\frac{2}{5}$

28. Mr. Hernandez received a $450 commission for the sale of a boat. This represented an 8% commission on the price of the boat. What was the cost of the boat?

F $3,600   H $4,499
G $4,075   J $5,625

29. Which of these inequalities means that 13 is greater than 4 times a number?

A $13 - 4 > n$
B $13 > 4 + n$
C $13(4) > n$
D $13 > 4n$

30. How many numbers in the box are equivalent to $\frac{3}{4}$?

| 75% | $\frac{12}{16}$ | 3.4 | 0.75 | $\frac{7}{28}$ |

F 1   H 3
G 2   J 4

31. Which group of integers is in order from least to greatest?

A $0, -11, -9, 2, 3, 15$
B $0, 2, 3, -1, -11, 15$
C $-9, -11, 0, 2, 3, 15$
D $-11, -9, 0, 2, 3, 15$

32. What rule is applied to the input number (x) to produce the output number (y)?

Input (x)	−1	−2	−3	−4	−5
Output (y)	4	6	8	10	12

    F Subtract 1 from x, then multiply by −2.
    G Multiply x by −5, then add x.
    H Add 5 to x.
    J Multiply x by x, then add 4.

In the diagram, two sides of square *ABCD* sit on the *x*- and *y*-axes. The sides of squares *ABCD* and *EFGH* are parallel. Study the diagram. Then do Numbers 33–42.

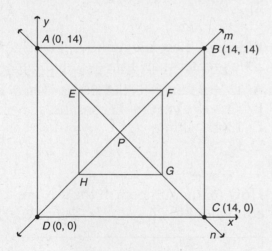

33. What are the coordinates for the point at which line m intersects line n?

    A (7, 7)   **C** (0, 7)
    B (7, 0)   **D** (7, 14)

34. Which describes the relationship between ∠*EPH* and ∠*FPG*?

    F corresponding angles
    G vertical angles
    H adjacent angles
    J complementary angles

35. What is the measure of ∠*BCP*?

    A 30°   **C** 90°
    B 45°   **D** 135°

36. Which is the correct name for figure *ABFE*?

    F parallelogram
    G rhombus
    H trapezoid
    J rectangle

37. Which angle is a supplement to ∠*BCD*?

    A ∠*BFD*   **C** ∠*FGH*
    B ∠*EAD*   **D** ∠*APC*

38. What is the area of triangle ∠*CDB*?

    F 98 square units
    G 64 square units
    H 49 square units
    J 24.5 square units

39. If square *ABCD* were flipped over the *y*-axis, what would be the coordinates for *B′*?

    A (14, −14)
    B (−14, −14)
    C (−14, 14)
    D (14, 14)

40. Angle *HGC* is this type of angle.

    F right
    G acute
    H vertical
    J obtuse

41. What is the ratio for the length of $\overleftrightarrow{AB}$ to that of $\overleftrightarrow{EF}$?

   A 1:2   C 2:1
   B 1:4   D 4:1

42. This word describes the relationship between $\overleftrightarrow{AB}$ and $\overleftrightarrow{BC}$

   F parallel
   G perpendicular
   H vertical
   J obtuse

Read this advertisement. Then answer Questions 43–46.

Use Clear Tone and save from 50% to 80% on calls to these countries!

Charges for a 2-min call from the U.S.

	Clear Tone*	Call Right**
Australia	$0.60	$3.00
Bahamas	0.60	2.40
Brazil	1.00	3.50
Britain	0.40	2.00
China	1.75	5.25
Cuba	1.70	3.40
France	0.60	2.40
Greece	1.00	4.00
Italy	0.80	3.20
Japan	0.70	2.80
Philippines	1.30	3.90
Poland	1.00	3.00
Sweden	0.70	2.10

* $6.25 monthly service charge
   28 cents for each additional minute.

** 15 cents for each additional minute.

43. For which country is Clear Tone's charge 50% of the Call Right's charge?

   A Australia
   B Brazil
   C Cuba
   D Greece

44. If you make ten 5-minute calls to Greece in one month, how much would you save using Clear Tone rather than Call Right?

   F $53.75
   G $19.85
   H $23.75
   J $32.50

45. Last month, Ming used Clear Tone to make four 2-minute calls to China and two 2-minute calls to Britain. Which of these is the charge that should appear on Ming's bill?

   A $7   C $14.05
   B $2.15   D $17.40

46. Flora buys a package with Clear Tone that gives her unlimited calls within her area code for $22 a month, including the service charge. The only long distance call she makes is a call to Poland once a week. If she keeps those calls down to 2-minutes each, how much will her yearly phone bill be?

   F $264
   G $ 74
   H $316
   J $176

47. If this pattern continues, which of the figures below will be next?

A

C

B

D

48. What value goes in the box to make the number sentence true?

$5.24 \times \square = 52{,}400$

F 10^2

G 10^3

H 10^4

J 10^6

Skills Inventory Posttest Evaluation

Use these answer keys to check your posttest. The evaluation charts match each problem in the posttest to a skill area. The charts will refer you to pages in this book that can provide information and practice to help you with problems you missed.

Answer Key—Part A:
Computation

1.	C	14.	G
2.	H	15.	A
3.	A	16.	G
4.	J	17.	C
5.	B	18.	H
6.	H	19.	D
7.	E	20.	J
8.	F	21.	A
9.	C	22.	J
10.	G	23.	B
11.	B	24.	F
12.	F	25.	D
13.	C		

Evaluation Chart—Part A: Computation

Problem Number	Skill Area	Text Pages
1, 2, 6, 7, 12	Decimals	32–44, 51–52
5, 8, 16, 22, 23	Fractions	48–63
4, 9, 17, 24, 25	Integers	68–72
3, 14, 15, 18, 21	Percents	82–86
11	Order of Operations	17
10, 13, 19, 20	Algebraic Operations	113–123

Answer Key—Part B:
Applied Mathematics

1.	B	25.	D
2.	H	26.	H
3.	B	27.	A
4.	H	28.	J
5.	D	29.	D
6.	H	30.	H
7.	D	31.	D
8.	H	32.	F
9.	A	33.	A
10.	H	34.	G
11.	B	35.	B
12.	J	36.	H
13.	C	37.	C
14.	G	38.	F
15.	D	39.	C
16.	G	40.	J
17.	A	41.	C
18.	H	42.	G
19.	D	43.	C
20.	G	44.	G
21.	B	45.	C
22.	J	46.	H
23.	B	47.	C
24.	G	48.	H

Evaluation Chart—Part B: Applied Mathematics

Problem Number	Skill Area	Text Pages
2, 3, 5, 6, 7, 8, 12, 30, 31, 41, 48	Number and Number Operations	12, 39–40, 50–52, 76–80
13, 15, 21, 26	Computation in Context	45, 64–65, 73, 81, 88–91, 124
1, 4, 14	Estimation	28–29, 35, 54, 146–151
10, 22, 23, 24, 35, 37	Measurement	145–157
25, 33, 34, 36, 38, 39, 40, 42	Geometry and Spatial Sense	130–142
17, 18, 19, 20, 43	Data Analysis	99–107
16, 27	Statistics and Probability	94–98
9, 11, 29, 32, 47	Patterns, Functions, Algebra	110–127
28, 44, 45, 46	Problem Solving and Reasoning	22–29, 64–65, 81, 124

Answer Key

Whole Numbers

Page 8
Row 1: 5, 6, 1, 14
Row 2: 16, 10, 4, 15
Row 3: 2, 11, 9, 4
Row 4: 7, 11, 0, 5
Row 5: 7, 15, 8, 17, 9, 4
Row 6: 7, 12, 8, 6, 3, 3
Row 7: 6, 8, 8, 12, 12, 10
Row 8: 10, 11, 2, 9, 9, 5
Row 9: 13, 10, 15, 7, 8, 13
Row 10: 13, 12, 16, 6, 13, 18

Page 9
Row 1: 2, 4, 1, 5
Row 2: 0, 2, 8, 3
Row 3: 9, 1, 3, 2
Row 4: 3, 3, 1, 6
Row 5: 1, 1, 0, 1, 6, 4
Row 6: 7, 2, 2, 2, 1, 3
Row 7: 4, 4, 6, 4, 1, 7
Row 8: 6, 5, 8, 7, 1, 5
Row 9: 5, 0, 3, 5, 8, 1
Row 10: 3, 6, 2, 4, 4, 3

Page 10
Row 1: 12, 16, 8
Row 2: 6, 32, 36
Row 3: 30, 15, 42
Row 4: 10, 28, 72
Row 5: 12, 4, 21, 27
Row 6: 49, 24, 9, 20
Row 7: 45, 35, 14, 24
Row 8: 16, 18, 40, 64
Row 9: 36, 56, 25, 48
Row 10: 63, 18, 81, 54

Page 11
Row 1: 4, 2, 7, 9
Row 2: 7, 8, 7, 4
Row 3: 9, 7, 2, 4
Row 4: 8, 9, 8, 8
Row 5: 9, 7, 5, 6
Row 6: 7, 6, 9, 6
Row 7: 2, 4, 2
Row 8: 2, 8, 6
Row 9: 6, 5, 3
Row 10: 5, 7, 0

Page 12
Row 1: 131; 1,394; 1,989
Row 2: 4,204; 242; 3,182
Row 3: 234; 2,856; 11,240
Row 4: 243; 130; 137
Row 5: 4,751; 5,947; 2,675; 3,002
Row 6: 2,063; 1,138; 4,351; 265
Row 7: 6,210; 7,200; 6,156; 31,812
Row 8: 81, 144, 43, 139
Row 9: 181 R1, 120, 98 R3, 19 R21

Page 13
1. 5^5
2. y^2
3. 9^3
4. 7^6
5. 25^3
6. 4^5
7. 8^4
8. 1^{10}
9. $5 \times 5 \times 5 = 125$
10. $2 \times 2 \times 2 \times 2 = 16$
11. $3 \times 3 = 9$
12. 1
13. $1 \times 1 \times 1 \times 1 \times 1 \times 1 \times 1 \times 1 = 1$
14. $4 \times 4 \times 4 \times 4 = 256$
15. $9 \times 9 \times 9 = 729$
16. $10 \times 10 = 100$

Page 14
17. 81
18. 64
19. 121
20. 144
21. 125
22. 1,000
23. 216
24. 27
25. 10,000
26. 1,000,000
27. 100
28. 1,000

Page 15
1. 320
2. 7,200
3. 847,000
4. 37,500
5. 127,000
6. 35,500
7. 1,570
8. 400
9. 54,000
10. 57,850
11. 10,000
12. 7,420
13. 134,760

14. 68,000
15. 952,000
16. 5,000
17. 960,400
18. 7,200,000

Page 16
1. 10
2. 9
3. 8
4. 13
5. 100
6. 12
7. 14
8. 2
9. between 7 and 8
10. between 10 and 11
11. between 2 and 3
12. between 8 and 9

Page 17
1. 3
2. 45
3. 392
4. 29
5. 60
6. 82
7. Yes.
8. Yes.
9. No. 24
10. $(5 + 5) \times 6 = 60$
11. $36 \div (6 + 3) = 4$
12. $(5^2 - 12 \div 3) \times 2^2 = 84$
13. $20 + (20 \div 4) - 4 = 21$

Page 18
1. 100
2. 400
3. 160
4. $79.40
5. $110
6. 6,000
7. 23,800
8. 16,000
9. 700
10. 1,700
11. 2,000
12. 12,000
13. $45
14. $140
15. $60
16. $11.40

Page 19
Answers may vary.
1. 9,000
2. 30,000
3. 200
4. 56,000
5. 1,000
6. 790
7. 200
8. 1,000
9. 800,000
10. 13,000
11. 6,000
12. 10

Page 20
1. C
2. G
3. D
4. F

Whole Numbers Skills Checkup

Page 21
1. A
2. G
3. D
4. J
5. A
6. H
7. C
8. G
9. C
10. F
11. D

Problem Solving

Page 23
1. C
2. G
3. A
4. F

Page 24
1. Theo had to drive 720 miles. He took a 20-minute break. He stopped for an hour for lunch.

2. Each girl will need a wooden ball, a bottle of paint, and a paintbrush. The balls cost 45¢, paint is 75¢ and paintbrushes are 89¢.
3. Green plants cost about $25 each.
4. An apprentice charges $96 a day.
5. How much did the oil cost per gallon?
6. How many miles does his car get per gallon?
7. What was the regular price?
8. How much did the last fundraiser bring in?

Page 25
1. subtract; $12
2. multiply; ≈ 15,000
3. add; $467
4. divide; ≈ 60 gal
5. multiply; 22,708 gal
6. add; 46 cartons

Page 26
1. A
2. H
3. A
4. G
5. C
6. G
7. C

Page 27
1. B; $34,500
2. F; 17,987 adults
3. A; 2 hours
4. J; 40 pages

Page 28
1-7: Numbers 3 and 4 should be circled.
8. D
9. F
10. B
11. H
12. B
13. G

Page 29
Answers may vary.
1. 380 miles
2. 100 miles
3. 210 miles
4. 900 miles
5. 500 miles
6. 8 gallons
7. 40 miles

Problem-Solving Skills Checkup

Pages 30–31
1. A
2. F
3. C
4. H
5. B

6. F
7. B
8. J
9. A
10. F

Decimals

Page 32
1. 15.06
2. 0.65
3. 40.4
4. 909.09
5. 200.005
6. 205,000
7. 0.300
8. 5.122

Page 33
1. B
2. G, H
3. B, C
4. F, J

Page 34
1. <
2. <
3. <
4. =
5. <
6. <
7. =
8. <
9. 4.735
10. 0.9
11. 0.824

12. 3
13. 3.13, 3.30, 6.0, 6.002
14. 0.46, 0.475, 0.477, 0.49
15. 1.04, 1.042, 1.048, 1.14
16. 6.089, 6.389, 6.523, 6.532

Page 35
1. 0.4
2. 4.9
3. 3.0
4. 0.9
5. 13.0
6. 10.0
7. 0.64
8. $9.00
9. 10.00
10. $17.46
11. 4.53
12. 10.10
13. 4.007
14. 11.196
15. 0.043
16. 10.286
17. 1.000
18. 0.976

Page 36
1. 47.75 m
2. 0.02
3. 5.3329
4. 0.2209
5. 0.205 g
6. 2.018
7. $0.75

8. $19.09
9. 137.13011
10. 63.02
11. 1.409
12. 0.6

Page 37
1. 14.041
2. 0.127
3. 21.375
4. 0.072
5. 4.943
6. 6.11 miles
7. 4.1915 grams
8. $24.97
9. 68 cents
10. 26.3991
11. 89.992
12. 8.16
13. 1.054
14. 10.015

Page 38
1. 0.1040
2. 3.35
3. 20.048
4. 4.48
5. 0.006
6. 0.0036
7. 0.000075
8. 0.0025
9. 432.5
10. 0.106
11. 0.0027
12. 0.0052
13. 9.1455

Page 39
1. 6.5
2. 0.079
3. 0.00367
4. 9.2
5. 0.127
6. 5.356
7. 1.57
8. 0.245
9. 0.054
10. 44.85
11. 0.000105
12. 11.28
13. 0.476
14. 0.0068
15. 0.00052
16. 0.000016
17. 0.2623
18. 0.000005

Page 40
1. D
2. H
3. C
4. F
5. 2×10^6
6. 1.322×10^9
7. 4.03×10^8
8. 3.057×10^9
9. 8.2×10^6

Page 41

10. D
11. H
12. C
13. H
14. 3.2×10^{-7}
15. 5.09×10^{-6}
16. 7.7×10^{-8}
17. 4×10^{-4}
18. 8.351×10^{-5}

Page 42

1. 0.021
2. 3.05
3. 6.13
4. $5.08
5. $30.23
6. 0.562
7. 0.3
8. 0.25
9. 0.023
10. 0.031
11. 2.041
12. $2.03

Page 43

1. 44
2. 600
3. 11.2
4. $863.00
5. 12,700
6. 31,000
7. 20
8. 21.17
9. 70

Page 44

1. 1.5
2. 1.75
3. 11.67
4. 5.22
5. 3.55
6. 5.71
7. 4.09
8. 14.83
9. 0.33

Page 45

1. 347.4 miles
2. $200
3. 16.22 mph
4. $4.10
5. 9 ft
6. 530.4 miles
7. $16.94
8. 20 roses
9. $8.69
10. $8
11. $46
12. $6.36

Decimals Skills Checkup

Pages 46–47

1. A
2. H
3. D
4. F
5. D
6. J
7. A
8. F
9. C
10. J
11. A
12. J
13. B
14. J
15. C
16. J
17. C
18. J
19. B
20. H

Fractions

Page 48

1. $\dfrac{7}{27}$
2. $\dfrac{20}{27}$
3. $\dfrac{15}{27}$
4. $\dfrac{2}{27}$

Page 49

Row 1: $\dfrac{9}{5}, \dfrac{9}{4}, \dfrac{9}{8}, \dfrac{7}{2}$

Row 2: $\dfrac{19}{9}, \dfrac{10}{7}, \dfrac{17}{6}, \dfrac{41}{10}$

Row 3: $3\dfrac{1}{3}, 2\dfrac{3}{8}, 1\dfrac{3}{4}, 1\dfrac{3}{16}$

Row 4: $2\dfrac{3}{5}, 1\dfrac{5}{12}, 1\dfrac{7}{8}, 2\dfrac{1}{2}$

Page 50

Row 1: 12, 30, 12, 21
Row 2: 40, 12, 4, 75
Row 3: 15, 6, 4, 1
Row 4: 3, 5, 6, 5
Row 5: $\frac{3}{4}, \frac{1}{2}, \frac{1}{3}, \frac{1}{3}$
Row 6: $\frac{5}{8}, \frac{2}{9}, \frac{1}{10}, \frac{2}{3}$

Page 51

1. 0.12
2. 0.7
3. 0.003
4. 2.9
5. $0.333\ldots, \text{ or } 0.\overline{3}$
6. 0.8
7. $0.0909\ldots, \text{ or } 0.\overline{09}$
8. $0.58333\ldots, \text{ or } 0.58\overline{3}$
9. 0.75
10. 0.25
11. $0.444\ldots, \text{ or } 0.\overline{4}$
12. $0.166\ldots, \text{ or } 0.1\overline{6}$
13. 0.625

Page 52

1. $\frac{7}{20}$
2. $\frac{3}{200}$
3. $\frac{21}{200}$
4. $\frac{9}{50}$
5. $\frac{3}{5}$
6. $1\frac{27}{50}$
7. $2\frac{2}{25}$
8. $35\frac{1}{5}$
9. $\frac{21}{50}$
10. $7\frac{13}{20}$
11. $3\frac{3}{25}$
12. $\frac{11}{25}$
13. $5\frac{2}{25}$
14. $\frac{3}{250}$

Page 53

1. <
2. <
3. <
4. =
5. =
6. <
7. >
8. >
9. $\frac{2}{4}, \frac{5}{8}, \frac{4}{5}$
10. $\frac{7}{12}, \frac{2}{3}, \frac{3}{4}$
11. $\frac{1}{2}, \frac{4}{7}, \frac{9}{14}$
12. $\frac{5}{12}, \frac{2}{3}, \frac{19}{24}$

Page 54

1. >
2. >
3. <
4. >
5. =
6. A
7. H

Page 55

1. C, D
2. F, G, J
3. D
4. F, G, H

Page 56

1. 1
2. $1\frac{1}{5}$
3. $\frac{1}{8}$
4. $\frac{1}{6}$
5. $5\frac{1}{2}$
6. $1\frac{2}{3}$
7. $\frac{1}{2}$
8. $3\frac{1}{3}$
9. $10\frac{4}{7}$
10. $5\frac{2}{3}$
11. $\frac{5}{21}$
12. $1\frac{1}{3}$

Page 57

1. 5
2. 8
3. 5
4. 19
5. 9
6. $1\frac{1}{2}$
7. $2\frac{3}{5}$

8. 7

9. $7\frac{3}{7}$

10. $3\frac{2}{9}$

11. $2\frac{1}{2}$

12. $\frac{7}{9}$

13. $\frac{1}{4}$

14. $4\frac{3}{4}$

15. $1\frac{2}{3}$

Page 58

1. 4
2. 8
3. 21
4. 15
5. 24
6. 20
7. $\frac{9}{20}$
8. $\frac{2}{5}$
9. $\frac{2}{21}$
10. $\frac{1}{6}$
11. $\frac{8}{9}$
12. $\frac{2}{5}$

Page 59

1. $\frac{4}{15}$
2. $\frac{5}{16}$
3. $\frac{1}{10}$
4. $8\frac{1}{3}$
5. 8
6. 5
7. 5
8. $\frac{3}{40}$
9. $\frac{1}{18}$
10. $\frac{1}{4}$

Page 60

1. 5
2. $1\frac{8}{25}$
3. 6
4. $1\frac{1}{6}$
5. $2\frac{10}{21}$
6. $\frac{1}{4}$
7. $5\frac{1}{2}$
8. $5\frac{5}{6}$
9. $2\frac{14}{15}$
10. $24\frac{1}{2}$

Page 61

1. $\frac{1}{15}$
2. $\frac{1}{4}$
3. $\frac{1}{9}$
4. $\frac{1}{36}$
5. $\frac{1}{10}$
6. $1\frac{2}{3}$
7. 16
8. $\frac{1}{2}$
9. $1\frac{1}{3}$
10. $\frac{3}{4}$
11. $\frac{4}{35}$
12. $3\frac{1}{3}$

Page 62

1. 75
2. 150
3. 49
4. 315
5. 105
6. 105
7. $27\frac{1}{2}$
8. $32\frac{2}{3}$
9. $27\frac{7}{9}$
10. $62\frac{1}{2}$
11. $21\frac{6}{7}$
12. $8\frac{1}{2}$

Page 63

1. $\frac{8}{7}, \frac{3}{4}, \frac{1}{7}, \frac{3}{37}, \frac{6}{13}$

2. $\frac{1}{4}$

3. 7

4. 5

5. $\frac{7}{15}$

6. $1\frac{1}{3}$

7. 3

8. 4

9. $13\frac{1}{2}$

10. 2

Pages 64–65

1. $\frac{1}{2}$

2. 7 volumes

3. 96 sq ft

4. 3 bushels

5. 22 senior citizens

6. $2\frac{3}{4}$ hours

7. $48.90

8. 64 ounces

9. $\frac{13}{60}$

10. 120 pounds

11. 6 piles

12. $\frac{7}{24}$

13. $\frac{1}{2}$ cup

14. 10 members

15. 1,312 women

16. B
17. H
18. C
19. F

Fractions Skills Checkup

Pages 66–67

1. B
2. J
3. C
4. F
5. E
6. K
7. D
8. H
9. B
10. H
11. B
12. G
13. D
14. K
15. A
16. G
17. C
18. J
19. A
20. J

Integers

Page 68

1. <
2. <
3. >
4. >
5. <
6. <
7. >
8. <
9. >
10. <
11. >
12. =
13. −5, −2, 0, 1
14. −8.03, −0.9, 0.25, 5
15. −33, −4.89, 17, 22
16. $\frac{-3}{4}, \frac{-1}{2}, \frac{1}{3}, 1$
17. −100, −65, 43, 82
18. −8, 0, $\frac{1}{2}$, 2.5

Page 69

1. $|8| = 8; -8$
2. $|-40| = 40; 40$
3. $|-9| = 9; 9$
4. $|25| = 25; -25$
5. $|17| = 17; -17$
6. 35
7. 62
8. 22
9. 7
10. 25

Page 70

1. 9
2. $^-9$
3. 1
4. 0
5. $^-11$
6. $^-6$
7. $^-6$
8. $^-18$
9. 0
10. 6
11. $^-7$
12. $^-8$
13. 0

Page 71

1. 9
2. $^-8$
3. $^-5$
4. 0
5. 17
6. 30
7. $^-2$
8. $^-10$
9. 12
10. 90
11. $^-15$
12. 54
13. 60
14. $^-100$
15. $^-110$
16. 70
17. C
18. F

Page 72

1. $^-25$
2. 6
3. $^-16$
4. $^-30$
5. $^-32$
6. 100
7. 40
8. $^-12$
9. $^-120$
10. $^-2$
11. $^-4$
12. 20
13. $^-3$
14. 10
15. $^-120$
16. $^-12$
17. 4
18. $^-3$
19. $\frac{-1}{4}$
20. 3
21. $^-4$

Page 73

1. owed money
2. July 14
3. charged him
4. $^-\$157.13$
5. $^-8°F$
6. 64,830 ft
7. $\frac{-2ft}{sec}$; 50 sec
8. 6 floors below
9. $^-17$

Integers Skills Checkup

Pages 74–75

1. A
2. H
3. A
4. H
5. C
6. F
7. C
8. G
9. C
10. H
11. C
12. J
13. B
14. H
15. D
16. J
17. A
18. F
19. B
20. J

Ratio, Proportion, and Percent

Page 76

1. 50:1 and $\frac{50}{1}$
2. 1:2 and $\frac{1}{2}$
3. 1:24 and $\frac{1}{24}$
4. 2:1 and $\frac{2}{1}$
5. 12:1 and $\frac{12}{1}$

Page 77

1. N
2. N
3. Y
4. Y
5. N
6. Y
7. N
8. Y
9. N
10. Y

Page 78

1. $\dfrac{\text{cm}}{\text{mi}}\ \dfrac{1}{200}=\dfrac{n}{1{,}000}$
2. $\dfrac{\text{rooms}}{\text{days}}\ \dfrac{2}{1}=\dfrac{25}{n}$
3. $\dfrac{\text{cookies}}{\text{calories}}\ \dfrac{2}{270}=\dfrac{5}{n}$
4. not a proportion problem
5. $\dfrac{\text{minutes}}{\text{pages}}\ \dfrac{5}{1}=\dfrac{n}{25}$
6. not a proportion problem

Page 79

1. $x = 3$
2. $y = 28$
3. $n = 5$
4. $x = 12$
5. $n = 5$
6. $x = 10$
7. $y = 60$
8. $n = 12$
9. $x = 9.6$
10. $n = 20$
11. $x = 15$
12. $y = 26$

Page 80

1. $\dfrac{\$31}{1\ \text{hour}}$
2. $\dfrac{18\ \text{packages}}{1\ \text{carton}}$
3. $\dfrac{\$40}{1\ \text{sweater}}$
4. $\dfrac{7\ \text{flowers}}{1\ \text{bouquet}}$
5. $\dfrac{\$2.50}{1\ \text{hot dog}}$
6. $\dfrac{40\text{¢}}{1\ \text{can}}$
7. $\dfrac{120\ \text{miles}}{1\ \text{hour}}$
8. $\dfrac{5\ \text{cards}}{\$1}$

Page 81

1. 12 in.
2. 382.5 mi
3. 12.5 ft
4. 8 cm
5. $11.20
6. 9.6 gal
7. $108
8. $4\dfrac{1}{2}$ qt

Page 82

1. $\dfrac{28}{100}, \dfrac{7}{25}, 0.28$
2. $\dfrac{75}{100}, \dfrac{3}{4}, 0.75$
3. $\dfrac{150}{100}, 1\dfrac{1}{2}, 1.50$
4. $\dfrac{84}{100}, \dfrac{21}{25}, 0.84$
5. $\dfrac{12}{100}, \dfrac{3}{25}, 0.12$

6. $\dfrac{30}{100}, \dfrac{3}{10}, 0.3$
7. $\dfrac{16}{100}, \dfrac{4}{25}, 0.16$
8. $\dfrac{200}{100}, 2, 2$
9. $\dfrac{4}{100}, \dfrac{1}{25}, 0.04$
10. $\dfrac{40}{100}, \dfrac{2}{5}, 0.40$

Page 83

1. $\dfrac{3}{500}$
2. $\dfrac{1}{800}$
3. $\dfrac{9}{400}$
4. $\dfrac{3}{10{,}000}$
5. $\dfrac{29}{800}$
6. 0.008
7. 0.00375
8. 0.001
9. 0.05875
10. 0.003

Page 84

1. 25%
2. 40%
3. 37.5%
4. $83\dfrac{1}{3}\%$
5. 50%
6. 62.5%

7. 70%

8. $33\frac{1}{3}\%$

9. 75%

10. 87.5%

Page 85

1. 50%
2. 30%
3. 25%
4. 87.5%
5. 6%
6. 440%
7. 80%
8. 350%
9. 600%
10. 4%

Page 86

1. 100
2. 150
3. 6
4. 35
5. 75
6. 8
7. 21
8. 2.25
9. 6.8
10. 10.5
11. C
12. G
13. D
14. F

Page 87

1. A 20%; B 375; C 75
2. D 80%; E 300; F 240
3. A 2%; B 35; C 7
4. D 50%; E 90; F 45
5. A 20%; B $180; C $36
6. D 25%; E 180; F 45

Page 89

1. percent;

   $\frac{15,000}{25,000} = \frac{n}{100}$; 60%

2. whole;

   $\frac{\text{employees over 10 miles}}{\text{total employees}}$;

   $\frac{265}{n} = \frac{25}{100}$;

   1,060 employees

3. percent;

   $\frac{\text{number that passed}}{\text{total number}}$;

   $\frac{9}{10} = \frac{n}{100}$; 90%

4. part; $\frac{\text{savings}}{\text{monthly earnings}}$;

   $\frac{n}{\$1,000} = \frac{15}{100}$; $150

5. percent; $\frac{\text{time at gym}}{\text{total free time}}$;

   $\frac{6}{30} = \frac{n}{100}$ = 20%

6. whole;

   $\frac{\text{people wanting to change}}{\text{number of people asked}}$;

   $\frac{5,240}{n} = \frac{25}{100}$;

   20,960 people

7. part; $\frac{\text{rent}}{\text{salary}}$

   $\frac{n}{\$2,460} = \frac{30}{100}$; $738

8. percent; $\frac{\text{number correct}}{\text{total questions}}$;

   $\frac{60}{75} = \frac{n}{100}$; 80%

9. percent; $\frac{\text{discount}}{\text{regular price}}$;

   $\frac{\$30}{\$200} = \frac{n}{100}$; 15%

10. part; $\frac{\text{amount of deposit}}{\text{total price}}$;

    $\frac{n}{\$16,400} = \frac{20}{100}$; $3,280

Page 90

1. $n = 4\% \times 30$
2. $10 = 2.5\% \times n$
3. $16\% \times n = 18$
4. $n = 19\% \times 65$
5. $n = 200\% \times 45$
6. $n\% \times \$340 = \$30.60$
7. $210 = n\% \times 600$
8. $128 = 40\% \times n$

Page 91

1. 1,720 parents
2. $600
3. 75%
4. 550%
5. $2,496
6. $288
7. $130

Ratio, Proportion, and Percent Skills Checkup

Pages 92–93

1. A
2. J
3. E
4. F
5. B
6. G
7. A
8. G
9. D
10. J
11. C
12. J
13. B
14. H
15. B
16. F
17. C
18. H

Probability, Statistics, and Data Analysis

Page 95

1. D
2. F
3. A
4. F
5. D
6. J
7. B
8. J
9. D

Page 97

1. C
2. F
3. D
4. G
5. D
6. H
7. D
8. H

Page 98

1. B
2. H
3. A
4. G

Page 99

1. Marcus
2. Stan
3. cook
4. 4

5. Sunday
6. 3
7. Monday
8. Sunday

Page 100

1. 3
2. 7
3. Saturday, day shift
4. $84
5. $1,584

Page 101

1. UPS Store
2. $250,000
3. $125,000
4. Subway and UPS Store
5. $30,000
6. ≈ $80,000

Page 102

1. B
2. H
3. C
4. J
5. C
6. H

Page 103

1. B
2. H
3. B
4. H
5. B
6. G

Page 104

1. Crunchy Chips
2. Frodo's Ice Cream
3. Health Nut Cereal
4. Tilly's Beans

Page 105

1. C
2. F
3. D
4. G
5. 338
6. 443

Page 106

1. 4.3 million
2. about 2 times
3. 133%
4. $33\frac{1}{3}\%$
5. A, C, and D

Page 107

1. C
2. G

Probability, Statistics, and Data Analysis Skills Checkup

Pages 108–109

1. A
2. K
3. B
4. H

5. C
6. G
7. C
8. H
9. A
10. G
11. B
12. H

Algebra

Page 110

1. C
2. H
3. C
4. J
5. 22, 29
6. 7
7. Y
8. a star

Page 111

1. ÷
2. −
3. ×
4. ×
5. −
6. −
7. ÷
8. −
9. ×
10. +
11. ×
12. ÷
13. ×
14. −
15. −

16. ÷
17. −
18. +
19. +
20. ÷
21. −
22. ×
23. ÷
24. ×

Page 112

1. 15, 33, 60
2. 23, 35, 99
3. 0, 3, −4.5
4. 16, 22, 5
5. B
6. H
7. Divide by 1 *or* multiply by 1.
8. Divide by 2.
9. Multiply by 2, then add 3.
10. Multiply by 7.

Page 113

1. 94
2. 0.03
3. 24
4. $\frac{4}{25}$
5. 1.27
6. −28
7. −17
8. 58
9. 280
10. 6
11. $1\frac{1}{4}$

12. $\frac{7}{12}$

13. 12

14. 180

15. $4\frac{9}{10}$

16. 2.02

17. 8

18. 5

Page 115

1. D

2. F

3. A

4. H

5. C

6. J

7. $\frac{n}{14}$ or $n \div 14$

8. $n + 2$

9. n^2

10. $n \div 2$ or $\frac{n}{2}$

11. $3n$

12. $3n + 7$

13. $n - 75$

14. $-6 \div (n - 2)$ or $\frac{-6}{n - 2}$

15. $(-6 \div n) - 2$ or $\frac{-6}{n} - 2$

16. $-4n$

17. $\frac{2}{5}n$

18. $13 \div n$ or $\frac{13}{n}$

19. $5n - 6$

20. $12n + 2$

Page 116

1. 15

2. 15

3. 12

4. 9

5. 2.5

6. 13

7. 11.76

8. 24

9. $5\frac{1}{8}$

10. -15

11. 16

12. 6

13. 0

14. -16

15. 3

16. 125

Page 117

1. B

2. H

3. B

4. H

5. $w - 15 = 12$

6. $45 > n$

7. $87 = 3n$

8. $14 < 6y$

9. $\frac{r}{4} = 18$

10. $7n = 224$

11. $96 - r = 28$

12. $n + p = 35$

13. $4x > 18$

14. $n \div 15 > 16$

Page 119

1. $x = 175$

2. $x = 492$

3. $x = 118$

4. $x = 12.7$

5. $x = 8$

6. $x = -4$

7. $x = 39$

8. $x = 2$

9. $x = 21$

10. $x = 216$

11. $x = 13$

12. $x = -5$

13. $x = 5.1$

14. $x = \frac{6}{7}$

15. $x = 4.86$

Page 120

1. $7ab$

2. cannot be combined

3. $12x^2$

4. $-6a^2$

5. cannot be combined

6. $16na$

7. $10b^7$

8. 2

9. x

10. $4t$

11. cannot be combined

12. xy

13. $3a^3b$

14. $8u$

15. $4y^2$

16. cannot be combined

Page 121

1. $y = 19$
2. $m = -585$
3. $p = \frac{9}{5}$ or $1\frac{4}{5}$
4. $b = 228$
5. $y = 21$
6. $r = 5$

Page 122

1. $x = 10$
2. $x = 8$
3. $x = 10$
4. $x = 6$
5. $x = 3$
6. $x = -1$
7. $3 - x$
8. $5 + \frac{1}{x}$
9. $2 - x$
10. $1 - 2x$
11. $x + 15$
12. $3x + 9$

Page 123

1. $x = 100$
2. $c = 1$
3. $x = 15$
4. $n = 12$
5. $b = 5$
6. $y - 3$
7. $3x^2 + 15x$
8. $44c - 4c^3$
9. $2a^2b + 2ab^2$
10. $3y^2z + 3yz^3$

Page 124

1. B; $160
2. G; $80, $165
3. A; $5
4. H; 621 lbs

Page 125

1. 5 years
2. 20 feet
3. 3.7 hours
4. $1,456

Page 127

1. C
2. G
3. D
4. G
5. D
6. F
7. $a > 27$
8. $b < -25$
9. $x > 3\frac{3}{4}$
10. $u \geq 4$
11. $y < 2$
12. $n \leq 16$
13. $a < 205$
14. $y < 54$
15. $x < 4$
16. $a > 7$
17. $y \leq 3\frac{1}{3}$
18. $y < 3$

Algebra Skills Checkup

Pages 128–129

1. C
2. H
3. B
4. K
5. B
6. F
7. A
8. G
9. A
10. H
11. C
12. K
13. C
14. K
15. B
16. G
17. C
18. J
19. B
20. H

Geometry

Page 130

1. C
2. F
3. $\cdot E$
4. $\overline{BC}$
5. $\overrightarrow{VW}$
6.

Page 131

1. right, B
2. acute, H
3. acute, C
4. obtuse, G

Page 132

1. B
2. H
3. C
4. H
5. 2nd Street
6. Avenue A and 1st Street
   or 2nd Street *or*
   Avenue B and
   1st Street or 2nd Street
7. C

Page 133

1. ∠ABE, ∠DEY, or ∠BEF
2. 135º
3. 45º
4. ∠FEY
5. ∠XBC
6. 180º

Page 135

1. complementary, 20º
2. supplementary, 155º
3. vertical, 50º
4. vertical, ∠5 = 150º,
   ∠6 = 30º, ∠7 = 150º
5. 55º
6. ∠ADE
7. 55º
8. 125º
9. 90º

10. ∠ABD, ∠ADB, *or*
    ∠CDB
11. angle ADC, angle DCB,
    or angle ABC
12. C

Page 137

1. D, G, H, L, P
2. C, D, E, G, H, L, O, P
3. A, J, K, N
4. C, O
5. I
6. G, L, P
7. B, M
8. L
9. B, F, I, K, L
10. F

Page 138

1. C, 20º
2. G, 25º
3. A, 90º
4. F, 60º

Page 139

1. none
2. E and F
3. G and I
4. 4.2 in.
5. 6.4 units
6. 5.7 units
7. 25 ft

Page 140

1. C
2. F
3. C
4. 10 units
5. H

Pages 141–142

1. (5, 2)
2. (5, −2)
3. (−7, 5)
4. (−2, −2)
5. Yes. right and up
6. No.
7. counterclockwise 270º
8. counterclockwise 270º

Geometry Skills Checkup

Pages 143–144

1. B
2. J
3. A
4. H
5. D
6. H
7. B
8. J
9. C
10. F
11. C
12. J
13. A

14. F
15. C
16. J
17. B
18. G

Measurement

Page 145
1. 18
2. 66.666…
3. 64
4. $32\frac{1}{2}$
5. 65
6. 32
7. 30º
8. $1\frac{3}{8}$ cup
9. 78
10. 55

Page 146
1. A
2. H
3. C
4. H
5. D
6. F

Page 147
1. B
2. H
3. C
4. G
5. 1 foot
6. 5 feet
7. 1 pound
8. 10 ounces
9. 1 pint
10. 1 gallon
11. 1 gallon

Page 148
1. 3
2. 30
3. 4.5
4. 3
5. 4
6. 9
7. 70
8. 11
9. 147
10. 6
11. 1 ft 3 in.
12. 2 lb 3 oz
13. 128 cups
14. 22,704 feet
15. 2 days

Page 149
1. g
2. mL
3. kg
4. g
5. 500
6. 20
7. 4.2
8. 250
9. $\frac{1}{2}$
10. 1,000
11. 750
12. 15

13. 250
14. 5,300
15. 2,150
16. 12,700

Page 151
1. left 3 places
2. right 5 places
3. right 3 places
4. right 3 places
5. right 1 place
6. left 1 place
7. 15.3
8. 140
9. 350
10. 24,000
11. 1
12. 640
13. 50
14. 6.290
15. 0.0035

Page 152
1. 1 meter
2. 1 yard
3. 1 gallon
4. 1 kilometer
5. 1 ounce
6. 1 inch
7. 1 kiloliter
8. 1 liter
9. 1 kilogram
10. 16.4 m
11. 0.8 oz
12. 20 km
13. 13.2 lb
14. 9.1 L

15. 1.8 m
16. 3.6 kg
17. 10 in.
18. 1,100 yd
19. 1.5 L

Page 153

1. 55'10"
2. 78 cm
3. 80 in.
4. 13 mi
5. 9 m
6. 13 ft
7. 36 mm
8. 64 ft 4 in.
9. 12 ft

Page 154

1. 12.56 in.
2. 31.4"
3. 62.8 cm
4. 18.84 mm
5. 3.93 ft
6. 20 in.

Page 155

1. 7 ft^2
2. 96 ft^2
3. 71 ft^2
4. 160 cm^2
5. 35 cm^2
6. 390 cm^2

Page 157

1. 25 in^3
2. 0.25 ft^3
3. 17.66 m^3
4. 70 ft^3
5. 512 m^3
6. 8 cm^3
7. 5 times
8. 25 ft^2
9. 6 ft^3
10. 110.08 units^3

Measurement Skills Checkup

Pages 158–159

1. A
2. H
3. C
4. F
5. A
6. J
7. A
8. G
9. C
10. H
11. A
12. J
13. B
14. J
15. C
16. G
17. E
18. J
19. B

Glossary

absolute value   a number's distance from zero on a number line. Absolute value is shown by placing a line before and after a number. Example: $|6| = 6$ is read as the absolute value of 6 is 6.

acute angle   an angle measuring less than 90°

acute triangle   a triangle with three acute angles

adjacent angles   a pair of angles that have a common ray
Example:

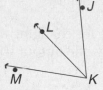

$\angle$ MKL and $\angle$ LKJ are adjacent

algebra   a branch of mathematics in which symbols are used to represent numbers and express mathematical relationships

algebraic expression   an expression in which a number is represented by a variable. Examples of algebraic expressions are $3y$ and $5m + 4$.

angle   a figure resulting from two rays meeting at a common endpoint called a vertex

area   the size of a surface, usually given in square units

average   the sum of a set of values divided by the number of values in the set; also the mean

axis   one of the number lines by which a point on a coordinate grid can be located. The x-axis gives the horizontal location and the y-axis gives the vertical location.

canceling   a process of simplifying fractions before multiplying

circumference   the distance around a circle found by multiplying the circle's diameter by π

commutative property   a rule that says if you change the order of numbers that are added or multiplied, the sum or product will not change
Example: $3 + 5 = 5 + 3$, and $2 \times 9 = 9 \times 2$

complementary angles   two angles that have a sum of 90°

congruent   exactly the same shape and size

coordinate   a number used to locate a point on a number line or on a coordinate grid

coordinate grid   a grid used to locate points on a plane by means of ordered pairs. The grid is formed by two number lines that intersect at right angles.

corresponding angles   angles that are in the same position and are formed when a line intersects two or more parallel lines
Example:

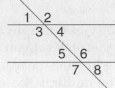

$\angle$ 1 corresponds to $\angle$ 5

cross products   the result of multiplying the numerator of one ratio or fraction and the denominator of another. Cross products can be used to find out if ratios or fractions are equal, or to find the missing term in a ratio or fraction.
Example:

$$\frac{3}{5} \times \frac{6}{10}$$

$$3 \times 10 = 5 \times 6$$
$$30 = 30$$

cube (n.)   a solid figure that has six square faces

cube (v.)   to use a number as a factor three times
Example: 2 cubed is $2 \times 2 \times 2$ or 2^3

customary system   system of measurement used in the United States that uses inches, feet, yards, pounds, ounces, quarts, gallons, and so on

data   information gathered by observation, questioning, or measurement

decimal fraction   a number less than one written in the base ten decimal form, commonly called a decimal

decimal point   a dot placed between the ones place and the tenths place that separates whole numbers from amounts less than 1

denominator   the bottom number in a fraction

diameter   a line segment that passes through the center of a circle and divides the circle in half

distributive property of multiplication over addition   rule that states if you multiply the sum of two addends, the result will be the same as if you multiply the addends separately and then add the products
Example: $3(4 + 5) = (3 \times 4) + (3 \times 5)$

dividend   the number being divided in a division problem

divisor   the number you divide by in a division problem

equation   a mathematical sentence that states that two expressions are equal

equilateral triangle   a triangle with three congruent sides and three congruent angles

equivalent   equal in value

exponent   a raised number in a power that tells how many times the base number should be used as a factor. For example, the exponent 3 in 10^3 tells you to use the base number 10 as a factor 3 times.
$10^3 = 10 \times 10 \times 10$

flip   see reflection

formula   a general rule, usually written as an equation, for finding the value of something. For example, the formula for finding the area of a triangle is $A = \frac{1}{2} bh$, where A stands for area, b represents the base of the triangle, and h represents its height.

function   a rule for changing a number that assigns exactly one output value for each input value

hypotenuse   the side of a right triangle that is opposite the right angle

improper fraction   a fraction whose numerator is greater than its denominator
Example: $\frac{12}{7}$

inequality   a statement that two expressions are not equal

integer   any positive or negative whole number, and zero

intersect   meet at some point

inverse operations   operations that undo each other. Addition and subtraction are inverse operations. Multiplication and division are also inverse operations.

isosceles triangle   a triangle with at least two congruent sides and angles

least common denominator   least number that can be used as a common name for fractions when adding or subtracting. See least common multiple.

least common multiple   the least number that is a multiple of two or more numbers. For example, multiples of 3 are 3, 6, 9, 12, 15, …, and multiples of 5 are 5, 10, 15,…, so the least common multiple of 3 and 5 is 15. The least common multiple can be used as a common denominator.

lowest terms   see simplest terms

mean   the sum of a set of values divided by the number of values in the set; also called average

median   the value in the middle of a list of values that are arranged in order from least to greatest

metric system   a decimal system of measurement in which the basic unit of length is the meter, the basic unit of mass is the gram, and the basic unit of capacity is the liter

mode   the value that appears most often in a set of data

multiples   all of the products of a given number and an integer
Example: Multiples of 4 are 4, 8, 12, 16, 20, 24, and so on.

negative number   a number less than zero

numerator   the top number in a fraction

obtuse angle   an angle with a measure greater than 90° but less than 180°

obtuse triangle   a triangle with exactly one obtuse angle

order of operations   the order in which to perform operations to solve an equation. First find the value of numbers with exponents, next do operations within parentheses, then work from left to right and perform multiplication and/or division, and finally, addition or subtraction.
Example: $3 \times 5 + (4^2 - 5) = 3 \times 5 + (16 - 5) = 3 \times 5 + 11 = 15 + 11 = 26$

ordered pair   two numbers that tell the x- and y-coordinates of a point on a coordinate grid

origin   the point on a coordinate grid where the x-axis and y-axis intersect (0, 0)

parallel lines   lines that are always the same distance apart; never meeting. The symbol for parallel lines is ||.

percent   per one hundred; a number expressed in relation to one hundred. The symbol for percent is %.

perimeter   the distance around the outside edge of a closed figure

perpendicular lines   rays or lines that intersect at a right (90°) angle. The symbol is ⊥.

pi   the ratio of a circle's circumference to its diameter, approximately 3.14 or $\frac{22}{7}$. The symbol for pi is π.

polygon   a two-dimensional closed shape with straight sides

population   the set that meets criteria from which a sample group is selected for gathering data

power   the product of factors that are all the same, often represented with a raised numeral. Example: 4 raised to the third power is $4^3 = 4 \times 4 \times 4 = 64$.

prime number   a number greater than 1 that has exactly two factors, itself and 1. Example: 3 is a prime number because its only factors are 1 and 3.

probability   the study of the likelihood or chances that an event will occur

proper fraction   a fraction whose numerator is less than its denominator

proportion   a statement that two ratios are equal

Pythagorean Theorem a statement that the square of the hypotenuse of a right triangle is equal to the sum of the square of the other 2 legs, or $a^2 + b^2 = c^2$ where c represents the hypotenuse, a and b represent the legs
$a^2 + b^2 = c^2$
Example:

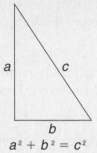

$a^2 + b^2 = c^2$

radius a line segment from the center of a circle to any point on its circumference

random sampling population sample chosen so that each member has the same chance or probability of being selected

range the difference between the greatest and the least numbers in a set of data

ratio a comparison of two numbers. A ratio of 5 to 3 can be written $5 : 3$, $\frac{5}{3}$, or 5 to 3.

ray part of a straight line that extends in one direction

reciprocals a pair of numbers with a product of 1.
Example: $\frac{3}{5} \times \frac{5}{3} = 1$, so $\frac{3}{5}$ and $\frac{5}{3}$ are reciprocals.

reflection a transformation resulting from flipping a point or shape over an axis. Also called a flip.

regroup exchange for an amount of equal value

regular polygon a polygon in which all sides are equal and all angles are equal

right angle an angle with a measure of 90°

right triangle a triangle with exactly one right angle

rotation a transformation in which a shape is rotated or turned a given number of degrees around a fixed point or axis

scale a number line on a measurement tool

scalene triangle a triangle with no congruent sides

scientific notation a system for writing very large or very small numbers that uses a base number between 1 and 10 multiplied by a power of 10. Example: 4×10^3 is the number 4,000 written in scientific notation.

similar figures figures that have exactly the same shape but not necessarily the same size

simplest terms an equivalent fraction or ratio written in the smallest or lowest numbers. For example, in simplest terms, $\frac{8}{10}$ becomes $\frac{4}{5}$.

slide see translation

square a rectangle with four congruent sides

square number the product of a number multiplied by itself. Example: $6 \times 6 = 36$, so 36 is a square number.

square root the inverse of a square number; the number that was multiplied by itself to produce the square number. The symbol for square root is $\sqrt{9}$.
Example: $\sqrt{9}$ is read as the square root of 9. $\sqrt{9} = 3$ because $3 \times 3 = 9$.

supplementary angles two angles that have a sum of 180°

term (algebra) part of an algebraic expression. Example: In the expression $4x + 3$, $4x$ and 3 are the terms.

term (geometry)   a number or an element in a sequence.
Example: In the sequence 2, 5, 8, 11, …, 2, 5, 8, and 11 are terms.

transformation   a change in the size, shape, location, or orientation of a figure

translation   A transformation made by sliding a shape without flipping or rotating. Also called a slide.

trend   a consistent change over time

unknown   see variable

variable   a letter or other symbol that represents a number (or more than one number) in an expression or an equation

vertex   a common point of two rays, two sides of a polygon, or three or more faces of a three-dimensional shape

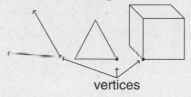

vertices

vertical angles   opposite and congruent angles formed by intersecting lines.

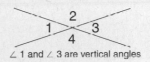

∠ 1 and ∠ 3 are vertical angles

volume   the amount of space occupied by a three-dimensional shape as measured in cubes

Index